THE LEARNING INDUSTRY

THE LEARNING INDUSTRY

EDUCATION FOR ADULT WORKERS

NELL P. EURICH

WITH A FOREWORD BY

ERNEST L. BOYER

LCF

**THE CARNEGIE FOUNDATION
FOR THE ADVANCEMENT OF TEACHING**

5 IVY LANE, PRINCETON, NEW JERSEY 08540

Library of Congress Cataloging-in-Publication Data

Eurich, Nell.
    The learning industry : education for adult workers / Nell P. Eurich ; foreword by Ernest L. Boyer.
        p. cm.
    Includes bibliographical references (p.   ) and index.
    ISBN 0-931050-42-1 (pbk.)
    1. Adult education—United States. 2. Continuing education—United States.
I. Carnegie Foundation for the Advancement of Teaching. II. Title.
LC5251.E79   1990   90-48700
374'.973—dc20

Copies are available from the
PRINCETON UNIVERSITY PRESS
3175 Princeton Pike
Lawrenceville, N.J. 08648

CONTENTS

Acknowledgments : vii

Foreword by Ernest L. Boyer : xi

*Trustees of The Carnegie Foundation
for the Advancement of Teaching* : xvi

Prologue: The Challenge of Change : 1

PART I: THE LEARNING RESOURCES

1. Classrooms for Adults : 17
2. Delivering Instruction : 37
3. The Intelligent Tutor : 71

PART II: THE ADULT STUDENTS

4. Training Technical Workers : 101
5. Educating Managers : 137
6. Updating Professionals : 185

PART III: THE UNFINISHED AGENDA

7. Missing Persons : 223
8. Educating Workers: Issues and Action : 255

Notes : 275
Index : 287

ACKNOWLEDGMENTS

For this report the editorial *we* is correct usage. It has been a collaborative effort from the beginning, both in research and writing. The topic is far too broad, the canvas too large to approach in any other way.

At the outset, each one of our staff of three selected areas of adult training in which he or she was most interested. Davis Jenkins, who oversaw the research process, started by exploring military training programs as well as delivery systems for learning. Sarah White Maeroff collected information on trades and technical fields and advanced professional training. Cynthia Greenleaf analyzed federal legislative programs and their operation on state and local levels.

We also commissioned papers from others more knowledgeable about particular providers or aspects of training. Ann Brassier, former director of training for the Office of Personnel Management, reported on programs in the federal government; Lee Teitel worked on partnerships in training, especially with community colleges; and several individuals from the national office of the AFL-CIO contributed papers and information on labor union programs. William Ellet, manager of *Harvard Business Review* publications, presented the first copy for the chapter on management training, which includes some of his own research, and Susan J. Shepard, who has expertise on the frontiers of the computer world, prepared the initial draft of the chapter on artificial intelligence as a learning aid. These two will probably still recognize their contributions, despite extensive rewriting.

Others will find it more difficult to recognize their contributions because we reorganized and omitted materials as the structure evolved. Julie Wilson did a draft on literacy programs; Felisa Tibbitts's study of South Carolina gave us a detailed picture of one state's training and education opportunities for adults; and Anne Galletta provided some materials on research about the learning process. Elizabeth Gee gave guidance and materials at the beginning of our inquiry into continuing education for the legal profession, and many others made similar suggestions. Their contributions have been absorbed in one way or another in the text, and we thank them. We had a tremendous amount of research that could not be used; it would have required a series of volumes. But as we make some sweeping generalizations, it is comforting to know that there are many facts behind them.

One stylistic problem has persisted throughout the work. Capitalized abbreviations have been a defeating hurdle. Their invasion of the language since the days of FDR is truly appalling, and since the advent of jargon from computer devotees, there is a real problem in translation and readability. We have made a special effort to stay with written words, not initials, but our success is not complete.

We are especially indebted to The Carnegie Foundation for the Advancement of Teaching for the opportunity to study and report on this important subject. It was the vision of The Carnegie Foundation's president, Ernest L. Boyer, that made it possible, and his encouragement sustained the effort. The Kellogg Foundation provided further support for the last year of the project.

To the many, many people among all the providers of adult learning who took time to see us and supply materials, we are most grateful. And for the work of one person who assisted through the final editing of the manuscript, Donald Lepley, we are deeply and personally appreciative. Without many minds, it could not have been done, even though I must accept final responsibility for what it says.

A last word of thanks is due my husband, Maurice Lazarus, who encountered the manuscript in its last year of preparation. To those days he brought his experience in business and education, his wisdom, and his comprehensive view when I was in danger of getting lost among the providers of adult learning.

—NELL P. EURICH

FOREWORD

BY ERNEST L. BOYER, *President,*

The Carnegie Foundation for the Advancement of Teaching

For years, Americans rather arbitrarily divided the human life span into a series of sharply defined stages. In this cycle, the successive periods were rigidly separate, one inexorably following the other like a string of freight cars clanking along behind the engine. First, were the years of early childhood, a time of carefree play. Then came the interval devoted almost exclusively to formal learning. Next, young adults entered the stage of work, a time when education was considered a thing of the past, and a time when individuals went through life drawing upon the dwindling intellectual capital they managed to accumulate during the increasingly remote time of formal schooling. Finally, came the years of retirement and leisure, more realistically characterized as "dignified decline."

Locked in this iron vise of custom, we behaved as if "real" education occurs only during childhood, something to get out of the way before the years of work. And this view of formal learning, as a pre-adult ritual, also had pervasive impact on how we organized the teaching and learning process. Schools and colleges scheduled courses mainly Monday through Friday, from nine to five, colliding head-on with the world of work. We scheduled long semesters, assuming the students had no other duties to perform and, with this rigid schedule, educational institutions excluded from their programs all but the young and unattached.

This segmented view of life may have been acceptable in a more comfortable yesterday, but major shifts on the social and academic scene are dramatically changing both the length of formal learning and the population to be served. Today, literally millions of adults are engaged in lifelong education, and in her report entitled *The Learning Industry*, Dr. Nell Eurich presents one of the most comprehensive studies of adult education in America ever prepared. She states that adult learning is, in fact, the largest and most rapidly growing education sector in the nation and that the success of this massive effort will profoundly shape the future of the country.

Dr. Eurich has limited her study to learning related to the workplace. This decision was made because there is so much going on in this important sector and because continuing education is so vitally important to the economic future of the nation. After a truly impressive survey of programs in business, labor unions, and the military, as well as traditional higher learning, Eurich urges the various sectors to collaborate more closely with each other and also concludes that teaching materials for adult learners profitably could be shared.

In one of the most provocative sections of her report, Dr. Eurich describes the profound impact new technology is having on the workplace. She argues convincingly that technology is not only displacing workers, it is also creating new kinds of work and will be the key in the delivery of adult learning in coming decades. In this regard, the author includes a fascinating chapter on artificial intelligence—the "intelligent tutor" which can, quite literally, combine instruction and work, with both proceeding simultaneously. It is a powerful new version of the old apprenticeship idea, one created by the technology revolution.

The move toward higher order skills at all levels of the workplace is an unmistakable trend that is feeding the demand for more learning. So the education industry continues to grow at an exponential rate, and in response, many large corporations are actively entering the education business. Consider, for example, that AT&T now puts its own basic course for electronic technicians on the commercial market. Big accounting firms and personnel employment agencies are teaching their clients—not just their employees. Bell South has opened its doors to the public, and many other companies are joining the industry of learning.

Dr. Eurich concludes that, in this hidden sector of American education, national leadership is essential. And yet, she finds no thoughtful strategy. Legislation regarding adult learning has generally taken a piecemeal approach, and the states are handed the resulting jigsaw puzzle to put together. Coordination is urgently required and the report recommends that all adult training and education programs at the federal level be put under the jurisdiction of the Secretary of Labor. This move, Dr. Eurich argues, would fix responsibility in one place—not five or six—and help alleviate confusion and promote coordination. *The Learning Industry* compellingly makes the case that, if America is to remain economically strong and vital, lifelong education is the key.

While reflecting on Dr. Eurich's comprehensive study, I was increasingly impressed that the time has come to view more formal education, not as a pre-work ritual, but rather as a continuing process from age five to eighty. It is time to rethink the conventional cycles of living and develop new and more flexible patterns of study that link work and learning at *all* levels of education.

To achieve this objective, it is clear that work skills must be well established while students are still in school. All students during the years of elementary and secondary education must become proficient in language and mathematics, learn to be productive, and be introduced to a variety of vocational options *before* they graduate from high school. American business and industry should be able to hire workers, confident that an adequate educational foundation has been laid.

At the collegiate level, students begin to specialize and, perhaps, complete a credential that will be linked to a career. But it also seems appropriate to suggest that increasingly students should be encouraged to interrupt their studies to be introduced more directly to the world of work. This new "step out" arrangement (to replace the old "drop out" stigma) would be a planned interruption of the college experience and would give students added perspective and maturity as they test career options.

Looking down the road, it also seems apparent that education will continue for a lifetime as adults intersperse formal and informal study throughout the working years—which is, of course, the focus of Dr. Eurich's study. Clearly, a new kind of industry-education partnership *is* emerging. Employers are providing work schedules that are more varied, and I anticipate that more and more labor contracts will include "agreements for continued learning," arrangements that will free the worker for several hours a week or more to take a course in his or her factory, store or laboratory.

I foresee a period when a growing number of working adults at all levels will be granted sabbaticals (just as college professors now are) either to refine their special skills or for more general intellectual and cultural enrichment. (Incidentally, some years ago, France enacted legislation requiring large firms to provide all workers, with five years or more of service, up to a year off, at half pay, for further education.)

I also anticipate more education for retirees. Increasingly, retirement will be thought of as an ideal period of life for further learning. And I feel confident that college and university residence halls will be used during vacation time to accommodate retirees, providing not only housing but the opportunity for learning and for activity in the arts as well. But older persons unable to come to the campus should not be written off. If education can go into the factories, why can't continued learning also go into the nursing homes and retirement villages? Why should a person, after a lifetime of productive work and experience, be allowed to vegetate intellectually simply because of the physical impairments of age?

What I'm suggesting here is a "right to learn" commitment in our national life, dedicated to the conviction that learning and human dignity walk together, hand in hand.

Could we imagine, for example, giving college graduates, along with their diplomas, a "Certificate for Continued Learning"—a kind of educational credit card, valid for life—entitling them to a certain number of additional courses at the issuing institution, or at any institution cooperating in the plan? Under this arrangement, at the time of graduation, students would be encouraged to develop, with their advisors, a program of further study—a kind of contract for lifetime learning.

While the individual would benefit from all of this, our colleges and universities would surely profit too. No longer would our campuses be reserved for youth and viewed with suspicion by the "grownups" in the outer world. Younger students, in turn, would look with less suspicion toward the world beyond the campus. The time must come when the campus, the workplace, and the community will truly mix—and college will be a place where people of all ages move freely in and out.

The design I've proposed assumes that business and industry, educational institutions and social agencies must be ready to accept recruits who will—at least to some degree—be earning while they learn. It assumes that we can rediscover the art of the apprenticeship, and see our young people enter the world of work as beginning artisans who are willing to be tutored, mixing experience with formal study, and who will, in time, refine their talents. It assumes that adults, given the opportunity, also will choose learning as a powerful and rewarding way to fill the leisure hours.

We have long affirmed a commitment to continued learning unqualified by considerations of race, sex, religion, or social status. We must now affirm with equal seriousness that our commitment has no strings attached in terms of age. Nell Eurich, in this landmark study, demonstrates, in a dramatic way, just how far we've come in the fulfillment of this inspired vision.

PROLOGUE
THE CHALLENGE OF CHANGE

A vast and still growing network of adult training is coming into the workplace, but it is neither fully recognized nor equitably distributed. It is not a cohesive system; instead, there is a wide variety of contributors, each serving its own constituency. Together, however, they are also serving the common purpose of trying to meet the nation's needs. As new partnerships develop linking the providers, the network of adult training grows stronger and more effective.

The United States is rich in learning resources, especially for its workers. We find educational opportunities for adults in the corporate world, in the military services, in government, labor unions, and nonprofit sectors, as well as in the expanding commercial market of training and retraining. This network is different from the educational scene we generally know; it does not yet evoke a common vision that is familiar to us. Its schools and its teachers are often unlike the images most of us carry from traditional classrooms. The adult training network has developed in a freer atmosphere with form and structure less limited by routine and calendar. It is more like education on demand or as needed.

But today the demand or need is becoming constant, encouraging the network's growth. The fact is that education has become a necessity, an absolute requirement, if workers are to perform adequately, find fulfillment in their lives, and contribute to our advancement as a country. Through technology and communications, a new world is emerging that continually calls for training. New tools are radically changing our work and lives, a new worker is appearing, and a much more diverse work force is taking shape. Each and all are factors in the growth of training for adults in the work force. If we are to meet the challenges facing the United States in the world economy, the knowledge of our workers will be a prime element.

A New World

America's leadership in the world market is called into question more and more as other nations assert their claims and industries jockey for position. In 1992, when the European Economic Community coalesces into one powerful market of 320 million people—or more if eastern Europe joins—new balances will be struck and old alliances broken. It is happening as East and West Germany unite and other countries seek their position in the changing configuration of states.

Multinational corporations cross many boundaries and belong to no one country; they embody the economic internationalism that transcends nations. Communications instantaneously connect world markets and affect products, people, and monies everywhere. Inflation in one country finds its counterpart immediately elsewhere, and unemployment has been characterized as a "time bomb, ticking away in the body politic of the west."[1]

For the United States to remain competitive in the new and intensely related economic world, high levels of productivity and worker competence are crucial. These two factors fuel our power and sustain our economic preeminence. And leaders of industry, realizing that "human capital" may be more vital for the knowledge society than physical resources, increasingly call for human resource development.

Though we may lament the economic jargon used for people,

at least they are regarded as essential to the bottom line and therefore worthy of investment. While many employers may remain to be convinced, more are emphasizing the educational and training factor as basic to the well-being of the company and hence their own self-interest. Business leaders are talking about their companies as learning organizations in which structure is modified to encourage and accommodate individual learning and contributions. More corporate leaders are sounding like Donald Petersen, retired chairman and chief executive officer of the Ford Motor Company: "Lifelong learning is the key that will unlock America's human potential. The value we place on learning will decide the future of our country."[2]

Similarly, as the states launch aggressive campaigns to attract business and industry, they are using educational resources as a main sales point. Some have formed consortia of colleges and universities to cooperate with business in research and training. Some have organized and subsidized vocational education to prepare the necessary entry-level workers. In the sharp competition among states trying to bolster their ailing economies, promises of educational resources available to the company are proving to be an effective enticement, perhaps second only to tax incentives. The governors are at center stage in the national debate on education, not only for their role in reforming the public school system, the foundation for America's workers, but also for their responsibility in helping to provide adult learning opportunities to keep pace with change.

New Tools and Training

Driving the demand and expansion of training for the work force is the technological—sometimes called the microchip—revolution that is drastically altering the old ways of doing business, as well as reaching into our daily lives and homes and, yes, even our ways of thinking and solving problems. Although this fundamental revolution started some 40 years ago with the advent of computers, and changes have been dramatic, the implications and applications of the new technologies are still to be realized.

Operations that take care of themselves without much human intervention—like robotics—are multiplying daily, rendering many skilled occupations obsolete and stimulating entirely new types of jobs and services. Technology comes with seemingly unlimited offspring: new materials, equipment, systems, processes, and practices are being introduced at an unprecedented pace. In fact, the great though intangible challenge is the rate of change, the speed with which new elements appear that can transform the nature of tasks and the products. Not only does change come faster, but it is constantly more far-reaching in its effects.

When the first Industrial Revolution occurred early in the nineteenth century, the worker had to learn to tend and use the new machines. Objects went off production lines into packing cases, and new forms of transportation took them on roads, rivers, and rails, and eventually by air. Discoveries supplied power to move objects and link people: steam and combustion power, electricity, telephone, and radio started connecting people and products.

Today we have new and radically different means of connection. To the uninitiated, it is magic of a higher order. Computers, television, satellites, and teleconferencing revolutionize the routines of working, even as they create new products like information and education. This time the agent of revolution, the computer, not only automates production with more continuity and control than earlier mechanized processes, but it also can tell us what is going on *inside* the process. According to Shoshana Zuboff's *In the Age of the Smart Machine*,

> The same technology simultaneously generates information about the underlying productive and administrative processes through which an organization accomplishes its work. It provides a deeper level of transparency to activities that had been either partially or completely opaque.[3]

And we may add parenthetically that it is the same remarkable technological ability that allows us to view and study the learning process as it goes on in human beings. When applied to this purpose, research is peering through what has been the opaque area of how individuals learn most effectively.

Computerized processes are well advanced in the workplace; they have already wrought a transformation and redesigned the environment. Whether in banks, retail stores, and hospitals, or on factory floors, a new age has been born. As it grows and develops, it never rests. Change is the one constant factor, which leads to the second sure fact: training must become retraining—a continual process—if we are to keep up with our own inventions and meet tomorrow's changes.

Each process or product introduced imposes a learning requirement on workers, from an incremental upgrading of skills to general retraining. Of course, automated processes can also *lower* the skills needed in positions, turning skilled workers into mere attendants. Or jobs can be eliminated outright, causing dislocation that often requires complete retraining for another type of work. For many who remain, however, the job becomes more interesting and knowledge-intensive, requiring additional learning. Whatever the effects, the change introduced carries educational requirements with it.

Major infusions of technology can alter an entire organization. In manufacturing companies, for instance, the new wave of computer-controlled flexible manufacturing systems requires more intellectually demanding skills in workers who operate them. Optimum performance also demands management systems that give workers more responsibility and initiative. Such flexible systems are incompatible with a rigid, top-down hierarchy. This means a shift to a more horizontal organization in which both managers and workers must learn to handle different roles.

As one corporate officer explains, changing to a "flat structure" in his company meant training professionals to take more responsibility, to sharpen analysis and judgment, and to improve communication skills. It meant cutting out some middle managers and placing professionals in closer contact with corporate offices. It is a leaner organization, and communication is more direct; each manager has more discretionary power and greater control over cost, efficiency, service, and productivity. In effect, managers have wider spans of control.

While managers and professionals adjusted to changing roles, the computerization of the same company required 10,000 employees to learn basic skills in programming and data processing and analysis. And the training spectrum goes still farther. The workers skilled in one part of the manufacturing process must now learn another: multiple skills are necessary as the production line becomes flexible. The answer to "deskilling" lies in the learning of multiple skills. With technical aids, workers' skills expand and their roles become not only more flexible—along with the system—but also broader and more valuable.

New technologies have further led to a quickened competition in the marketplace. Companies must continually expand their offerings of goods and services and improve those they already offer or risk losing business to competitors. Intensified competition is forcing organizations to shorten "cycle time," the elapsed time from the conception of a new product or service to its delivery for sale. Initiatives to expand the product line and reduce cycle time generally emphasize teamwork across functional lines and enlist employees at all levels to think in terms of innovation and market responsiveness. Management does not will these new ways of working and thinking into existence. They must be taught through informal and formal means, and they are aided tremendously by telecommunications with satellite delivery that can quickly reach the marketing and sales people and customers.

Too often companies fail to prepare employees for this rapid process; the training itself takes time and it must obviously take place in advance of the expected outcome. Longer-term goals cannot be reached via short-sighted preparation: the time taken in training will prove to be essential to winning. But as competition accelerates the rate of technological change under way, the question is whether we can even keep up with training for the work force, not to mention provide it in advance of demand.

The New Worker

Training programs will need further adjustments and delivery methods to fit the new life-styles and values that individuals are bringing to their jobs. A new kind of worker emerges, coming with changing attitudes toward work. According to Daniel Yankelovich, people want more self-expression and a wider range of choices; they want to feel a part of the work effort, to find self-fulfillment, and to have opportunities for growth. Not valuing money alone, and not holding the attitude that work is a sacrifice or a necessary evil, the new worker seeks creativity and participation in the process. Yankelovich, seeing the change as a "huge rise in individualism in the workplace," points out that the "powerful surge in entrepreneurship" captures these desires and values and embodies the essence of autonomy and individuality.[4]

Certainly the entrepreneurial spirit may be at work in the great numbers of small businesses being created. The changing corporate structure that gives more responsibility to the worker may also accommodate the desire to participate more fully and see the results of one's work. Indeed, employers are recognizing the new workers and in pronounced ways adjusting jobs to fit their needs.

New patterns are interrupting the uniform, standardized routine of work for eight hours a day in centralized locations. "Flextime" schedules permit job sharing and part-time assignments; other arrangements allow the four-day week with ten hours each day. Milwaukee's local government is a leader in such innovation. The county executive, David F. Schulz, says the city is responding to a trend that is evident everywhere. "There has been a sea-change. Employers value their employees more. We're fitting the job to the employee and not the employee to the job."[5] Incidentally, for more than a decade, Milwaukee has given government workers tuition subsidies to keep abreast of their fields.

As hours shift, so does the location of the job. New means of communication free employees to do their work at home and electronically submit it. For many types of work today this is not only satisfactory, but some say that concentration and productivity improve. Forward-looking employers might well ask whether it is necessary to expand physical facilities in the central office or whether it would be smarter to give more employees computers for the home.

Changing hours and changing places for work will mean that more alternative routes are needed for educational advancement. Independent, highly motivated workers may be expected to find their own ways. But for all the others, training programs must be both easily and constantly available. Flexibility in work hours can also be used to accommodate training periods and fit them regularly into time schedules.

A Diverse Work Force

The educational task before us is awesome. Demographic facts indicate that two-thirds of the people who will be working in the year 2000 are already in the work force today.[6] This means simply that the majority of adults now employed must have opportunities for retraining or new learning if jobs are to be maintained and productivity improved in this decade.

Further, as Americans live longer and wish to go on working, many find themselves outdistanced by the pace of change. All too often the people forced into early retirement are those who have fallen behind, yet they may have years of productivity left. Such tragic circumstances point up the importance of retraining for mid-career workers.

In addition, new entrants into the force will include increasing numbers of minorities—the population segment growing most rapidly. The number of women, presently approaching half the work force, will also rise, although predictions do not call for as great a rate as in the 1970s. It is clear that training programs will need to be adjusted particularly for the widening diversity of people and their various educational levels. On the whole, those who will be entering the work force are not well matched to the types of jobs being created.

For the new jobs expected, forecasters say that more than half will require education *beyond* the high school level.[7] Since most of the new workers will be coming from minorities, of whom many are high school dropouts, the challenge to the schools and postsecondary institutions is immediate. Basic school reforms are under way, but they are late in coming. As a result, much remedial training is required, and it will continue to be needed at work force entry levels as well as in the ranks of older employees. Far too many adult workers are illiterate or operating only marginally and with difficulty. Without the basic skills there is nothing on which to build, no foundation for learning more.

Yet among those employed we also have large numbers of persons with postsecondary education. At least it can be presumed that they have some basis for learning. Twenty-six percent of all employed adults hold a college degree, and another 20 percent have studied one to three years beyond high school. Therefore, close to half of America's work force has had some college experience, up from 37 percent in 1978.

If it is true that those with education generally want more, there are many who will welcome additional opportunities for training and take advantage of them. Nearly half the work force stands ready with some preparation and probably motivation for learning more. It is the other half, including the new entry-level workers, who deserve our first attention and more effective programs. The dichotomy between those who have had advanced

educational experience and those who have not reflects the dangerous social and economic schism in our country. What has been
called *The Forgotten Half*[8] constitutes the greatest challenge for
training efforts for the work force.

Altogether the range of people in need of learning is very wide
and long, extending from those who require instruction in basic
skills to the technologically sophisticated professionals, and from
workers of many types who must add another skill to managers
and executives who must learn new ways of dealing both with people and with new processes and new organizational structures. The
challenge is tremendous. But it can and must be met.

A Look Ahead

While acknowledging the value of general studies and the liberal arts, we focus in this study primarily on the connection
between education and the world of work, a connection vitally affecting the economic future of the nation and the well-being of our
people. Fortunately there are great resources upon which to draw
in building the adult training network.

There is considerable diversity among those who provide
worker education and training, and they operate more or less independently of one another. Each has its own history from which
a distinctive training program has emerged for its own purposes.
Yet our cross section of examples from the different providers reveals that they do, in fact, have much in common. Aside from
orientation programs introducing workers to the special company
or institution, and some highly sensitive training that pertains to
research or a new product or instrument, the curricula of the various providers resemble each other remarkably.

Much of the learning is generic in nature; it is not company-
specific or proprietary to a particular organization. Basic training
for an information systems technician is similar whether for an industry, a government office, or the military. Therefore the course

is often transferable. Superior instruction can be shared and so reduce mediocrity as well as redundancy.

At the very least, each provider could profit greatly from analysis of other training programs and methods for instruction. Models of best practice can be found in government classrooms for civilian or military personnel as well as in corporate classrooms or new course materials in the marketplace.

Education in many forms and formats *is* available and effective for America's workers, who are going back to school in growing numbers. No one needs to argue further for continuing education; it is a fact of life. Many parts of a powerful training network already exist. Our study aims to examine them and suggest their extension through various delivery methods needed to meet the goals ahead.

To simplify the discussion, we do not differentiate sharply between education and training. It may be legitimate to consider education a broader-based and longer-lasting kind of learning distinct from training, which tends to come in shorter and more narrowly focused packages. But the lines blur too easily in common usage, as in medical training or medical education. It becomes laborious to distinguish constantly and adds little to the broad view of adult learning opportunities. In our examples, the nature and purpose of the training discussed will be clear from the description itself. Further, we use "work force" broadly to include all workers—laborers, technicians, managers, professionals, and executives—regardless of levels.

There is naturally a high degree of selectivity in the examples given; our choice was based on whether a program was typical and fairly indicative of the larger scene or whether it was new, suggesting a trend or a model that could hold promise for others. In summary, then, this report on learning for the workplace might be thought of as a guided tour, presented in three parts.

First we consider the resources for adult learning in the United States with a focus on the major providers outside the traditional education system. The outsiders are legion, with untold numbers of people engaged in programs supported by large, effective organizations and institutions trying to educate their workers. We show their size and scope, their overall contribution to the task of training and retraining the work force.

Higher education enters specifically as we cite segments of the postsecondary system for their job training. Community colleges, vocational education, and proprietary schools appear for their contributions as well as the professional schools of universities. Aside from these references and comments on career-oriented training in colleges and universities, we do not analyze the traditional educational establishment. We include only its direct role in job and career training for the work force.

Because the task is very great indeed, and the providers cannot meet the challenge either singly or together, we devote significant attention in chapter 2 to the technological resources that can extend educational opportunities and reach more workers. These innovative instructional delivery systems use new media and take advantage of computer networks and satellites to deliver training anyplace in the world. In this section we analyze each medium, give examples of its use, and chart what seem to be its limitations as well as its effectiveness for instruction.

One new development emerging from research laboratories deserves special attention in chapter 3: artificial intelligence as an aid in training and education. In the teaching of some subjects it is a most intelligent tutor, and applied differently it helps to create an expert system that can stand beside the worker and provide guidance and answers to problems encountered. It is a new type of on-the-job training, and it may offer great possibilities in the future.

In the second part of the report, we turn to the workers and describe what training opportunities they have. We look first at the skilled trades and technical fields, presenting workers in construction where apprenticeship is strong, office administrative assistants, information systems technicians, and those encountering the new factory with computer-integrated manufacturing systems.

Each of the fields chosen is vital to a healthy economy, each represents a large segment of the work force, and each has been directly affected by technological changes that transform their tasks and make further education a necessity.

In the next chapter, we move to view the education of America's managers, the group that historically has received the greatest attention and share of training dollars. What is their curriculum, and is it effective for the challenges they face and the decisions they must make? The old question of whether management is an art or a science resurfaces, and it remains unsolved.

And finally in this section, we turn to the advanced professionals and what is being done to update their knowledge, which is subject to obsolescence ever more rapidly. The problems of engineers and computer scientists receive first attention, but closely following are the expanding programs to bring the latest information to physicians and attorneys and to bankers and accountants. As professional people, they supply essential informed leadership.

For these segments of the work force—skilled technicians, managers, and professionals—we draw examples from the various providers to see the contributions from each toward the opportunities available. We note, for example, the labor unions' role particularly for apprenticeship and for skilled technicians; we describe management training in the corporation, the military, and government; and we add professional associations to the mix of providers for the professions.

The third and final part of our report deals with those whom training programs fail to reach or adequately serve. They are what we call the missing persons. These are people outside the economic system and the opportunities it offers: workers displaced by changing industries, unemployed youth, immigrants and refugees, and those on welfare rolls. They share the common denominators of poverty and often illiteracy. They constitute a distressing failure of a democratic society that prides itself on "the general welfare" of its people.

In the last chapter, we conclude that the issues examined call for public responsibility and action. We call for strong federal policies and support, and more effective state programs. Private sector initiatives and more and more partnerships among the providers must be encouraged. Government participates in some of these collaborative ventures with other sectors, and yet cooperation is not prevalent in state and federal programs themselves. Separate legislation designed piecemeal for certain purposes and assigned to one federal department or another discourages cooperation with other programs. Efforts toward interagency coordination in Washington, D.C., have not worked. After an anlaysis of programs and current legislation, we suggest how some programs might be better coordinated and reach more people among the millions who need training in order to enter or reenter the work force and lead productive lives.

Problems are apparent, to be sure, but so are possibilities. It is not a bleak horizon. Common sense dictates some recommendations; others are more complicated and require the further consideration of people engaged in providing training. Above all, our national leadership must take decisive action.

Worker education is already a headline issue, primarily because people are worried about the United States' competitive position in the world economy. Their emphasis is not on learning as a pleasant and personally enriching experience but on the growing realization that improving productivity is directly and inevitably related to the skill of the work force. It is not the first time that economic change has driven educational reform and expansion. Today's impetus is not unusual.

It is significant, however, that powerful forces have entered adult education. Many are recognizing the imperative need to improve and extend learning for the work force, and some are taking action. New alliances appear as collaboration among sponsors develops. The network grows and alternative ways of learning are invented to give training when and as it is needed.

PART

I

THE LEARNING
RESOURCES

1

CLASSROOMS FOR ADULTS

There is no way to assess accurately either the monetary value of the various training programs in effect for the work force or the total numbers of adults enrolled from time to time. At best, estimates suffice. But the totality of resources becomes apparent as the major providers or sponsors of education are described with the general types of training given. Details of programs are in subsequent chapters.

Here we start with those outside traditional education and in the order of their magnitude: corporations, the military services, government programs for civilians, and labor unions. Next comes the profitable side of the learning industry expanding in the sale of training. And then we consider those segments of the educational establishment that contribute most directly to training for jobs and careers, such as community colleges and technical institutes, trade schools, and the universities' professional schools. Their contributions are important both in their own preparation of workers and in their expanding alliances with other sponsors to offer training.

Colleges and universities, of course, provide fundamental education in the arts and sciences apart from the requirements of specific careers, but that is another book. This report simply refers to the graduates' choice of major fields, and recognizes that large numbers of older adults are reentering traditional classrooms for job-related reasons.

Corporate Sponsors

By far the greatest amount of training and retraining takes place in corporate classrooms.[1] Expenditures are estimated from $30 billion annually upwards. Our guess is around $60 billion for formal training—without the wages of employees while they study. If wages are included, the amount would double. Lately, however, even those estimates have been outdistanced by SRI International in a study on corporate education and training. If informal on-the-job training is included, their report suggests, more than $200 billion is annually expended.[2]

It becomes a numbers game, once again depending on what is counted, but on any count, corporations appear to be the largest providers of adult education. SRI says, "About 70% of the retraining of U.S. workers takes place in corporate education and training programs." That is an exceedingly high percentage, but it includes learning on the job, which is not only the most prevalent form of training but may also be the most effective.

Whether the training is given in the company or sponsored by it outside, significant numbers of workers have access to it. The American Society for Training and Development says that some 14 million workers are served each year,[3] which is far more than the number of students enrolled in four-year colleges and universities. At the other end of the scale of estimates is the total number of 35.5 million individuals receiving formal, employer-sponsored education. The higher figure, coming from the 1989 annual survey of *Training* magazine, is based on companies employing 100 or more people.[4] Translated, the higher estimate means that about one-third of the work force is getting training. That leaves the majority of workers still to be reached, but at least many adults are learning under their employers' auspices.

Further analysis finds them concentrated mainly in large companies and certain industries. More training is obviously necessary in high-tech industries and manufacturing companies that require high levels of knowledge and research, and as the technologies spread into other industries applying them, more workers there require additional training too. This is happening in financial services, public administration, communications, utilities, and other kinds of service industries.

Smaller numbers of trainees are found in smaller companies and in fields that are not changing so much. Yet it is in small, private businesses with fewer than 500 employees that job opportunities are generally growing, and it is here that some 48 percent of the total work force is employed. This presents a serious challenge, since small companies lack the funds and programs for training. Hence a very large number of workers are denied opportunities for improvement.

Similarly, workers in different job categories get varying degrees of attention and opportunities for training. Managers, technological professionals, and other technicians, as well as sales and marketing personnel, receive more training than those in clerical and other positions that commonly require less educational preparation. The American Society for Training and Development indicates that employees aged 25 to 45 get more than two-thirds of the training, and white males dominate in numbers served. Women get a surprisingly large amount, according to this report, but Hispanics and African-Americans, whether male or female, generally receive much, much less.[5]

An encouraging note for production workers, cautiously added by the *Training* magazine report, suggested that the old model of training emphasis was cracking. As management layers were disappearing in the new company structure, and production workers were assuming more duties, there were signs in 1989 indicating more formal training for the blue-collar worker: "More production workers *per organization* are getting trained and each one is receiving more hours of training." In fact, the report stated that the increase in the number of hours over the last two years had brought production workers to the *average* of nearly 34 hours annually—the same as the average for senior managers in formal training. Office and clerical employees, however, remained low in comparison and received "a pittance compared with the rest of the groups."[6]

Among the recipients of training in the lower echelons are workers who lack the basic skills of reading, writing, and arithmetic. We discuss the problems of the illiterate later, but here, in considering education sponsored by industry, we must point out that most companies are doing very little. They try to avoid the problem altogether by not hiring those who are ill-prepared. But we should not fault employers too severely for not correcting society's ills: they react after all to the first demands of business. Assessment of their own workers, however, reveals that the problem already exists within their ranks. Furthermore, low literacy levels glaringly reveal themselves as new technologies require higher skills.

It comes as no surprise to learn that manufacturing industries that offer the most remedial instruction are emphasizing math skills needed in the statistical control of processes. Computers do not deal well with inaccurate input; if they recognize it, they reject it, but if they don't know it, they will process it and reach erroneous results.

Many studies have been made of late about the extent of remedial training going on in corporations. There are great differences here too, partly due to poor definition of "basic skills." But allowing for the confusion, it seems that about one-third of the larger companies offer their workers such help.[7]

Moreover, as the labor pool shortage worsens and more applicants come from undereducated minorities, companies can expect to strengthen their teaching programs for new employees. The growing burden should not be too onerous financially since training costs are written off in large part as an expense of doing business. It does mean, however, broadening corporate curricula and more emphasis on lower levels of workers. And it is an additional handicap for U.S. companies competing with others abroad.

The overall view reveals inequalities, and many of those most in need of training are not getting it. Nevertheless, the corporate world is contributing heavily to adult training, and their efforts are not likely to diminish simply because their own self-interest is at stake. Companies on average spend about 1 percent of their payroll on training programs,[8] but this proportion can go considerably higher depending on the nature of the company, its needs, and the philosophy of its leadership. Some have guidelines for investment policies in training. One enlightened company, Motorola, spends almost 2.6 percent of its payroll and requires all divisions to spend at least 1.5 percent of payroll; it also recommends minimum hours of training for each employee.[9]

The corporate contribution has added value since it offers training connected to a job—in the context of employment—and capitalizes on worker motivation. Moreover, corporate instructional programs are likely to be well-conceived and organized for stated and clear objectives. For these reasons, learning in the workplace for most workers usually takes precedence over outside school instruction. And companies provide the greatest amount of training in-house where they have more control over the training format and environment.

Adult training generally profits from being attached to employment and the place of work. After all, individuals may spend 15 years from the age of six onward in the educational system, but they spend 40 or more years in jobs, earning a living. New skills and knowledge must be acquired over the latter two-thirds of a person's lifetime, when he or she is working. So if we wish to reach adults to upgrade skills and abilities, it is best done in connection with their work.

The Military Services

In expenditure and numbers served, the second largest provider of adult learning is the military. In fiscal 1989, the military was scheduled to spend nearly $18 billion on formal training for officers and enlisted personnel at its many schools and training bases.[10] This sum included pay and allowances for trainees, trainers, and administrators, and the cost of operating and maintaining training facilities, as well as related equipment and construction. It also included training for reservists, but it omitted the cost of training maneuvers and on-the-job training. J. D. Fletcher of the Institute for Defense Analysis claims that if the costs of all military training—formal and informal—were added up, the sum would exceed the reported cost of formal training by a factor of three or four, approaching $50–70 billion.[11]

Compared with all other major providers of adult learning, the military is most organized, as one would hope, and training progresses in rank and file with the nature of responsibilities. From basic training for all recruits and officers (except those commissioned by direct appointment), the steps are clear and assigned for preparation in special duties. Training usually accompanies a change in assignment and is almost always required to qualify for a promotion in rank.

The system for officers is not unlike the corporate structure that provides for managerial training from supervisors to first-line managers to middle and senior levels to top executives. And for high-ranking military officers, too, the curriculum broadens to help their professional development in leadership, military science, and advanced political and technical fields that are taught in the war colleges and at civilian institutions. Unlike policy in many companies, however, the military's training progression holds for all officers across the board; few exceptions are made.

While enlisted personnel generally work in more specialized skills and training is so directed, they too have functional training that cuts across job specialties. The basic and technical training of recruits and officers amounts to the bulk of formal military training; only about 30 percent is for subsequent retraining.[12] Total participation in formal training (measured by the military in training loads) means that 250,000 members, both active and reserve, of the four services undergo training on an average day.[13] That is a very good daily average for forces totaling nearly 3.8 million in active and reserve ranks.[14]

Military terminology makes another distinction that could be of interest to corporate trainers and other providers. Courses are divided into "collective" training vs. individual training. The former, given for groups—a squad, aircrew, or battalion—is an exercise in teamwork where all members learn cooperatively. Since corporate curricula include numerous courses to teach teamwork, trainers might well analyze the military's collective approach, particularly for performance goals that are not based solely on discipline.

In addition to formal training, the military offers support for service members to advance their skills, obtain a diploma or degree, or satisfy an interest during off-duty time through what it calls "voluntary education"—in the civilian world, continuing education. In fiscal 1987, nearly 780,000 military personnel were enrolled in undergraduate and graduate courses through voluntary education, and more than 410,000 took noncredit courses including language training and basic skills.[15] Among the outcomes that year were:

- 12,500 high school diplomas or GEDs
- 19,300 associate degrees
- 6,000 baccalaureate degrees
- 7,000 graduate degrees.

In a number of ways, the military also makes it easy to take courses or earn academic credit. The Defense Activity for Non-Traditional Education Support (DANTES) administers testing and programs to enable service members to earn college credits for knowledge gained outside the classroom, including skills acquired in military training. The Community College of the Air Force grants degrees based on military training and on courses taken at accredited postsecondary institutions throughout the country.

Some civilian institutions also have opened doors to assist military personnel: the Servicemembers Opportunity Colleges is a consortium of more than 400 institutions that have minimized residency requirements, recognized nontraditional achievement through measurements such as the College-Level Examination Program, and eased the transfer of college credits.

Each service also has programs permitting selected persons to study full-time toward degrees, and most services reimburse tuition fully. But all require a payback of service from the beneficiary. Under the new G.I. Bill, which took effect in 1985, active-duty personnel can receive education benefits of $300 per month for 36 months. In return they must agree to complete three years of service and take a pay cut of $100 per month for 12 months. Reservists are entitled to $140 per month for 36 months in exchange for six years of service. Since the bill took effect, the services have witnessed a surge in the numbers signing up for these benefits. In fiscal 1987, about 69 percent of eligible military members—those on active duty, reservists, and veterans—sought the benefits.[16]

Educational opportunities are a powerful recruiting tool for the armed forces. They honestly pay off on their promises and do it so well that they create problems for themselves. Colonel Joseph Shanahan, chief of training policy for the Department of Defense, says that "the more training the military gives a person, the more marketable that person becomes in the civilian sector."[17] The services are not only losing highly trained technicians to industry but also the instructors who trained them.[18] Each year 300,000 men and women return to the civilian work force, where employers eagerly hire them because their training has been targeted to specific performance goals, and they are accustomed to discipline and work standards.

In a sense, society recaptures the public expenditure for their training. But there remains a serious problem for the military in a never-ending battle to keep its forces trained for the fast-changing technological weapons and devices of modern warfare. The challenge to the military is perhaps even greater than it is for the general work force.

The Federal Government

The federal government spends far less for the training and education of its 2.1 million civilian employees, but still has extensive programs throughout its agencies and departments around the world. Seven thousand people comprise the training and development community that serves federal workers. The latest official estimate (fiscal 1986) for the total annual expenditure is $580 million.[19] No one is sure. Some say the number is more than $1 billion.

One reason for the difficulty in precision is that training is not a primary mission of the government any more than it is in the private corporate sector. Therefore, training expenditures are often buried in budgets for operations. The numbers supplied, which the agencies choose to report to the Office of Personnel Management, often reflect only part of the whole. Furthermore, much of the training that goes on in federal agencies is not centrally managed. The training director of the Veterans Administration, for example, says that the costs reported in the department's training budget are for only the small number of programs it manages centrally, while most programs take place in its hospitals and are therefore folded into the operations budget.

The Grace Commission's *Report of the President's Private Sector Survey on Cost Control* (1981) referred to the general ignorance of the total spent but acknowledged that developing a system to gather accurate cost data might not be worth the expense. Confusing categorical breakdowns complicate the picture. The government defines long-term training as lasting at least 121 days, but it usually refers to for-credit courses taken at a college or university by advanced professionals. This kind of training is on the decline; it remains important only at a few departments, including

Defense, Commerce, Health and Human Services, the National Aeronautics and Space Administration, and the Veterans Administration.

Otherwise, the training scene is quite extensive. A computerized directory, administered by the American Society for Training and Development, lists 20,000 courses from some 20 government providers. Courses range from animal husbandry to regression analysis, with every kind of technical, administrative, and generic skill in between. In fiscal 1986 there were at least 1.8 million instances of training, averaging around 30 hours each.[20] That figure approaches the 40 hours annually required by some of the largest U.S. corporations.

Still, education and training are not a high priority for federal agency and department administrators. Because of the loss of many of the most qualified civil servants during the Reagan administration—what has become known as the "Beltway brain drain"—this is a serious problem. And training is not high on the list of recommendations of the privately funded National Commission on the Public Service.[21] Perhaps the civilian agencies should look at the success of their colleagues in the military who are using education (and other means) as an enticement to recruit the best and the brightest.

Labor Unions

While their training programs are little known to the public, the labor unions are major providers of adult learning. Apprenticeships are probably the most recognized, serving more than a quarter of a million workers each year. Depending on the trade, apprenticeships can last from one to four years. They combine on-the-job training, classroom instruction, and independent study. On completing the courses, apprentices become journeymen, a most respected title among the trades.

After that, no further training is required, but labor officials estimate that as many as 8 percent of their journeymen join in some sort of improvement training each year.[22] These officials readily agree that more should be participating because of the continual introduction of new technological tools and new materials. But the pattern of ongoing learning is not well established, and at the end of a day's work the classroom is not especially inviting.

Money for these programs comes from negotiated wage contracts, and the sums can be very large indeed. The construction industry alone spends half a billion dollars a year on training apprentices and journeymen.[23] A handful of unions and employer associations in this industry have set up national training trust funds. The Plumbers and Pipefitters Union and the National Contractors Association, for example, set up such a fund in the early 1950s. In the years since, more than $53 million has been spent in training union members in addition to the millions given each year to local apprenticeship training committees. The plumbers also spend $54 million a year operating a national system of 330 local schools that provide apprenticeship training and journeyman upgrading in welding and other technical skills. The sheet metal workers, bricklayers, painters, and ironworkers unions have established similar funds.

Massive layoffs in the steel, auto, and communications industries have led their unions to push for retraining programs in their national contract negotiations. Their efforts have resulted in training funds administered jointly by the union and management, often in an organization created for the purpose. These we discuss in detail later, but their general size and scope mentioned here are impressive.

Under the UAW-Ford fund since 1983, some 45,000 employed and unemployed union members have had training at 35 locations throughout the country. The Communications Workers of America—another leader in this movement—and the International Brotherhood of Electrical Workers have joint programs with AT&T that served more than 35,000 workers between 1986 and 1989. These programs have tremendous potential both in the sums of money available and in the numbers of workers reached.

The UAW-General Motors "Nickel Fund," for example, generated $250 million in one year.

Most of these funds furnish training in basic skills, literacy, technical fields, and other areas to improve union members' job prospects and advancement opportunities. Some integrate support for educational institutions, like the Communications Workers' agreement with Mountain Bell. That contract allocates $7.6 million over three years to support a network of community colleges and vocational-technical schools in which workers can receive career counseling, technical training, and for-credit instruction. Some 28,000 workers, both employed and laid-off, are eligible for these benefits.

As major sponsors of adult training, labor unions are even harder to assess for total numbers. Except for the national efforts, training programs belong to local jurisdictions, and reporting mechanisms to AFL-CIO headquarters are nonexistent. Besides, the labor movement is not a monolithic organization that operates nationally from a central office.

Although this situation complicates our assessment, it does not hide the fact that extensive and valuable programs are available under union leadership. And they should step up their efforts to increase cooperative training programs that can help millions in the work force not only to maintain their jobs but also to advance through education. Moreover, just as training programs reflect the self-interest of employers—whether corporate or military—so they can serve the self-interest of the labor movement in a period of declining membership due to job loss. The antidote is more training to promote multiple skills that will enable the worker to keep the job.

A Profitable Business

Around the major providers of adult training another segment of the learning industry is developing with vendors and third parties servicing the other trainers and the public. Supplies of learning materials and seminars and gurus from the private sector multiply daily. Anyone with an idea and salesmanship can join the multitude. Estimates claim that ten times as many vendors are selling training services today as ten years ago. "One database for trainers lists 91,000 seminars available for corporate use," says one report.[24] The topics range from the physical to the metaphysical, from behavioral skills and attitudinal change to every conceivable aspect of management, from esoteric scientific interests and technical fields to the sublime and the ridiculous.

Some subjects provoke humor, such as the newly announced courses on how to "Cut Your Corporate Clutter Quickly," which instruct on cutting paperwork with separate strategies for management and support staff. These are video training programs with participants' workbooks and a facilitator's guide, all for $449 from the Encyclopedia Britannica Educational Corporation's training and development division. But when one thinks of the overwhelming amount of paper being regurgitated by technical means, the idea may not be so funny.

To be sure, there are many excellent products and programs. Moreover, outside consultants, among the vendors, can play an objective and knowledgeable role in planning for courses and their delivery. Many very big companies are also swelling the vendor ranks. Not only have print publishers like McGraw-Hill and John Wiley & Sons moved into electronic and technological aids for instruction, but also large corporations are selling training to each other. While competition is severe and products naturally vary in quality, this part of the learning industry has real potential in helping to bring America's work force into the next technological age.

Educational Institutions

A look inside the established educational system for its contribution to workers' training reveals the community college as the dominant provider. The least traditional and newest child on the block, with a 50-year history of astounding growth, is the major contributor to adult learning for job-related purposes. While total enrollment at four-year institutions remained about the same over the decade prior to 1986, two-year colleges grew phenomenally to an enrollment approaching five million. An equal number attended on a noncredit basis, so their grand total was nearly ten million adults, most of whom were in studies directly applicable to the work force.

Situated within commuting distance for most of its students, the public two-year institution offers postsecondary education to many adults for whom other doors are closed. Those who lack time or money or sometimes academic strength find opportunities here. By and large, community colleges have added remedial and developmental courses as necessary to compensate for failures in the lower school system. They are more flexible in scheduling course hours and welcoming part-time students of all ages. And their cost is modest compared with other postsecondary institutions. Tuition and fees at public community colleges averaged $660 in 1986–1987 as against $1,414 for in-state students at public four-year institutions.[25]

It is to these two-year colleges that minorities turn for training. They enroll in growing and disproportionate numbers. Hispanics, for example, are six times more likely to be enrolled in a community college than in a four-year program.[26] In California's community college system, 38 percent of the one million students represent minorities.[27] And slightly more than half the people enrolled in credit courses in all community colleges are women.

The concentration of minorities and women in these institutions constitutes a divisive trend that a democratic society must not overlook. Other training opportunities are not eequally available to these people—a fact that should give pause to our makers of public policy. Other educational enclaves are closed to the minorities that are becoming the majority of our population in many parts of the country. Furthermore, most community college students do not transfer to four-year institutions but go directly into the work force, usually in entry-level jobs. Without more advanced training their futures in this technological age are limited: they are more apt to be in single-skill jobs that become dead ends. The system is askew.

Nevertheless, community colleges are doing the yeoman's job for the work force. And many older adults are reversing direction as they return to school from the workplace. Their choice of subjects and skills is extensive, from database management to many technical fields and liberal arts. Overall, however, just over 25 percent of graduates take their associate degrees in business and management. The pattern of choice reflects that of graduates of four-year schools and suggests that the work force is getting an inordinate number of people "schooled" in business. Other popular subjects are computer and information sciences, engineering technology, and health sciences—again similar to the fields chosen for more advanced degrees.

Besides training individuals for entry-level positions, community colleges have further expanded their mission to serve local community needs by acting quickly to cooperate with business and industry in their areas. On a very large scale, they are providing customized training for employees, tailoring courses to fit the particular company's needs. Since it will be recalled that many workers in small companies lack training programs, these courses for local businesses are especially valuable. Moreover, the colleges are attracting attention from large national corporations too, which see the advantages of training near their operations in many states. In community colleges throughout the country, General Motors has sponsored such a program for auto mechanics servicing computerized systems in cars.

Community, technical, and junior colleges are a large part of the complex for vocational education in the country, and they receive more than a third of the public funds allotted under the Carl D. Perkins Vocational Education Act.[28] But there are other types of institutions contributing as well. The *Digest of Education Statistics*,

1988 lists 8,956 vocational and technical institutions considered noncollegiate. Most are private, including 6,329 proprietary or for-profit schools and 1,797 nonprofit institutes. In many instances they offer courses comparable to community colleges, though usually of shorter duration and more intense.

The trade or proprietary school, because of its private ownership and profit-making goal, is at best a stepchild of the education system. Of late it has been under severe criticism for unethical recruitment and even fraudulent practices. Some charges are no doubt true, but the child deserves defense. Further, our purpose is to examine the extended family of training opportunities for adults in the United States—wherever they may be and under whatever auspices. Training can be a remunerative business, and many trade schools are thriving with healthy profits, large enrollments, and effective programs. Dorothy Fenwick, executive director of the Accrediting Commission of the National Association of Trade and Technical Schools, believes that 80 percent of the schools are probably sound, that not much is known about 15 percent, and that 5 percent are no doubt fraudulent.

Regardless of the scandals, proprietary schools are giving specifically job-related courses to some 1.5 million adults. Many are supplying the short skill courses and behavioral discipline needed in the work force, in some cases exposing their students for the first time to disciplined work and study habits, promptness and courtesy, and a certain level of social skill.

One of the chief advantages of a trade school, according to Janice Parker, president of the Taylor Business School in Chicago and a veteran of vocational education, is that it requires more than just skills training. A Taylor student must dress for school as he or she would for work and maintain the decorum of the workplace in the classroom. Resumé preparation, dressing for interviews, insistence on punctuality, civility, and performance are hallmarks of the good trade school. For those who lack economic and social advantages, such behavioral orientation can make a decisive difference in getting and holding a job.

Supporters of trade schools point out that personalized attention and insistent discipline are "hand-holding" that community colleges or other public training programs cannot afford; yet these are especially valuable aspects in training students who have failed in public schools. Visits to a number of well-regarded, privately owned schools confirm that quality training is available in many classrooms.

Taken together, the two-year colleges, vocational-technical institutes, and trade schools are making a worthy and practical contribution to the lives of millions of adults, most of whom are or will shortly be in the American work force. In many instances, their skills and knowledge will be geared closely to the occupational need.

On different levels, of course, colleges and universities are sending graduates into the work force with specific career and professional preparation. As mentioned earlier, baccalaureate degrees in business and management far exceed any other field, and on the graduate level theirs has been a bullish market for a decade. Much of the increase is attributable to an influx of women. In 1987, women received nearly 38 percent of the M.B.A. degrees awarded.[29] Over the period from 1978 to 1986, the number of female M.B.A. graduates rose 115 percent.

The upward movement of business enrollments and graduates has been accompanied by an expansion in the number of institutions offering such degrees. A Ford Foundation report estimated that in 1958 about 125 institutions were offering M.B.A. degrees, with nine schools accounting for half the degrees awarded.[30] In 1988, the generally accepted estimate of schools offering graduate business degrees was 700, although only 233 were accredited by the American Assembly of Collegiate Schools of Business. The work force clearly has an ample number of potential managers.

Such, however, is not the case with engineers. The National

Research Council noted a 10 percent increase in engineering doctorates between 1986 and 1987,[31] but the numbers include a significant number of foreign nationals. Foreign students earned 51 percent of the doctorates given in engineering in 1987, compared with 29 percent a decade earlier. Of course many remain in the United States and so help to alleviate our shortage. Many people of Asiatic origin, for example, work in research laboratories and teach engineering and other sciences. But we are still not producing sufficient numbers of engineers and other badly needed scientists. For the professional people in these fields who are already in the work force, advanced training is essential, and programs carrying information on the latest discoveries are a fast-growing part of the educational delivery system.

Among the fields that have shown greater increases over the last decade are the computer and information sciences and communications—areas obviously vital to our economic development. Students are choosing subject matter with the job market in mind. Career or occupational choice continues to dominate the degree market. Although the liberal arts offer an ideal foundation for educational growth and certainly for adaptability in learning new fields, the fact remains that most graduates of postsecondary institutions are selecting studies that they believe will lead directly to employment.

As adults move on and off campuses studying part-time, their courses too are usually job related. In fact, most employers' tuition refund programs limit reimbursement to costs incurred for training pertinent to the job. This policy adds force to enrollment trends; jobs and advancement are healthy motivators. Professionals are returning periodically for recertification or advanced knowledge. The audience for higher education has profoundly changed: it is simply younger and older adults. Higher institutions are free to offer education and training to those who want to learn, regardless of age boundaries. The percentage rise is remarkable for all age groups, particularly those above 30, and all are above the ages thought—in the past—to be appropriate to the undergraduate years (see table 1). A recent College Board study states that almost half of all degree-seeking students are at least 25 years old, with those over 35 following close behind. The classroom has a more mature audience.

Table 1   Adults Enrolled in College

Ages	1970	1985	% Rise
25-29	1,074,000	1,953,000	82
30-34	487,000	1,261,000	159
35 +	823,000	1,885,000	129

Source: *Digest of Education Statistics 1988*, National Center for Education Statistics, U.S. Department of Education, Office of Educational Research and Improvement, Table 119, p. 143.

Unsurprisingly, with the heavier enrollment of adult students, part-time study is increasingly popular, whether in four-year or two-year institutions. Part-time students account for more than 40 percent of the total 12.3 million college enrollment, and a large percentage of those part-timers are women over 30.[32] Indeed, two-thirds of the college population over 34 are female.[33]

Part of the explanation for this new landscape lies in social and economic changes in this country during the past four decades. The move toward a service economy, with fewer well-paying man-ufacturing jobs, has meant that enormous numbers of people who earned quite good incomes from those jobs have had to start over again in mid-life, finish high school diplomas, and learn new skills and attitudes. Returning to campus is an obvious way to pick up many of the skills needed in high-technology industries. In the pro-cess, postsecondary education is changing dramatically as it serves more and more workers at all levels of employment.

The Task Before Us

America has extensive programs to educate the work force. Yet when evaluated against the present and continuing challenge of the technological advance, no educational provider—not the large corporations, the military, the government, the labor unions, the growing vendor group, or the colleges and universities—is adequate to the task. Each faces severe handicaps.

Colleges—community colleges included—and universities are hampered by obsolete equipment and entrenched curricula, as well as teaching patterns not adjusted for adults. They frequently lack up-to-date information as research moves quickly past the current technologies and faculty knowledge. The military has difficulty in training people for technological instruments that develop faster than instruction manuals can be written and instructors trained. Corporations are hard pressed to keep up with their own inventions and products ready for market. And labor unions grope to find their way in the new work environment.

Even when the major providers' training programs are considered together, the total resources in place cannot meet the need. More than just having continuous training available, we must expand the ways in which we educate and offer people the opportunity to learn. Today courses and information are available in standard classrooms, by correspondence and independent study, computer-assisted instruction, television, teleconferencing, satellite delivery, and many other means. There are massive databases full of information to be summoned by tapping a keyboard. With such means at our disposal, is there any reason why we cannot educate our work force more effectively? New systems and types of training are emerging from inventive sources, and those holding the most immediate answer for adult training needs may be the new delivery systems designed to take learning opportunities well beyond our present classrooms to adults wherever they may be.

2

DELIVERING INSTRUCTION

The magnitude of the task of educating and retraining America's workers requires the full use of delivery systems and the technological aids that are developing. Certainly traditional instructional methods alone cannot accomplish the task. Nor can the major providers just described do it unless they dramatically extend the reach of their classrooms and send instruction to many more workers. To offer people continuing access to learning, education has to be constantly available to them through convenient and economical means. Such availability is the promise of telecommunication delivery systems that reach homes, offices, classrooms and libraries, and factory floors.

Ironically, these technologies spring from the very revolution that has helped make issues of work force training so pressing. Revolutions always create new problems when they resolve old ones, but this time the new tools are capable of addressing the problems they've helped create. Telecommunication media can carry the message—in this case, instruction—and they can aid the *process* of learning as well.

Because their use is vital to solutions of the problems in training and productivity, we devote this chapter and the next to an analysis of various media and their use today. Some educational delivery systems have proven that they are as effective as traditional teaching for certain purposes, and some have far surpassed ordinary teaching in terms of the time spent in learning and the student's rate of retention. We report on these results. Other programs included are newer, more experimental, and have yet to be tested. The potential gain could be enormous *if* we supply content of quality for the media and select the technological means wisely for the goal.

Reactions to new technology in education have commonly been extreme in one direction or the other: some reject it out of hand because it is unfamiliar and upsetting to their entrenched routines and procedures in teaching, while others leap forward to embrace a new form—often only hardware—before it has been given substance. So it happened in the 1950s when television was hailed as having unlimited promise for classroom instruction and when teaching machines were tried, but soon went into schoolroom closets.

Today the story unfolds differently. The technologies are more powerful, their possibilities are greater, and we are more sophisticated about their presence among us. One of their greatest assets is their ability to interact with the person who is learning, to guide and suggest next steps, to correct mistakes, and measure the person's progress. Some technologies are exceedingly clever in teaching the process of problem solving. And many accommodate learning that is self-paced and individualized, features that have become characteristic of nontraditional approaches and that are particularly suitable for adult learners with crowded schedules who must study when they can.

Telecommunication is hardly novel. It is simply the communication of information in spoken, written, or coded verbal or pictorial form by electrical means using wires or radio waves. The tools are familiar to everyday life in America—the telephone, television, videotape, satellite and cable broadcast, and the computer. Linked in a system, they can erase barriers of time and space with the push of a button or the flip of a switch.

Although we live with them daily, and technological delivery systems for learning are extensive in the United States, we are not yet accustomed to thinking of them as a profound educational resource for the work force. Nevertheless, big corporations are using their own networks to take instruction to their employees and customers worldwide. Universities are joining cooperative networks that provide courses especially for employed professional workers. We describe these developments and others in some detail to indicate the possibilities for extending the benefits to more people. Learning can be there for anyone, anytime, anywhere—depending on the choice of media.

The possibilities seem limitless, but crucial questions remain: Which technological aid is best suited to the specific purpose or instructional goal? What combinations of the media will help to meet the objective? And most important, will the content be of sufficient quality to ensure that we are not simply extending mediocrity?

In table 2, we present an evaluation of the effective uses and limitations of the different media. Some common points are omitted for the sake of clarity and brevity. Any one of the media, for example, can be supplemented by texts, instructional manuals, and assignments if a course is intended. And all can be mixed for more effective use. Similarly, some media are more adjustable for particular subjects than others. A dividing line, for example, is whether the medium is designed to deliver mainly passive instruction or whether it permits genuine interaction with questions and answers. The cost factor also varies widely. Because of the complex variables, we could not make the cost estimates more specific, but all the delivery methods save the cost of sending employees to trainers and vice versa.

To assess where we are today in the use of the different media, we describe each with examples that show the stage of development and its effectiveness for some but not other purposes. We furnish considerable detail so that providers of adult learning can

ON AND TION	AUDIENCE AND SCHEDULING	COST
er with other uals; informative	Unlimited audience; reaches widely scattered employees	
c ction	Time limited to viewing schedule	Costs can be high for production and broadcast time
	Use at any time with television and videocassette recorder	Cost lowers with reuse and mail distribution
		May be less expensive to produce, but depends on quality
n ussion	Adaptable for diverse groups of students Permits flexible scheduling	
ce of tutor or facil- ing site e large single student		
discussion tional allowed via tele-	Wide distribution	
by group size nt	Broadcast time inflexible	Expensive for small group Requires equipment; if satellite used, receiver sites needed
speak and dem- play screens s can be pre- d interactively	Covers wide geographic area Long-distance telephone data communication	
persons per ses-	Limited by real-time frame	Equipment expensive: student needs telephone-computer hook-up
ctive via personal telephone; in- n common	Serves geographically dispersed persons Crosses national boundaries There is time to consider response Free of time limitations	
contact	Psychological barriers to comput- ers and to working alone May be delay in response	

Table 2 Evaluation of Media for Distant Teaching and Learning

		CONTENT	PRESENTAT PARTICIP
TELEVISION BROADCAST	**Effective uses:**	Uniform material ensures consistent training	Lecture by teach experts Graphics and vis clips
	Limitations:		Presentation stat Passive; no inter
VIDEOTAPE *Same as television with these differences:*	**Effective uses:**	Can be reviewed in whole or part	Stop and replay
	Limitations:		
TUTORED VIDEO INSTRUCTION *Same as video-based instruction with these additions:*	**Effective uses:**	Subject review with tutor, particularly for students with poor language skills	Student interacti Encourages disc
	Limitations:		Requires presen itator and mee Group must not Not effective for
VIDEOCONFERENCE	**Effective uses:**	Can use time-sensitive materials, but also many subjects	Lecture or panel Graphics, etc. op Some interaction phone links
	Limitations:		Interaction limite and time elem Rather passive
AUDIOGRAPHIC CONFERENCE	**Effective uses:**	Useful to teach problem solving, also troubleshooting skills and maintenance procedures	Participants can onstrate via dis Complex graphi pared and use
	Limitations:		Small number of sion is best
COMPUTER CONFERENCE	**Effective uses:**	Suitable for wide variety of subjects, including problem solving and discussion	Completely inter computer and tense interactio
	Limitations:		No voice or visua

investigate those delivery systems that seem most appropriate for them.

Television

Much of distance learning revolves around the video image. Over almost 50 years, the technology of television reception has developed from ghostly figures on a tiny screen to the new high-resolution color picture. It can now include exceptionally clear stereo sound and be interference free, thanks to cable. High-tech video delivery systems can be used alone or mixed and matched to suit—satellite, cable, microwave, and general broadcast. Telephones can be tied in to make the communication two way in real time. A variety of parties—proprietary systems, commercial broadcasters, public television, and so on—compete to occupy the 80 or so channels available on the average television set. Local stations and private companies have their own mobile satellite uplink units capable of originating broadcasts and the downlink to receive.

In urban and rural areas alike, "satellite dishes" for business and personal use have popped up across the landscape, pointed toward the orbiting satellite of choice. Of the 2.4 million satellite dishes at American private homes in 1989, an estimated 60 percent are in rural areas. Above, an arch of satellites in geosynchronous orbit offers an abundant supply of data, talk, pictures, news, sports, entertainment, and increasingly, education and training for work.

For some time, a number of universities have been sending live video and audio classroom lectures to students at corporate sites by means of an Instructional Television Fixed Service (ITFS), one of 28 channels reserved by the Federal Communications Commission for nonprofit educational broadcasting. In the late 1970s, for example, California State University at Chico began delivering master's level computer science courses to Hewlett-Packard facilities in northern California. Some years later, the company extended the coverage to its other plants by satellite; eight courses went to remote locations in California, Colorado, Idaho, Oregon, and Washington. To offset some of the cost, Hewlett-Packard suggested inviting other companies into the program. Chico agreed, and a variety of companies and organizations began to receive the Chico program by satellite: General Dynamics, MCI, Bently Nevada (a manufacturer of safety systems for large rotation machinery), Alcoa Laboratories, Texas Instruments, and the U.S. Naval Weapons Center at China Lake, California.

According to Leslie Wright, associate dean at Chico, the program is designed to enable a student-employee to earn a master's degree in computer science in two and a half years. Chico offers ten courses each year and also has four core courses on videotape for self-paced study. Some professionals take selected courses only to keep their knowledge and skills up to date.

On the East Coast, the University of Maryland has a long track record in distance learning that started with correspondence courses for the troops in World War II. Through this method and with some classroom learning and examinations, many people got their degrees and credentials. True to form, the university has continued distance delivery, adopting the newer method of instructional television. In 1980, technical courses went to engineers and computer scientists in local high-tech companies and government agencies. In the beginning, Maryland awarded credit to students at remote sites only for courses broadcast from a "live" classroom. But distant students are now allowed to tape courses. The cost is the same for students on or off campus. In addition, Maryland offers an array of noncredit, professional development courses tailored to the needs of its corporate clients on such popular topics as interactive communications networks, hypersonic aerodynamics, and software warranties.

Annual enrollment in the instructional television programs varies between two and three thousand, and the system offers more than 20 corporate and government clients some 50 courses per semester for graduate credit. The university also uses a satellite uplink to send instruction nationwide to students at designated locations.

In 1986, the University of Maryland established a site in a public building in Montgomery County, Maryland, to serve employees of local, smaller and medium-sized high-tech companies. Each receiving business or agency pays a yearly fee to the university based on the organization's size. This move to include smaller companies deserves high praise because all too frequently they have been bypassed or simply overlooked. The usual target audiences are employees of big corporations where many may enroll and financial returns are both greater and steadier.

Chico and Maryland both started with limited geographic coverage and then expanded nationwide. There is no technical reason why such systems cannot expand beyond the United States. The National Technological University, discussed in the chapter on updating professionals, was inaugurated on a nationwide basis, but it has not sent its advanced engineering courses abroad. In fact, it has refused to accept applications for admission from Canada and Mexico.

At the present time, however, the largest number of educational television-based systems in the United States serve limited geographic regions within states, and they are usually focused for particular audiences. There is the West Central Illinois Education Telecommunications Corporation, known as CONVOCOM, a nonprofit corporation consisting of public and private colleges and universities, public television stations, and businesses. The system offers two-way videoconferencing and course delivery to and from six cities, providing courses to businesses and the public. The state of Pennsylvania has PENNARAMA, a statewide microwave network connecting major cable television systems with the state's colleges and universities. One of the oldest of such networks in the nation, it offers college credit courses, continuing education, teleconferences, seminars, and special audio services to any facility—school, business, home, community center, or library.

Pennsylvania State University recently introduced a computer network linking the College of Agriculture at University Park with the state's 67 county offices. Using VAX hardware and software from Digital and 550 Apple Macintosh personal computers, it is breaking new ground for the extension service in educational use. Agents throughout the state relay to rural residents information they receive about agriculture, horticulture, home economics, family living, energy management, and youth development. Called the Pennsylvania Education Network, it paid for itself within 18 months after implementation. Annual savings through electronic mail alone amount to $240,000 in telephone and mail costs.[1]

The college has further contracted with the state's Department of Education, which uses the network to reach 750 educational organizations with various services including a database. Their operation is dubbed PENN*LINK. University Park is an active center for instructional technologies and distance delivery. Dispatched by satellite to all campuses of the university, graduate and undergraduate courses travel about the state. Beyond the borders, Penn State offers acoustical engineering to civilians in the Department of Naval Personnel at their workplaces in Key Port, Washington, and San Diego, California. The first master's degrees were awarded in the spring of 1989.

Two-way video connections enable faculty at University Park and the Hershey Medical Center, about 90 miles distant from each other, to teach jointly in the interdisciplinary fields of bioengineering and food sciences. Such a connection also serves two campuses for advanced degrees in adult education. For the application of media generally, Penn State is a leader, and increasing numbers of faculty recognize that "credit is credit and a course is a course, regardless of location."

Oklahoma has four continuing higher education systems serving schools, industry, colleges, and communities. Another system, the National University Teleconference Network at Oklahoma State University, acts as a broker for some 200 postsecondary institutions across the United States. It serves members' technical needs for satellite use and generally provides noncredit continuing professional training on an extremely wide variety of subjects. There is a fast-sales aura about the operation, but without a doubt it is bringing people together nationally and providing materials for hospitals, businesses, and community agencies—beyond universities.

Many states are turning to telecommunications to address continuing education needs. Kentucky and Maine are erecting elaborate systems; North Carolina and Virginia are expanding existing networks; Massachusetts, Maryland, Ohio, and other states are studying the feasibility or planning further development. At Utah State University, an Intermountain Community Learning and Information Service is being established to serve rural Utah and three other Western states. Networks proliferate within states and across the country. Visualizing the systems described and adding those of many states not mentioned, along with corporate and broadcasting networks, would reveal an interlacing nationwide pattern of unbelievable dimensions. The physical resources exist to deliver learning opportunities to anyone with a television set in any or all of the 50 states.

But there are difficulties. Although instructional television delivery is feasible and economical, it does not answer many needs. An obvious problem with conventional television as an instructional medium for the workplace or independent adult learning is simply timing. A live ITFS broadcast of an engineering course, for example, operates under rigid time constraints. On a public access television system, like a public broadcasting or commercial channel, a program must be presented within a certain time slot even if it isn't live. Because they claim relatively small audiences, educational programs usually find their slots between bedtime and sunrise—not the most propitious hours for viewing.

Videotapes

The advent of the videocassette recorder brought time control and added flexibility to television-based education. Having the ability to tape and view programs, learner and teacher are no longer restricted by time and place. Any place with a videocassette recorder and a television set can be a classroom. A tape can be delivered by mail, borrowed from the library, or rented. A tape can be stopped and restarted, rewound and reviewed. It can be viewed by an individual or a group. It can be produced to the exact requirements of the best teacher or corporate training program.

Videotaped instruction through a television set is a good medium for certain kinds of education and training. Studies have found, for example, that mathematics and the sciences can be taught equally well in a classroom or by television.[2] Because every viewer receives the same material, lessons that stress uniformity in subject matter are readily conveyed in this medium. Repeated use of many tapes of a single presentation guarantees uniformity from one class session to another or among instructors. Videotapes can be made and distributed quickly at little cost. Or they can be elaborate productions, depending on the particular requirements and resources.

Video training tapes are now available on just about every subject imaginable, from "Effective Public Speaking" to "Vasectomy by Electrocautery." They are essential to many businesses that need to ensure timely and uniform distribution to many widely scattered employees. Taco Bell, a division of PepsiCo, expects in the near future to include most of its 2,700 restaurants in regular mailings of its training tapes. Fast-food giant McDonald's has long relied on video-based instruction to help foster the food and service consistency that is its hallmark. From its training tapes, employees learn, for example, the proper methods for frying potatoes as well as the corporate ideology.

Unions are using video to package and distribute information to their worker members. Some of these are educational, like a videotape recently produced by management and the union at the U.S. Postal Service to train shop stewards to cope with mail handler grievances.[3] Others are designed more to indoctrinate, as with a series produced by the Sheet Metal Workers' national training fund (jointly administered with management) to introduce apprentices to the purpose of apprenticeship, the role of unions and contractors in their lives, and the importance of their industry to the national economy.[4]

Insurance companies use both taped and live video training on topics ranging from complex new financial instruments to the essential art of getting and keeping clients. New England Mutual Life, a Boston-based insurance company with 3,500 agents around the country, makes videotapes available to its independent agents for home viewing—a successful training fit with the needs and work styles of the agents. Allstate Insurance, a 55,000-employee company headquartered in Northbrook, Illinois, maintains a continuously operating two-way video, two-way audio network to train agents and keep them up to date. Massachusetts Mutual Life Insurance Company uses an interactive video system to improve and standardize training—a strategic need given the high agent turnover in the insurance industry. The Travelers has built a $20 million education center in Hartford, Connecticut, where training facilities include satellite broadcast reception and transmission facilities. Along with video and videotape training, Travelers offers videodisc kiosks where employees can browse through information on everything from new products to profiles of agents and company history.

Because they deliver information one-way, a television or videotape presentation is often much like a traditional lecture. In fact, courses very often are simply stand-up lectures captured on camera. This is not necessarily bad unless the teaching is poor. At least the student does not have to be in the classroom or lecture hall, and the lecture can be viewed as often as needed. Furthermore, the video lecture can be carried far beyond the model of a single teacher speaking a lesson, perhaps using a chalkboard. It can include interviews with other experts, documentary footage, graphics, and special effects that add new dimensions to the subject matter. For example, "The Mechanical Universe," a program produced by the California Institute of Technology with support from the Annenberg School of Communications and the Corporation for Public Broadcasting, uses dynamic computer graphics to help students visualize and understand concepts of physics that are difficult to explain in words and static diagrams. "The Mechanical Universe" also features dramatic reenactments that bring to life historic scientific discoveries described in the lesson.

While such imaginative subject matter, perhaps delivered by several expert teachers together, can make the televised course much livelier than the common classroom lecture, it remains a one-way delivery method with no opportunity for a student to interrupt and ask a question. This fact alone limits its usefulness in many learning environments. Nevertheless, it remains valuable for uniform presentations intended to convey a standard body of knowledge to the audience. And its potential for indoctrination is apparent: a cleverly designed television course can be as effective as commercial advertising—without fear of interruption from the learner. Small wonder that companies engage its power to introduce employees to their distinctive corporate cultures, and to rivet the public's attention to a new product.

Tutored Video Instruction

Corporations, especially in cooperative instructional programs with universities, have added the human element to the classroom receiving the course. To overcome the passive nature of the video medium and still permit distant delivery, a tutor or discussion leader meets with a small group of students to view unedited tapes of classroom lectures. When a student has a question or comment, the leader stops the tape and the group talks about it. Questions that cannot be answered are referred to the lecturer for follow-up.

Tutored video instruction (TVI) can combine the best of both lectures and small classes: the lecture provides depth and continuity in the subject matter, while the tutorial discussion responds to individual needs. In the corporate setting, the tutor is not expected to be an authority, but the person selected would presumably have some knowledge about the subject and the ability to guide the discussion carried on by the students.

Experiments with TVI show that students learn best when they stop the videotaped lecture frequently. Optimal interruptions seem to come every ten minutes or so, lasting from three to five minutes—something clearly impossible with a television broadcast or classroom lecture. It is most effective when students and a tutor watch together; it is less effective for a single student—with or without a tutor. TVI students are less likely to fall behind in their work than students actually hearing the lectures in the professor's classroom. Interestingly, the effectiveness of TVI is not closely related to the quality of the lectures, suggesting that tutor-guided discussion teaches more than the lecture itself.[5]

In the following example, TVI developed as a direct response to corporate adult training needs. Originally, Stanford University sent its engineering courses (via ITFS) to employees at Hewlett-Packard and other neighboring electronics plants close enough to receive the broadcast. But then Hewlett-Packard wanted to give its engineers in Santa Rosa, California, about 100 miles north of Stanford, the same educational opportunities. The desire to make instruction available to their employees beyond the delivery radius was the same motivating force that led Chico to move to a satellite for extended coverage. But, in this case, videotapes of Stanford lectures were mailed to Santa Rosa along with class notes, homework assignments, and other materials distributed to on-campus students. The students returned the tapes and homework to Palo Alto a week later.

The Stanford faculty chose the tutors from the professional engineers at Santa Rosa based on their ability to lead discussion groups and their interest in reviewing the subject matter. Advanced knowledge in the particular subject was not essential. When necessary, on-site tutors telephoned faculty after the TVI sessions to discuss problems and get supplementary materials. The students had the same homework and examinations as students on campus; the same grading standards applied to all work done by the TVI students, the on-campus students, and those taking the course by live ITFS alone.

After two terms, Stanford evaluated the experiment. The grade point average of TVI students was "comfortably above that of both the on-campus students and the students studying by closed circuit television." Moreover, students with marginal qualifications for admission to the Stanford degree program did well using the TVI approach. Other Stanford experiments showed that students who used TVI on campus outperformed students who attended only the regular lectures. Further, it was found that TVI classes were attracting a large number of students whose first language was not English. Later studies at Hitachi Central Research Laboratories support the hypothesis that TVI is particularly suited to students whose English is deficient because presentations can be "slowed down" and clarified.[6]

A pioneer in this and other educational innovation, Hewlett-Packard is a company playing for global stakes in electronics and computing markets. Commenting on the company's experience with TVI, John A. Young, president and CEO, has said:

> We in industry have also experienced benefits we did not foresee.
> . . . What we had not expected were group problem-solving skills
> that have emerged from the program. Tutors, especially, have
> gained invaluable team-building and management skills. . . . The
> professor still plays the vital role of developing, structuring, and
> presenting the course material. The only significant change here
> is the number of students who have access to the professor's in-

formation. In being able to reach more students, the professor becomes more productive but no less effective.[7]

The main additional expense is for taping classes, which is not costly. Moreover, the tapes are available for review and make-up purposes, even for on-campus students. Finally, off-campus TVI sessions can be scheduled at an employer's convenience so that the student-workers' productivity is not unduly eroded.

Stanford now offers a full master's degree program in engineering through TVI to employees at Hewlett-Packard and other companies. And the technique has been extended to Stanford's honors cooperative program, which is available to Hewlett-Packard employees at their work sites throughout the United States and in Europe. The company uses TVI to offer courses from other universities as well.

The measurable merit of the TVI approach has attracted adherents from a variety of providers. Columbia University's School of Engineering and Applied Sciences uses it to deliver graduate courses to AT&T's Bell Laboratories and other technical professionals at their places of work. Harvard Medical School has used it to teach physiology. It has also proven to be very effective for courses given to prisoners.

Videotape can be combined with other media to create packages that are labeled *telecourses* because they are usually disseminated, at least in part, over television or video systems, and they are structured like the typical college course. Textbooks and study guides accompany the programs; sometimes audiotapes and computer software are included, as in ComputerWorks, an introduction to the use of computers in business that comes with interactive computer exercises on 15 floppy disks. The study guide presents an orderly lesson plan, instructing the student on which segments of the video program to watch for lectures and demonstration, what readings to do in the textbooks, and what exercises to complete.

Adults who, for whatever reasons, cannot attend classes often take telecourses. For a few, like the handicapped or geographically remote, telecourses may be the only access to higher education or advanced job training. Frequently they are the choice of adults who have been out of school for some time and who like the idea of taking a course in the comfort of their own homes. A person may find that "I can do that" and will then be confident enough to enroll in on-campus programs. Some colleges, realizing the drawing effect of telecourses, are using them for recruitment. Students do not usually take telecourses as self-study, although they could. More often they meet in infrequent class sessions or communicate by telephone or mail with the teacher and sometimes other students. Such courses can be efficient and convenient, but for subjects that require coaching, development of complex ideas, or hands-on guided practice, they are rarely suitable.

The theory behind the telecourse method is that thoughtful course design and production compensate for whatever a student misses by not being in a classroom. Ideally at least, telecourses can feature the best lecturers and incorporate the most interesting ideas on a given subject. One or more excellent teachers may be brought together just to create one course. Unlike conventional course development, a telecourse is usually a team effort involving a project manager, editors and writers, audiovisual technicians, and instructional specialists who work to ensure the pedagogical soundness and aesthetic appeal of the product.

Videoconferencing

In a videoconference, television and telephone technologies combine. Audiences at various sites view and participate in live proceedings from one or more broadcast studios. Students can call in questions and comments by telephone. Though videoconferencing is referred to as interactive, this can be an exaggeration. If a satellite is used, the conference can have a very large audience scattered over many remote sites. This technique achieves economies of scale but involves too many participants for real talk. And as a live event, it has a set duration that further limits comments or questions from the audience.

Videoconferences can be large or small, special events or regular exchanges. They may encompass a geographic region, a nation, or half the globe. The Microelectronics Center of North Carolina (MCNC) in Research Triangle Park is an innovative educational and industrial entity supported by the state. MCNC's communications system, linking several universities with various industrial sites, is designed with videoconferencing and electronic training delivery. Student-workers interact with faculty through video and telephone and through computer exchange.

The medium is particularly good for reaching many people with material that is timely and up to date in a particular field. For example, Texas Instruments, as part of a push to educate a potential market for its current and future artificial intelligence products, has held annual AI satellite symposia. This series features presentations, panel discussions, and demonstrations by leading authorities on the role of AI and knowledge workers in business. Broadcast throughout North America, Europe, and parts of Latin America, the first two symposia reached more than 85,000 managers, engineers, and technologists in hundreds of companies, laboratories, universities, and government agencies.

Texas Instruments' experience shows how videoconferencing can be improved for training purposes. Symposium number one was the usual stand-up lecture format, but in number two the company combined tapes of informal interviews in relaxed settings with live question-and-answer sessions, and interspersed visits to manufacturing and research sites with brief technical talks. The third symposium, in April 1987, created a benchmark on two counts: it reached 65,000 persons, and its innovative use of video technology earned first place in *BusinessTV* magazine's 1987 video conference awards. In the following year more than 300 colleges and universities and 700 companies and government agencies, including 40 percent of the *Fortune* "100," tuned in. People participated from offices and plants, from classrooms and hotel conference rooms where they gathered. All that is needed is the downlink equipment, which typically can be rented for $1,500. Texas Instruments charges no fee to receive the broadcasts and sells videotapes of the event later at nominal cost.

At the present time, videoconferencing is generally exploited in more targeted training situations, on a more modest scale, and on less global topics. For example, an increasing number of large corporations use it to deliver timely new information to employees in sales, marketing, and service. While the medium is probably used most frequently for this kind of top-down training, it need not be so. Domino's Pizza reverses the direction and encourages local employees to contribute. The company sends a mobile satellite uplink by truck to any of its stores in the United States where an employee has come up with a valuable idea for saving time, cutting costs, or improving customer service. The tip is then broadcast throughout the company. In a markedly different example, physicians and medical students in the four largest teaching hospitals in South Carolina regularly get together through videoconferencing to discuss case histories.

Although this method is effective in delivering some kinds of information, it does not allow for the kind of intense, spontaneous interaction with people and information that can engage the learner with a problem and inspire him or her to think critically and creatively. As one video producer candidly points out:

> Problem-solving training doesn't belong on the medium, not if the point is to be flexible and to work with real problems. The dialogue is very important in that kind of training. You don't have that in a teleconference. You must remember that interaction is fairly limited and narrow. You can't establish comfortable rapport between trainer and student. You can't call a break when the group looks tired, or stop the program early or late, or have an unplanned evening session. And if there is a lot of reference ma-

terial for trainees to work with during the program, they will more than likely get lost and confused. You have to keep these sorts of limitations in mind when designing teletraining.[8]

Audiographic Conferencing

Audiographic computer teleconferencing enables individuals separated by distance to use computers for live communication of printed words, graphics, and other still-frame video images that can appear on a computer screen, while the participants speak to each other by conference telephone. When a person speaks, types, draws, or points to a place on her computer screen, she can be heard by the other participants, who can also see her drawing or her visual explanation. These features make the combination a powerful medium for group problem solving, especially on technical topics where engineering schematics or other complex images come into play.

AT&T uses audiographics in conjunction with videoconferencing to give both employees and customers technical training on the use and maintenance of its products—a learning area where the hands-on aspect of audiographics helps. AT&T, having developed the technology at its Bell Labs, is one of the biggest users of such conferencing and comarkets it with the Optel Corporation as a commercial product, the Optel Telewriter. Three networks for training special audiences come from their National Teletraining Center in Cincinnati, Ohio, and the number of sites served nearly doubled in one year.

In 1984, Dan Goroff, an assistant professor of mathematics at Harvard University, together with other instructors from his department, formed the Cambridge Teleteaching Group. Their goal was to create sets of all the screens and graphics needed to teach entire courses via audiographic conferencing. The products, called Socratic Series Courseware, were designed to be taught by other teachers and consisted of prepared text and graphics templates on diskettes, student guides, and teacher manuals. Their first course taught college calculus to students in cities throughout the Northeast under the sponsorship of Harvard's Extension School.

Goroff claims from this experience that the interaction among students and teachers physically separated from each other but joined in an electronic class is usually more intensive than in an ordinary classroom. Both students and teacher quickly adapt to the protocols of the electronic class. He believes that the inability of users to see each other is an advantage because it focuses attention on one's computer screen and the subject. Since the students can also control the screen images that are the common object of discussion, the teacher is not limited to lecturing but can direct students in assignments. So, for example, the calculus courseware includes a screen template with an x : y axis on which an instructor can draw two points and ask a student to calculate the slope of a line connecting them. If the student makes a mistake, the instructor can give immediate feedback, as in a one-on-one tutorial, and the group benefits from the tutorial.

Because of the potential for intensive interaction among participants in an audiographic conference, the number of participants is best kept low, to no more than 10 to 15. The medium uses telephone lines as the means of transmission, so one can take part in an audiographic conference from just about anywhere there is a telephone—given, of course, the necessary computer equipment. For example, the Boston University Medical School has used the technology to teach courses in anatomy to students at a university in Beijing, China. Audiographics are expensive, both in the cost of the Optel Telewriter and the telephone charges. Nevertheless, the technology now commercially available gives a taste of what will be possible and more affordable one day.

Studies by AT&T[9] and others have revealed no significant differences between the amount of information adult students learn through teletraining and through classes where the instructor is present. This might be expected since the method of teaching is essentially the same. But the important message is that adults apparently learn certain material equally well with distance delivery systems, and these systems can bring instruction to many more persons.

Asynchronous Computer Conferencing

As in an audiographic conference, participants in a computer conference communicate by means of computers linked through modems and telephone lines. But there are significant differences. First, communication on this basis is limited to text and graphics entered or created on a participant's computer; there is no voice communication. Second, computer conferees usually send and receive information at different times, or asynchronously. Third, computer conferences are often less formal groups. The members of a conference are people who use the medium to share ideas and information on a particular subject. It may be a class, but it is more often a professional or personal interest group. Often a participant's only means of contact with the group is the computer. On the face of it, audiographics—and just about anything else—would seem a better way to learn. For interesting reasons, however, the opposite is in fact the case for most adults who use the medium.

Computer conferencing systems usually permit messages to be communicated in two ways. Text, and sometimes graphics, may be addressed privately to some other person with access to the system; this is essentially electronic mail. But messages can also be placed where they will be read and answered by any number of group members. Messages are saved and displayed for others to read in the order in which they are received, creating a transcript of the proceedings.

An informal conference—a forum or a special interest group— may be held for users of Apple Macintosh computers or for students in an American history course. Subgroups accommodate those with a particular interest, like a single computer programming language. Most conferences have a moderator who performs administrative tasks, like admitting new members and maintaining data files, and who oversees the discussion. The moderator may be recognized as a teacher if the conference is also a course, and in any case, the moderator is seen as a "wizard" of sorts. Fierce loyalty can attach to a moderator, a teacher, or the conference, and a dynamic very similar to school class pride develops if the group is together long enough.

Since the members do not all communicate at once, a computer conference can feasibly involve many more participants than any other kind of interactive class. A conference devoted to artificial intelligence topics on the CompuServe Information Service network has averaged 5,500 members representing the United States, Canada, Europe and Britain, and Japan over a three-year period. It offers 800 information files and turns over some 400 messages a week. Members join and drop out temporarily as discussions vary or their schedules dictate. And because of the specialized subject area, this is a relatively small conference. CompuServe itself now has more than 500,000 members—the largest such on-line service in the world.

On-line exchanges have the open quality of a small group discussion. Communication is usually informal, and messages are evolving a text structure of their own. For example, keyboard symbols are coopted to indicate the body and speech cues that would be present in conversational settings. It is common to see experienced users fill their messages with :-) for a smile or BTW for "by the way." It is not, however, a free-for-all: members exchange formal documents like papers, proposals, presentations, and bibliographies.

This hybrid text communication, a kind of conversational writing, is one of the reasons, researchers at the University of Arizona believe, that students who use computer conferencing to learn a foreign language show greater achievement than their counterparts in traditional classrooms. They excel not only in their ability to write and read the new language but also in their conversational skills—despite the fact that they are only typing at, not speaking directly to each other. Several other factors probably also contribute to the system's remarkable success. Students like conferencing, and while they often enter the course without knowing they will be using computers, they have no fear of them. Students spend an average of three times longer on the system than required! They tend to help each other more and to forget that the teacher is also on line.

Like audiographic conferencing, this method has the advantage of acute concentration on the issues being discussed. Moreover, the approach stimulates at least as much intellectual give-and-take, and some say much more because it allows time for reflection. The computer stores all comments in sequence, and participants can enter the discussion at any time and review any part of the proceedings. Before sharing their thoughts, they can consult other people or sources and refine their comments. Those whose command of English is not perfect need not feel pressured. They have time to prepare what they want to say. These features permit a higher level of participation and richer commentary than is often feasible in face-to-face encounters. Evaluation of a system used by employees of a large pharmaceutical company revealed that "heavy participants" who averaged four and one-half hours per week on line actually saved ten hours a week of verbal communications time.[10]

For the adult learner, an important advantage of computer conferencing over other distance technologies is its convenience. Because the network and its central host computer, where the conferences are stored, are available 24 hours a day, participants can send and receive information whenever they choose, regardless of time zone or personal schedules that may be heavy or erratic. And since all that is needed to subscribe to a conference is a terminal, a modem, and access to a regular telephone line, a person can take part from just about any location. Even those who travel in their jobs are able to tap into these electronic "networks of minds"[11] by logging on with portable computers from their hotel rooms.

The Pan American pilots' union, for example, established an "electronic union hall" through which its peripatetic members can stay informed of contract talks, safety reports, and such matters.[12] The union provides some training over the network and has plans to step up training use. Members can tap into the system from wherever they are using laptop computers, and the union pays for the communication costs.

Such systems open up learning opportunities for the person at home with family obligations, the physically handicapped, and the geographically isolated. Not even speech or hearing is essential, as illustrated in the courses in American history taught to students at the National Technical Institute of the Deaf by Norman Coombs, a professor at the Rochester Institute of Technology. Coombs himself is blind, but that doesn't prevent him from using his computer; a voice synthesizer reads messages to him. An individual with restricted keyboard ability can use spellcheckers and other smart software to create quite suitable messages.

Paradoxically, computer conferencing offers teachers and students separated by time and distance opportunities for the intensive and intimate sharing of ideas that is characteristic of a small seminar, but it can be continued as long as the participants want, and new subgroups can be formed to meet special interests. Learning without a classroom no longer means solitary "correspondence study" deprived of contact with the teacher and other students. Experiments by the Army in giving a course to reserve officers showed that those who used computer conferencing had a lower drop-out rate than those who used the correspondence approach. One reason posited for this was ongoing support from the instructor on line.

Rather than passively wait for knowledge relevant to the problems being faced now, the working student can actively seek advice on alternative solutions, tapping into the knowledge and experience of others. In the process, the distinction between student and teacher becomes blurred; each participant in a computer conference is a student in search of knowledge, and each is also a teacher with knowledge to offer others. Writing about a computer conference in a large corporation, Shoshana Zuboff notes:

> Mastery of one's subject area and the ability to share knowledge effectively became recognized as new sources of power and influence. . . . People became known as experts in their subject areas based on the content of their contributions, and less attention was paid to their formal job designation.[13]

Teachers are not made obsolete by computer conferencing just because every learner is also a potential teacher. Their roles, however, are changed. Rather than serving as a source of knowledge and controller of discussion, as in the traditional classroom, the online teacher is a guide to information and moderator of exchanges. For adult learning, this may well be a better role for the designated teacher. There is a good chance that students' needs for learning will be met and the individual will feel that he or she is a respected person rather than a youngster in class. Research on courses so taught shows that, while in a typical classroom the teacher contributes 60 to 80 percent of the conversation, in computer conferencing the teacher accounts for only 6 to 10 percent.

A carefully designed course can be delivered with near perfection, students' participation and progress can be monitored, and interaction between the teacher and student can be quicker and more frequent. Team teaching is also easy to carry on. At New York's New School for Social Research, through Connected Education, Inc., a course called "Issues in International Telecommunications" was taught from Tokyo by Masasumi Takada, a commentator for Radio Japan; from Washington, D.C., by Jerome Glenn, head of a group concerned with telecommunications in the Third World; and from New Jersey by Paul Levinson, director of the program. In such a case, the teachers are not limited to the faculty of universities or the ranks of corporate and military trainers; they can be anyone with expertise in any organization.

The suitability of these learning networks to the lives of busy adults is borne out by the success of a program for top executives offered by the Western Behavioral Sciences Institute (WBSI), a think tank in La Jolla, California. Begun in 1982, the International Executive Forum gives policy-level executives the opportunity to discuss socioeconomic and political issues of first importance. Fellows include executives from major companies like United Telecom, Pacific Telesis, Digital Equipment, and Polaroid. Their classmates are military flag officers, officials from the National Science Foundation, state governors, and others. The program has also attracted participants from England, Sweden, Saudi Arabia, Switzerland, Canada, and Mexico.

Each class of 25 students starts with a week-long seminar at La Jolla, where they meet their faculty leaders and are introduced to the computer conferencing method. When they return home they are well acquainted with each other and the procedure. The institute has garnered distinguished and diverse faculty members because they can teach from any location and at any time that fits their full schedules. The two-year program has six-month terms with different themes: The Private Sector and the State; Technological Progress and People; the Management of Scarcity and Abundance; and Globalism and Interdependence. It is a true learning network—no degrees and no academic credit—since its participants are usually well established in their careers and need no more credentials, only further learning.

The curriculum pointedly rejects quantitative courses and the case study approach of business schools. Instead, as the catalog emphasizes, the objective is to help leaders "emerge from the program with the ability to balance short-term profitability against long-term viability." Confronting complicated problems and concerns in an ongoing atmosphere has advantages over the short, intense course format usual in classroom continuing education. Moreover, since time zones are no hindrance, fellows worldwide can communicate evenings or weekends at any hour. The Department of Defense recently awarded WBSI a contract to create a similar computer conferencing program for War College graduates who must continue their education as part of the competition for promotion.

Large corporations, of course, have tremendous computer networks, but they are not yet tuned particularly for conferences that provide employee education; instead, they are generally directed toward business operations. A prime example is Digital Equipment's international network connecting over 50,000 nodes in 33 countries with more than 100,000 users. The largest nonmilitary network in the world, it grows by about 50 percent a year; even more startling is the growth rate in data applications—300 percent per year. Manager Peter Brown explains the company's internal transformation: "Many things we used to do with paper are now done electronically. Everything rides on the network from the time a customer orders something."[14]

Besides data, the network carries more than 1,300 computer conferences on company business, products, and so on. It may be a rather fine line to draw between conferences on products and personnel training that would include the former. The point is that systems are in place and their use could easily be expanded for teaching purposes. After all, the exchange of information is a large part of education. Research at Digital has shown extensive use of their system for information on esoteric subjects and topics outside the employee's regular concerns. Users query experts with specific questions; it is not unlike a graduate seminar in which students share ideas and probe questions of interest to them and their peers.

A similar situation exists for researchers and scholars who are linked in computer networks that serve their special interests and allow exchange of ideas and data. BITNET, which connects scholars at more than 700 institutions worldwide, has recently offered a course on Einstein's theories. But its "conferencing" does not usually include instruction. Many such networks have emerged—but not for training.

In the United States, a "data superhighway" has been proposed to link regional networks with supercomputers across the country and permit access by researchers from universities, industry, and government. It would create "collaboratories" so that scientists could view and control complex machines many miles away as well as exchange data. Driven by the desire to bolster the nation's technological leadership, the organizers want to develop fiber-optic communication links "that are thousands of times faster than today's commercially available networks." The plan, which may take five years to develop, has legislative support as well as endorsement from the National Science Foundation, government agencies, and leading computer scientists.[15] Development of the comprehensive network was announced in June 1990.

Is it too fanciful to suggest an "educational superhighway" for adult training to improve the work force? Computers are prevalent in the workplace, and they are on the desks of many workers. The Home Builders Association has been considering computer conferencing to tie together its institutes scattered throughout the country. People would go to the centers to participate in training courses. Although there is the obstacle of cost of equipment purchase, especially for lower income people, learning centers on campuses and in storefronts or elsewhere could provide the necessary access.

A second, perhaps more difficult obstacle to learning through computer conferencing is the requirement of strong reading and writing ability. So it is not accessible to those who lack the basic skills. This will limit its use to people with more advanced abilities, probably in higher-level jobs. But if the computer itself can be used more effectively to teach those basic skills, then many more people can join and learn from computer conferencing.

Other barriers are psychological. The fear of computers many adults have may prohibit them from learning with or through them. And perhaps a greater source of resistance is the notion of learning outside the classroom. The belief that education takes place in the classroom, and usually involves competition with others, is ingrained in us. So, for adults who have not had the chance to go to college, the experience of going to class on campus is often important, carrying an aura of achievement and respectability.

Once adults experience the power of collaboratively seeking and sharing ideas, they are likely to gravitate toward technologies that help this kind of learning. But people have some hurdles to cross before they can feel comfortable with the technology; after that, the danger is that they will become addicted to it.

A Mix of Technologies is Best

It is clear that no one technological method can do everything any more than one method of personal teaching in the classroom can be appropriate to all subjects and circumstances. The all-important point is to select a combination of methods that promises to be most effective for the purpose or goal of the course. If the purpose is to give all students the same body of knowledge, a lecture format may be best, and it can go to any number of people on television or videotapes. But if discussion and involvement of students in solving a problem or considering an issue are needed, then audio contact or a conferencing method is required. Analysis of the various means leads to one conclusion: a mix of technologies is best.

Barriers of geography, language, and economics were surmounted by a project combining videotapes and computer conferencing. BESTNET (Bilingual English and Spanish Telecommunications Network) is an electronic consortium of more than 20 colleges and universities in the United States and a dozen in Mexico. The Western Behavioral Sciences Institute and San Diego State University launched the project in 1985 with grants totalling $790,000 from the Fund for the Improvement of Postsecondary Education and Digital Equipment Corporation.

BESTNET offers college credit courses to Hispanics throughout the Southwest and Mexico. Lectures and lab demonstrations in subjects like calculus, physics, and computer science are delivered in Spanish on videotape; class discussions are carried on by computer conferencing, with labs on college campuses and in community centers where adult students can come to view tapes and log onto the computer. A test of the effectiveness of the combined delivery method compared BESTNET student performance with San Diego classroom students. The former, many of whom had less background in the course material, did as well as their traditional classroom cohorts.[16]

Another example of mixing technologies for more effective instruction, a Rochester Institute of Technology program, shows the evolution from a regular classroom setting. The program, which gives the first two years of engineering courses to students 50 miles south of Rochester at Jamestown Community College, began by shuttling faculty back and forth. The expense and time constraints prompted the institute to send videotapes rather than professors, and student performance suffered. Then the institute set up an audiographic conferencing system to connect faculty and students. Through videotapes they see lectures and demonstrations by the institute's best faculty for the basic engineering subjects, while the audiographic system enables them to interact with those faculty in discussing problems and working them out. Jamestown students, many with two-year degrees in technical fields and employed, have the rich opportunity to complete two years of study toward the bachelor's degree before moving or commuting to Rochester to finish the work.

New combinations of technologies are multiplying daily under the aegis of large corporations seeking more cost-effective methods that bring good results. With employees scattered around the country and around the world, corporations are fast developing their own satellite networks. Because the growth is phenomenal and they constitute a "flagship" for others to consider for training purposes, we review their present status as a group.

Corporate Satellite Delivery

In 1988, there were more than 40 corporate-owned satellite networks, delivering to nearly 12,000 sites.[17] A year later 61 were in operation, and projections call for 141 by 1992.[18] Most of them are launched for business communications, not to carry instruction for workers. But with the networks in place, companies soon realize their value for training. So it was with the very active Automotive Satellite TV Network, serving more than 3,000 dealerships. Its parent company, Westcott Communication System, added the new Law Enforcement Television Network which, in five months, had more than 1,000 police departments as monthly subscribers for training purposes. Support materials with pre- and post-tests go by mail to accompany the programs. Westcott plans to announce soon a third network to carry training for a different group of workers.

Similarly, the J.C. Penney Company has expanded its corporate use by selling telecommunication services to other companies. Penney not only saves millions in reaching buyers and other employees at 700 locations via satellite, but its videoconference system has also become a money-making venture.

Other corporations are more explicit in the division of use, namely, whether it is primarily for education or general business matters. For example, in 1986, when Digital Equipment Corporation launched its video network with 18 receiving sites across the United States, 100 percent of the programming was devoted to corporate communications, none to training. Two years later, after a deliberate effort and with almost 100 downlinks in the United States and Canada, 80 percent of the programming was training and only 20 percent corporate communications. Digital expects that the ratio will continue to shift as demands increase for the network, but it has already proved its value in training.

In one instance the company tried a pilot program called "Tech Line" to test the feasibility of replacing teams of instructors traveling to Digital facilities to instruct repair and maintenance employees. The money saved by not putting instructors on the road and the positive response to the program from customer services employees convinced the company to use the satellite.[19] It is a simple formula: fewer instructors can reach a much larger number of students.

IBM, a pioneer in networks carrying instruction to customers and sales employees, is reorganizing and extending its delivery. Rather than separate systems, the Corporate Education Network now carries courses for advanced professionals from the Technical Institutes at Thornwood, New York, as well as training for other employees, marketing, and customers. It is used less for management education, which remains more traditional in classroom structure. IBM's curricular reform movement, however, is remarkably basic: professional development teams are designing new courses that combine subject-matter experts, writers, audio-visual experts, and so on with an instructional-systems designer who puts the entire course package together—an approach for a superior product, and IBM sees good business in education.

The high-tech industries, facing intense competition and strict time frames, have been at the forefront of using satellites for disseminating information and education. AT&T, Hewlett-Packard, and Texas Instruments were early users, as were the Boeing Company, Rockwell International, NCR, and others.

Time is money, of course, and the financial services industry is another leader in satellite-based dissemination of training on everything from new products and services to the latest SEC regulation or to an analysis of national economic trends. Deregulation of the industry has contributed to the rising market for information as well. In 1981, Merrill Lynch & Company began to use satellite broadcast for distributing information, and the company now sends 160 training and general information programs a year to 452 branch offices. Following the lead were Aetna Life and Casualty (which offered first a course on effective business writing), John Hancock, IDS-American Express, MONY, and the Illinois and Georgia Banking Associations. Chase Manhattan Bank uses video-conferencing to link more than 2,500 of its employees in eight countries for live discussions of perspectives on the bank's current and future global strategies.

Because satellite broadcasts can be produced in a central location, a corporation can control the information it chooses to deliver to its employees and ensure its consistency and confidentiality far more than it could if it relied on many instructors and scads of printed material. Moreover, the company can choose its best instructors and take them almost instantaneously to the employees.

It is more than a novel way of doing business; it creates a global network for instruction or, at minimum, information. Just as technological delivery systems bring information about the solar system and other planets back to us on earth, giving scientists the materials for learning, so also satellites in their more restricted travels can carry information and materials for learning that the work force needs in its everyday tasks.

Evaluation

The technical means are here and ready; repeatedly, research has demonstrated their effectiveness in learning, retention, and the application of the training in performance. Without using these technological gifts, our nation's work force cannot be brought up to date and kept there. The task is simply too big for accustomed ways and traditional procedures in education.

But one caveat is necessary: technologies are only *tools*, not *content*, and delivery without quality is of no value. In fact, the danger lies in creating splendid equipment to transmit inferior learning materials and poor instruction. Many of the examples we have used show that quality can be attained; it is coming from universities, corporations, and the military services. These models must set a standard for use.

Equally vital is another caution: the technology must be selected to enhance the instructional purpose. Many media are available from which to choose. Some technologies are more successful than others for particular purposes, and these differences are not difficult to ascertain. They become fairly clear as one matches the methods and their combination with the specific training purposes. Chances are that a mix of technologies will be most successful.

Providing learners with convenient access to information is important and basic, but enabling them to engage actively with other minds is the real catalyst for learning, for rendering the raw material of information into the finished product of knowledge. Hence, with all the talk of technology and long-distance learning outside the classroom, the power of people getting together in person to share ideas and learn from each other should not be ignored or forgotten. But, given the scale now needed, it cannot be done in the traditional ways.

Finally, while the latest technologies are applied as wisely and as extensively as possible to meet learning needs, it is well to remember how little is known about how individuals learn. There are further lessons to come from artificial intelligence and research efforts to model human learning and reasoning.

3

THE INTELLIGENT TUTOR

Artificial intelligence is a powerful resource of a different order in training and education. Such intelligent computer tools can not only take over and perform some jobs, quite independent of human help; they can also teach. They can work as colleagues with us, interacting as assistants or intelligent resources for expert information that contributes directly to performance on the job and, therefore, to productivity. The computing that replaces workers in some tasks can be used to train people for other jobs, both new high-tech tasks and more familiar but redefined jobs. Many observers assume that intelligent computer-assisted instruction systems will become the preferred choice for interactive training systems within a decade.[1]

In this chapter we give a progress report on the use of intelligent computer tools, what they can and cannot do, and how their application effects change in training patterns. Examples show their efficacy and suggest further possibilities. It may be that they can teach some skills more effectively and efficiently than people can. And in any case, they provide additional means for upgrading workers. Research into making the machines smarter may also eventually change the way *people* teach because of what is being discovered about the learning process itself.

Artificial intelligence (AI) is defined as the task of engineering some aspects of the human thought process. It does not try to imitate the human mind any more than a plane attempts to imitate a bird. In fact, Harry Tennant, chief scientist at Texas Instruments' Artificial Intelligence Center and one of the leading researchers in the field, points out that replicating human thought is not necessarily a good idea: people have done some extraordinarily bad thinking! But to reach their goals, AI researchers have had to improve their understanding of the human thought process itself, and their work to that end has contributed to the fields of cognitive psychology and linguistics, revealing a great deal about how people learn.

Unlike conventional, "number-crunching" computer programs that move inexorably and blindly from beginning to end, or else crash, AI programs can reason about the data they already have and the data they are given during a session. They can be designed to cope with uncertainty and incomplete information as those situations occur when a user is interacting with a program.

Expert systems, a derivative AI technology making rapid progress in real-world applications, including instruction, are so named because they can capture the expertise of a human being highly trained and experienced in a particular domain. Within certain constraints, for example, the specialized knowledge *and* ability to apply that knowledge that sets expert mining engineers apart from their colleagues can be captured and made available by means of the computer. A mining engineer thus becomes a consulting expert system, so to speak. And drawing on the person's knowledge does not depend on the expert being available—or even being alive.

The use of AI computing in a continuous, interactive learning environment for adults on and off the job is an exciting prospect. Intelligent computers are moving out of the experimental stage and becoming a tool for teachers and trainers alike. Intelligent computer-assisted instruction is being used in some school and university classrooms, workplaces, and government and military training facilities—in small but growing numbers.

Harry Tennant believes that AI has great potential for training and assisting the work force. At Texas Instruments' fourth symposium on "AI and the Knowledge-Worker Productivity Challenge," he commented:

> As we move away from an industrial economy and toward an information-centered economy, more and more of the work force is going to be composed of knowledge workers [those who create, modify, or distribute information]. The question is, what can be done to help them? Artificial intelligence is one answer. It won't fix the entire problem, but it is making contributions in several areas: creating and managing information, helping workers keep technically current, enhancing creativity, and contributing to the motivation of knowledge workers.[2]

Educators in industry at every level are beginning to pay attention to the development of programs that can teach more effectively and with measurable outcomes. Instructional designers and trainers in the classroom are under mounting pressure to show results. And they are under additional pressure to incorporate new subject matter into their courses. Workers have to be trained for new jobs more quickly, under tightening budgets. The complexity of changing tasks frequently calls for extra skills but allows little time to acquire them. Even if the process or instrument being introduced has built-in guides and assessment features to aid the employee, more basic understanding and background knowledge can be invaluable. Intelligent computer-assisted instruction brings that added dimension. Now let us look at where we stand in the development of intelligent tutors.

Reality or Hype?

Every new human endeavor is surrounded by prophecies that are riduculously optimistic or pathetically pessimistic, and the development of intelligent computers is no exception. Dramatic, glamorous systems with unlimited abilities are still the sole property of magazine and marketing headlines and probably always will be. AI research is not likely to unveil a system that will teach as effectively as a good human teacher. An unfortunate media and marketing hucksterism has created exaggerated expectations for intelligent computer applications. This is unfortunate because it has misled many people and discouraged them from seriously investigating the potential of intelligent computer-assisted instruction (ICAI) in training contexts. Fortunately it has not discouraged everyone, and significant, realistic progress is being made.

Two AI and education researchers, Gordon McCalla and Jim Greer, have formulated a statement of purpose that summarizes a generation of ICAI research. The mandate is, they say, "to draw the best from both traditional computer-assisted instruction (CAI) and reactive learning environments, and to construct systems that emulate a real teacher working individually with real learners." They elaborate:

> The fulfillment of this mandate would serve to make the computer a viable partner in the teaching/learning enterprise. The necessity of the human dimension in instruction cannot be overlooked, however. It is naive to view ICAI systems as teacher substitutes seeking to make teachers obsolete. A more realistic view of ICAI might be a set of teacher's assistants that patiently offer advice to individual learners, encourage learner practice and stimulate learners' curiosity through experimentation. This would potentially make the teacher available for more creative endeavors, or for helping learners overcome subtle or difficult problems beyond the capability of ICAI. Intelligent computer-assisted instruction will facilitate individualized instruction either within an existing school setting or in a more decentralized setting.[3]

Research and Use

Serious research goes back at least 15 years. Intelligent tutoring systems have been in use for some five years, though admittedly not in many places, teaching substantial portions of the curriculum for certain subjects both in school and on the job. In general, their design is organized by an AI computer simulation of human problem-solving behavior. The systems permit the learner to explore the subject matter, and they offer coaching. They also make an immediate evaluation of a student's approaches to the problem, including analysis and response to errors or patterns of error.

Diagnosis of student errors is a major research area. Cognitive scientists are investigating the mental models that students are believed to build about the subject matter in any learning process. The aim is to make sure that these models are accurate representations of the subject and do not merely instill more and more "facts" about it. This process may actually foster creative thinking because it gives the learner deeper understanding of the relationships among the facts the student is absorbing.

In some instances, research in intelligent systems is endorsing what we have long believed: namely, that person-to-person tutoring is the most effective way to teach, at least for some purposes. Socratic dialogue has remained the paradigm for discussion and exploration of issues; but here it also proves most effective for learning skills in mathematics, logic, and computer programming. Carnegie-Mellon University (CMU) researchers found that tutored students need only 11 hours to learn as much as their fellows in a classroom setting learn in 43 hours. The experiment was conducted during instruction in LISP, a computer programming language. Results showed that the tutor made the most significant contribution in the problem-solving parts of the instruction.[4]

The LISP Tutor and Geometry Tutor. Given this evidence and much more from general education research showing tutoring to be superior for a variety of subjects, CMU researchers set about building an intelligent computer-assisted instruction (ICAI) tutor that would be as effective in teaching LISP as a human tutor. They succeeded in combining AI technology with a psychological theory of skill acquisition. The result, the LISP Tutor, became established at the university in 1984, and a version of it reached the commercial market the following year. It has been used successfully with technical and nontechnical undergraduates and with industry and government computer programmers. John R. Anderson, a developer of the LISP Tutor, also worked on the Geometry Tutor, an ICAI system that has been integrated into a Pittsburgh, Pennsylvania, high school geometry classroom to teach proof-solving skills.

Learning results reported for the LISP and geometry tutors are good. Time savings are in the range of 40 percent. Learners using both systems acquire much better problem-solving ability with ICAI. School students using either tutoring system generally improve their performance by one grade: a C student in a conventional class can perform at a B level with the help of the ICAI tutor.

PROUST.   An equally notable ICAI approach is PROUST, a programming tutor for the Pascal computer programming language developed by Elliot Soloway and his colleagues at Yale University. PROUST is capable of high-quality analysis of "bugs" (errors) in student assignments. But in field tests, some student programs deviated so drastically from PROUST's or its developers' expectations that they could not be analyzed at all. The developers of PROUST aim to refine it so that it will also suggest additional programming projects for students to tackle so they can get practice where they need it.[5]

A General Tutor.   Other research is looking less at error analysis and more toward general uses. Marijke Augusteijn of the University of Colorado at Colorado Springs has completed a prototype with the support of Ford Aerospace and Communication Corporation and her university's Office for Space Science Technology. Augusteijn and her team have designed an intelligent tutoring system that is subject-matter independent—within certain limits, any subject can be engineered into the tutor. One important limit is the system's inability to accommodate conceptual knowledge.

The tutor, like most advanced ICAI, can present material at different levels of difficulty and take a student's individual learning style into account. It can coach the student through a problem-solving exercise. And as it performs remediation based on its own analysis of the cause of the student's errors, it goes farther in adjusting to individual differences in learning.

To do this, the Augusteijn team takes its model from David A. Kolb's theory of experiential learning. One application of the theory is well known as McBer and Company's Learning-Style Inventory, a model that sees learning as a four-stage cycle: concrete experience, which is immediate and subjective; reflective observation; abstract conceptualization or thoughtfulness; and active experimentation, the application of what has been learned. In other words, the learner must get involved in the new area, reflect on the experience, create hypotheses that integrate the result of that reflection in a logically sound manner, and apply the resulting implications for action or hypotheses to problem solving. The adaptive aspect recognizes that individuals have different emphases among the four learning orientations, and the inventory actually measures degrees of preference. One individual may favor abstraction over hands-on experience, another may learn more comfortably by receiving information and reflecting on it, and so on.

Developers see this adaptive capability of intelligent systems as especially important in the world of industry, where trainees have very different educational backgrounds. For example, a trainee with a humanities background tends to learn differently from a trainee who is an engineer. The system will modify its presentation of material after determining the learner's style, thus permitting something quite close to the best one-on-one instruction.

Given that students in school or employees on the job can acquire certain skills faster and more effectively with ICAI, what are the limits to its use? Theoretically, any tutorial strategy can be implemented, but some educational approaches are easier to represent. For example, as mentioned above, ICAI tutors do not yet handle instruction of conceptual knowledge. A hierarchical model of learning, which sees knowledge as acquired in phases, is commonly used now because such an organized structure of knowledge is well suited to current technology. Thus, applications concentrate on skills like word processing, programming languages, geometry and other math, and some aspects of physics—diverse on the surface but hierarchical underneath.

As Bank Street College's Seth Chaiklin and Carnegie-Mellon University's Matthew Lewis pointed out in a 1987 evaluation of ICAI and general educational goals, "We have to be clear about how our systems interact with current educational goals."[6] This advice pertains to researchers, teachers, and instructional designers who might otherwise run amok fielding ICAI only for the sake of using very high technology. ICAI is very good for some things; it is not, however, the total solution to all training problems.

The University of Saskatchewan recently established a laboratory for advanced research in intelligent educational systems that relates research and development to useful application. It brings together Canadian and American leaders in AI, cognitive science, and instructional systems. Emphasizing application, not just research, the work is intended to foster communication between the people who develop systems and the people who use them.

Gordon McCalla, lab director, exemplifies the project's concern for bringing education into the ICAI development process. His work has included intelligent tutoring systems and knowledge representation in expert-system environments. Expert systems can not only instruct like intelligent tutors, they can also handle more complex situations in problem solving and usually explain the reasoning process used. They can serve as both monitor and mentor.

An Expert System: Aldo

Campbell Soup Company's use of an expert system as a training tool and intelligent coworker is typical. At the center of any Campbell plant around the world is the huge cooker that sterilizes the food. Any malfunction of the cooker causes an extremely expensive disruption of the plant floor and shipping schedules. Plant engineers handle the minor problems encountered in operation of the cookers. But intimate knowledge of their design, installation, and operation is rare and virtually impossible to transmit in regular training.

In the mid-1980s, Campbell's expert cooking vat engineer, the man whose factual and experiential knowledge of the giant soup cookers made him a strategic corporate engineering maintenance asset, planned to retire. The company worked with Texas Instruments to capture Aldo Cimino's expertise in a personal computer-based expert system that would function side-by-side with field maintenance engineers. The software, the Cooker Maintenance Advisor, is now a proven tool that saves time and money by distributing knowledge to the maintenance engineers when they need it. It also helps train new maintenance staff members. Employees have affectionately dubbed the software "Aldo in a Can." While no one can claim that *all* of Aldo's expertise was captured, much of his knowledge and experience remains for others. Aldo can enjoy his well-deserved leisure, and Campbell maintenance engineers consult the expert system when a problem arises rather than having to rediscover all the tricks of the trade Mr. Cimino accumulated over 44 years.

The key element here is "consult." The worker is not using the expert system to search for data, such as the time to reach the boiling point of cream of mushroom soup in cookers of various sizes. Instead, maintenance engineers interact with the system, often in a question-and-answer format, to troubleshoot a problem such as temperature deviation in a vat when everything appears to be functioning properly. They do not need to be sent for training every time a small change is made in a vat. They use their intelligent mentor.

Knowledge Engineering

An expert system must capture both the factual knowledge of a subject area and the general intelligence about the subject that a human teacher possesses. Much of the preliminary work on such a system is what is called "knowledge engineering," which operates on the principle that expert performance on a task rarely conforms to any rigorous algorithmic process. A knowledge engineer may be the human expert in the subject area, or someone from the same discipline who is also experienced in AI techniques, or a programmer who gathers information from the experts. The knowledge engineer is charged with identifying the details needed for the system, organizing them in a way the system can use, and then planning how the system will function.

Insight into the instructional power of ICAI may be gleaned from overview of the kinds of knowledge that are engineered. It is much more than mere facts; it is the composite subject knowledge and psychological expertise of one or more teachers that is the great strength of these systems. Today's best ICAI developers share these thoughts:

> There is a great deal of knowledge that expert teachers use in the instructional process. Domain knowledge, knowledge of the content to be taught, is crucial, but is only one small part of the teacher's knowledge base. Domain knowledge must be integrated in such a way that appropriate questions, tailored to individual learners, can be posed. Similarly, queries from learners must be answered within the context of the learner's ability to understand. The teacher may act as a mentor engaging in Socratic tutoring, may offer guided practice (as in apprenticeship), or may offer explanations at appropriate times in the instructional process. The teacher diagnoses learner misconceptions by watching for familiar error patterns. Remedial actions are then designed according to the individual learning needs of the student.[7]

Although remarkable progress has been made, significant problems remain. One difficulty lies in inadequate understanding of how people learn. In fact, researcher William Clancey writes that "there is no need to consider strategies for teaching if we do not understand what the student is doing."[8] Despite recent research and theories on the subject, cognitive scientists cannot yet model the student's knowledge. Among those addressing the problem are Elliot Soloway at Yale, John Anderson at Carnegie-Mellon, and John Seely Brown and Richard Burton at Xerox's Palo Alto research center. They are beginning to prove the usefulness of certain techniques, but this will be a crucial research area for the near term and probably longer.

Researchers are looking to educational theory and research for an appropriate cognitive theory. Piaget's developmental theories and the schema theories are difficult to model; statistical models of learning are computable but do not offer sufficient insight into the learning process. Much research and development lies ahead.

State of the ICAI Art

Using current AI technology, an intelligent tutoring system with the following characteristics is considered feasible now and may be built soon.[9] It will have subject area knowledge that it can peruse and manipulate, some experts on the forefront of research claim. It will use either a flexible, responsive teaching strategy or more indirect coaching. But even more, it will understand its user's language and grasp the user's misconceptions about the subject involved.

It will have what researchers call the capability to understand natural language. When the student types more or less natural sentences, questions, and commands at the keyboard, the system will understand most of the student's words and syntax—within a circumscribed subject area, of course. One of the many problems in getting computers to understand natural language is that users often are ignorant of the meaning of the everyday words they use. Computers, far from removing the need for literacy and general education, may well increase it in this instance.

Critics point out that the major difficulty lies not in getting the system to produce an acceptable natural language response, but to *understand*. Furthermore, the subject area covered will have limited parameters. Nevertheless, such dialogue will free the student from rigid and complex command sequences to focus on content rather than form. Pictorial and graphic images can also be used easily to reinforce learning and add variety to the lesson.

The system will do more than compile a record of student errors; it will diagnose errors to the level of finding the misconceptions underlying a student's poor performance, then adjust its instructional style accordingly. The program will not learn in a very sophisticated sense, but various programming techniques can disguise this shortcoming and offer the student a satisfactorily individualized response. Finally, a knowledge engineer will be able to use the system to find out more basic information quickly about student-teacher interaction.

The Need for Teachers in Research

More insight into the performance of good teachers is essential for building the next generation of ICAI systems. Teachers themselves must join as models and as colleagues in the effort. In research, there has been relatively little emphasis until now on how people teach or on designing teaching expertise into the systems. Such expertise does not mean the representation of knowledge on the subject but its actual presentation to the student. As one research team has stressed, "Without an appreciation for how much tacit knowledge underlies good instruction performed by human instructors . . . it is easy to visualize the potential without really knowing what might be required to make it a reality."[10]

The profound implications of ICAI challenge teachers and instruction researchers to keep up with the infusion of advanced computing in their fields. McCalla's comments reflect the opinion of other researchers. "Education practitioners should become more familiar with ICAI technology," he says, and this means learning about the systems generally as well as the strengths and weaknesses of particular ones. Both potential and improbable developments should be understood, the better to avoid hyperbole. Most of all, the cognitive theories forming the basis of ICAI require further study and experimentation to determine their validity. "Ultimately," he writes, "teachers will mediate the implementation and conduct the evaluation of ICAI systems. Consequently, teacher input at this early stage in ICAI development is essential."[11]

The Military on the Bandwagon

Trainers in institutions such as the armed forces have progressed to these methods ahead of the educational establishment for a variety of reasons including, no doubt, the different emphases of the two groups. Performance in a specific job is the goal of military training; the goals of school are traditionally more general, and work toward them less constrained by time and economic pressures. Training in the armed services is usually conducted within a clear framework of time and cost, so the motivation to teach people quickly and effectively at the lowest possible cost drives the search for better methods.

Some of the most interesting work in ICAI and intelligent job assistance by means of expert systems is going on in the military. This is encouraging when one realizes that on an average day in 1988 some 210,000 people on active duty and some 45,000 members of the National Guard and the Reserves underwent some type of formal training. These figures exclude all job-site training, factory and unit training for new systems, team training for performance of specific missions, and all field exercises.[12]

The Air Force's PETITE/IV. The Training Development Branch of the Air Force Communications Command, a leader in instructional technology applications, has made significant progress in interactive videodisc training, in the use of software authorizing systems, in both conventional and computer-assisted instruction, and in ICAI particularly for training in a variety of maintenance jobs.

Problems with older training technologies led the branch toward intelligent computing. While interactive video tools proved useful for training maintenance technicians who required skill training of a drill and practice variety, they were found to be unsatisfactory for instruction in troubleshooting. Regular maintenance is a skill incorporating prescribed routines, but troubleshooting is an activity that involves the use of higher level intellectual skills.[13] Skill in diagnosis or troubleshooting is what sets the experts apart in many fields, and the trainers wanted to find ways to create expertise. The branch has developed the prototype electronic technician intelligent tutor with interactive video (PETITE/IV). The project tests the feasibility, cost, and effectiveness of the ICAI technology. Its first purpose is to give instruction in a shorter period of time to produce expert electronics maintenance technicians.[14]

PETITE/IV is a most suitable example of AI and cognitive science applied to the adult training environment because the Air Force problem is similar to what business and industry are facing. Equipment is changing, job descriptions are changing, and both require cost-effective changes in workers.

For electronic troubleshooting, PETITE/IV's developers faced complications. Their thinking can be summarized as follows: electronic equipment is becoming more reliable, which is good, but reliability means that experience acquired on the job is declining because fewer repairs are made—which is bad from the trainer's point of view. Moreover, because of higher reliability, equipment is designed and often delivered without backup. This bodes well for capital investment but ill for the trainer, who needs a backup system for instruction. If, on the other hand, modular units are provided for repair, they are unsuitable for training on specific parts.

Furthermore, because of improved reliability the repair job

tends to become less specialized while at the same time modern equipment is much more complex and complicated. When the equipment fails and there is no substitute, the pressure to get it repaired is much more intense. Clearly the Air Force selected a training problem for its ICAI experiment that is absolutely crucial to performance. In an emergency, a military airplane cannot wait for equipment repair or replacement. Electronic experts are essential.

Too much conventional training is "monkey mechanics," in the phrase of the Air Force: follow the documentation, step by step, until you find the problem, and then follow the repair documentation, step by step, until it is repaired. If the first diagnosis is incorrect, it will not be discovered until the repair procedure fails to restart the system. Training people to do a task that way does not train them to *think* about the equipment they are working on. Furthermore, documentation increasingly fails to cover every possible problem of complex systems, and too often the explanation is mystifying to all but the initiated.

One instructional approach might be to give the technicians interactive video and let them practice, practice, practice. The medium is very good for this kind of training. But an attractive and better alternative to repeated practice of limited skills is to teach the technicians to think, to develop conceptual abilities and skills so that their training extends across many kinds of systems. The result: more people can learn better skills in a shorter time.

The 1988 branch report on the PETITE/IV prototype waxed enthusiastic both about the performance of the intelligent tutoring system as designed and about two unanticipated benefits. First, the developers found that technicians enjoyed training with the system. They found working with an AI computer system interesting. Second, the trainers became more deeply involved in the instruction design than they had been with conventional or interactive videodisc training. The AI system development technique of knowledge engineering turned out to be a very useful approach to course content development that could probably be extended to other instructional designs because it compelled trainers to think carefully and speak articulately about their knowledge.[15]

The Navy's STEAMER. The Navy provides a different kind of example—created, installed, and working. STEAMER is an interactive simulation-based system developed for the Navy Personnel Research and Development Center to train engineering officers in the operation of steam propulsion systems. The project has included specialists in computer programming and AI who work with such research centers as the Massachusetts Institute of Technology, Xerox's Palo Alto research center, and Symbolics, Inc., a small company devoted to AI computer hardware and software. Such team members might be expected in an artificial intelligence and instruction project, but in this instance the project also included Terry Roe, a retired boiler technician with 22 years of experience in propulsion operations. While many of the systems described are still under refinement, STEAMER is essentially complete.

One report on the project expresses the scope of the knowledge problem confronting the Navy. "When you spend from 50 million to a few billion dollars for a Navy ship," the authors observe, "you also get an extensive user's manual. One form of this manual contains a list of procedures, called the Engineering Operational Sequencing System, for operating the plant. This set of manuals, which would fill a good sized book case, contains all of the procedures needed to run the ship's propulsion system."[16] As anyone who has seen the manual or documentation for a simple software program knows, they are seldom intelligible. Imagine a bookcase full of them!

STEAMER uses graphics to simulate the physical systems. The computer screen shows representations of dials, control panels, pipes, pumps, and the flow of steam or water. A pump, for example, is green if it is operating and red if it is turned off. The graphics permit students to control, manipulate, and monitor simulations of dynamic systems at many different hierarchical levels. The graphics also allow students to view aspects of the steam system that cannot ordinarily be seen in a real power plant, like the flow rates in pipes and the variables that affect flow. This helps them build an accurate mental model of the system at work. Students can develop and test their own hypotheses about the steam propulsion system—and find out whether they are right or wrong at less cost and in greater safety than if they were experimenting with a real ship.

STEAMER can be an adviser or mentor, a facility somewhat different from the guided tutorial of the LISP Tutor. STEAMER's instructional approach, combined with the interactive graphics, seems to be a successful way to train in environments where the important learning is understanding the dynamics and principles of a physical system rather than acquisition of data about abstract subject matter. This instructional approach has been widely adopted. It is used, for example, in airline pilot training.

A Trainer's Prediction

Coming first and faster than some other AI computer application efforts are expert systems that help workers do their jobs. These are the mentors or colleagues that function as a resource in time of need—like "Aldo in a Can." They support people's ability to improve their performance, virtually on their own, in a particular task area, and thus they can directly aid the quality of the work and the level of productivity. They are a modern type of on-the-job training.

The potential impact of these mentor systems is so great that expert Paul Harmon claims they will soon transform training. A "simultaneous decline in 'memory or theory-oriented' instruction in training environments" will accompany their proliferation. [17] These expert systems are attractive mainly because techniques that help an employee in the performance of a task are more cost effective than training the employee to memorize a procedure or its theoretical basis—especially when the procedure soon may be outdated.

An instructional technologist in a business environment is most concerned with developing instruction that yields a very specific performance level—training that enables the worker to get the job done at minimal cost. Harmon reports:

> I've been engaged in analyzing human performance problems and developing solutions for the last 15 years. I've worked on a wide range of problems at major corporations, including management education programs, sales training programs, programmer training programs, accounting programs, and a wide variety of programs to provide instruction for all kinds of operational and clerical personnel. . . . One-fourth of all problems I have encountered have been amenable to job aid solutions.[18]

The technology for developing and delivering intelligent job assistance is in place. These aids are spreading as an adjunct to training that relieves the training load and also ensures high job performance. Such assistance can later be integrated into an ICAI system as the expert or knowledge-base component. A smart job assistant is, in a sense, the subset of an ICAI system that possesses the subject area knowledge and rules about applying that knowledge. It has neither a tutorial segment nor a capability of modeling the student and his or her instructional history. It is an expert system that asks questions only about the specific situation and offers recommendations: "Does the robot arm activate when the power switch is turned on?" No. "Check fuse." And a good system will, for example, display a color graphic on the monitor showing the layout of the fuse box with the arm fuse highlighted in some manner. It happens that the subject area knowledge component with procedure and rules about a task is one system that can be built well today, but capturing deep knowledge in a system remains difficult.

Conventional, simple job aids have long been around: the telephone directory, a pocket calculator, the airline flight schedule. For several decades, performance aids have technologically provided job instruction, especially for highly specific maintenance. But now there are satisfactory aids for more intellectually complex jobs. As noted earlier, procedure manuals with complicated written instructions are useless to the average worker and even the technician; they are simply incomprehensible.

For instruction on these products it seems more effective to have a human tutor or teacher than a manual. Neither may be feasible, however, and neither approach can cope with the large numbers of workers who need the introductory training. Intelligent job aids, like Campbell's Aldo or the expert systems appearing in the insurance industry to help in everything from handling forms to decisions on underwriting, permit skilled persons to record their knowledge in a portable, interactive system that assists and trains individuals as they learn and perform their job assignments. Examples from industry outline an image of the shape of things to come.

Applications Increase

Honeywell Inc. has developed an expert system called MENTOR, designed to guide a service person with experience in air-conditioning maintenance through the performance of preventive care and low-level diagnostics. It accomplishes an important training task "on the job." Honeywell's Building Services Division uses MENTOR in field work. Control Data uses an expert system to bring the expertise of head operators, systems analysts, and customer engineers to help an operator in difficulty restore normal operation.

Mueller Associates has developed a radar diagnostic and training expert system for a client. The intelligent job aid diagnoses problems in the transmitter unit of a large shipboard radar system. Acting as an adviser, it offers test procedures for troubleshooting the transmitter and an interactive tutorial training program. It has graphics of test equipment, and users can match a waveform on the computer screen with the waveform they are actually seeing on an oscilloscope. "Studies have shown," the developer points out, "that the most significant factor affecting the availability of the radar system is the training and performance of the service technicians."[19] Mueller's system makes the instruction of 20-year veteran field engineers available on-site to Navy service technicians—an accomplishment no other training form can offer.

In civilian use, there are fully tested training systems at many industrial sites throughout the United States. The Recovery Boiler Tutor, for example, was built by J. H. Jansen Company, a steam and power engineering firm near Seattle, Washington, under the sponsorship of the American Paper Institute. It can provide the user, a control room operator, with multiple explanations and tutoring geared to that person through an interactive simulation. Operators have reported using the system up to 70 hours over three months to practice coping with emergencies. The system's developers observed that the operators "handle the simulation with extreme care, behaving as they might if they were in actual control" of a pulp mill boiler emergency.[20] The Recovery Boiler Tutor is in use in more than 80 plants in the United States, Canada, and Europe.

On a rather less technical but no less demanding front, Arthur D. Little, Inc. has developed an intelligent job assistant for the banking industry called Platform Manager's Assistant to aid in complex jobs. They help customers with often difficult transactions, they give information about the bank's services, they sell the bank's products, and they are often the front line in resolving customer difficulties. The new system evolved from work to improve officers' performance in an environment increasingly complicated by expanding bank services. And it significantly improves the officers'—and the banks'—performance.[21]

Multiple purposes can be served at one time, as can be seen in two programs of the U.S. Defense Advanced Research Projects Agency (DARPA) and IntelliCorp, Inc., a small AI software company. DARPA's internal administrative project management will have two knowledge systems. One will automate the generation of orders and documents that distribute money and authorize contractual obligations in the agency's name. Currently, the agency generates more than 1,800 orders annually and requires a full-time staff of seven senior employees. The intelligent system is expected to reduce delays and the potential for human error on initial orders, and it will free time for senior staff to spend on more productive projects.

The other system will give some 100 DARPA program managers a way to track and account for the financial data relating to their projects, including the ability to determine the types of questions and refinements necessary to maintain proper control. Given the scope of the tasks these systems will handle, it is important to note that DARPA plans to use both systems as training tools for new employees. Furthermore, the new control methods will help track mismanagement and overruns on defense contracts. This should be of interest to Congress and the public.

Computer-Assisted Instruction

While we watch and wait for advancing research and applications of intelligent systems like ICAI and its colleague in expert systems, the use of the more familiar and older computer-assisted instruction (CAI) continues to spread on campuses and in workplaces. It too acts in some ways as if it were a knowledgeable tutor guiding individual students or employees. While CAI is less flexible, less qualitative in evaluating student performance, and generally less clever than ICAI in offering dynamic options for the learner, it has proved its worth. Its advantages include effective, low-cost delivery for instruction in many subjects from the obvious arithmetic lesson or science course to courses in English grammar, foreign languages, history, and musicology. It facilitates individual learning at one's own pace. It can also be portable instruction, taking the teacher to any person anywhere with the proper computer (very often now an inexpensive personal computer).

Costs of program development vary widely; a ratio of 200 hours of development time to one hour of instruction time is not uncommon if the course is prepared from scratch. On the other hand, software authoring systems are available that let trainers "plug in" their material and fine-tune it for computer use, thus greatly reducing development time and cost.

For teaching drill and practice material, CAI has advantages over the usual classroom routines. In an exercise, learners get instant feedback on their answers. During this repetitive process, the computer has infinite patience, drilling even the slowest learner with no evidence of frustration or boredom. If the CAI program is a good one, the computer may generate a different instructional sequence for each student's individual pattern of response. As CAI specialist Greg Kearsley has pointed out, "For any course that involves students with diverse backgrounds or ability levels, computer-based instruction can be very worthwhile."[22] Nevertheless, the ability to respond to learners' needs is still limited.

Kearsley has developed a good checklist of what CAI is and is not good for at the present time. Computers are not especially good for teaching a subject that depends heavily on text or static graphics. A book or a simple printed form presents text more cheaply and more conveniently. Also, people do not read straight text as fast or as well on a computer monitor as they do on a printed page. Graphics are very effective in CAI, but good computer graphics are expensive to program and the hardware to display them is still costly. Careful thought must go into the choice of computer or printed page when it comes to some kinds of pictures. For example, photographic slides or videotape may be better for presenting realistic images.

A frequent criticism of CAI systems is that they developed in a theoretical vacuum.[23] This claim is not entirely valid. Most CAI programs have incorporated some concept of learning and teaching, although often these have been merely the common approaches used in school and training classrooms: present the material in a small segment, query the student's grasp of it, and move on to new material or remedial practice depending on the test results.

Some concepts are more challenging, like those that involve the student in programming a computer. Conjecture has it that instruction in problem-solving strategies can come from working with programming tools that guide the student toward efficient methods. Other instructional tools, widely used in adult training, are games and simulations based on the subject. A variety of programs, for example, is available to teach management techniques through simulation of a corporation in action. A program called PORTSIS (derived from portfolio analysis) is available for learning and practice in finance. Students track, maintain, and evaluate investment portfolios. PORTSIS helps the teacher judge the student's investment decisions and strategies. Other CAI systems use simulation to teach pilots, to instruct in electrical wiring principles, and so on. Here again the student is plunged into an activity that takes advantage of the computer's interactive capacities. Learning is the bonus derived from doing.

CAI in the Marketplace

Advanced computer-delivered instruction has come a long way from rigid electronic "workbooks" tied to expensive computer hardware. Individuals, consulting firms, and companies both large and small are developing and marketing courses. Some are entirely computer based; others are for practice and review following a traditional training session. Some are developed by a training facility for a specific situation, and literally thousands are available for purchase off-the-shelf at rather low cost. It is easy to find CAI material for adult education and training in areas from business education and technical and scientific subjects through languages and basic office skills.

An example is a series of courses from Datapro Educational Services, a unit of McGraw-Hill, aimed at the adult learner who needs ongoing professional instruction. The series on information technology consists of 5 computer-delivered courses and 13 seminar courses. The live and computer courses need not be taken together. The cost of a computer course can be as much as $600, while seminars cost up to $900 plus travel and accommodations. An IBM or compatible personal computer is the only hardware requirement.

On other educational levels, Digital Equipment Corporation's VAX software source book includes educational packages ranging from the Engineering Science Program Exchange to clerical skills training. The exchange is a library of more than 80 CAI items covering specialties from civil to nuclear engineering. At a somewhat lower level, the source book lists a program called Handsight that monitors the skills of a person using the computer keyboard and gives therapeutic exercises for systematic errors. According to its developers, for $900 users can achieve touch-typing skills in 15 to 20 hours. Friendly Handsight, by the way, prints out a certificate of achievement and "presents" it to each successful student.

There is no doubt that computer-aided instruction is effective in the common CAI format. The earliest systematic review, in 1972, found a median increase in student achievement of 40 percent in CAI drill and practice lessons involving more than 10,000 different students. Later studies have found very similar results for schools using CAI. A major review of CAI in the military found an average training time saving of 32 percent—a significant reduction if the trainee is being paid during training time. Equivalent or better student achievement was found in 47 of the 48 evaluations reviewed. While some methodological questions can be raised about each of these evaluations, nothing has appeared that puts the results in grave doubt. They support the belief in the instructional and economic advantages of using computer-driven teaching models for certain nonconceptual learning tasks.[24]

Remedies for CAI's deficiencies may be found in the advanced research accompanying the ICAI development described earlier. It could be said that whatever CAI can do, ICAI can do better—and it can do much more. The strides being made in learning how people learn will benefit both the older, more prevalent system and the newer intelligent aids.

Summary

Advanced computing means that people will work differently and be trained differently. For the first time since the days of master and apprentice, work and training need no longer be separate events, and being untrained for a task need not signal a productivity bottleneck for employers and insecurity for workers. Work and training will be integrated and ongoing. It is fortunate that new intelligent systems come close to implementing apprenticeship with quality. Labor union leaders should take note and should help finance their development and application, which can provide superior instruction based on the worker's need, knowledge, and ability.

It is a further blessing that instructional technology may keep up with—or at least closely follow—the revolution in business and manufacturing processes. The greatest challenge is for workers to get the training promptly and so perform well enough to hold their jobs. Some may imagine a Frankenstein's monster and withdraw, but that would be a crippling choice. To earn a living, people must work with the new instruments that will aid their self-training.

The concept of training by intelligent computers is rapidly penetrating both civilian and military thinking. Had this study been done a few years ago, we could have mentioned the ICAI systems under development in a short chapter. There is no way that could now be done, and even these examples may be seriously out-of-date before publication. Today we must be satisfied with an overview. In August 1988, Raj Reddy of Carnegie-Mellon told the annual meeting of the American Association for Artificial Intelligence that some 8,500 corporate expert systems of all types were in development. How many of these projects will eventually find a place as assistant trainers is impossible to say. But imagination is not necessary to see that technologies for learning are here and developing.

The examples given are a representative sample of the intelligent aids to learning available in the workplace today and an indication of what is on the immediate horizon. ICAI is being increasingly combined with more conventional instruction delivery modes like interactive videodisc. It can be moved into the training environment and act as an adjunct to the instructor. The worker can get training in the basics and then go to work with an intelligent job aid that will carry the very best kind of training with it—interactive, on-site, and drawn from one or more specialists who would otherwise be inaccessible.

Aside from the data of individual researchers like John Anderson and his Carnegie-Mellon team or those on the STEAMER project, it is difficult to find long-term evaluations of ICAI performance in the field. They are out there, but the systems in use are simply too new. A significant number of evaluations, however, are under way, and reports appear with increasing frequency in the literature. National meetings address the topic. In June 1989, the Fourth Rocky Mountain Conference on AI took as its theme "Augmenting Human Intellect by Computer." The program emphasized computer-supported work and education.

Unlike the burgeoning market for computer-assisted instruction, AI products are just entering the commercial market, and they are not making their entrance in an organized fashion. They come from many sources: small, entrepreneurial companies, large corporations, universities, and the military. They come from research that is exploring minds, how they operate and learn, individual differences, and many aspects that cut across disciplines. Logic, mathematics, psychology, philosophy, engineering and computer science, and the arts and literature are all being asked to contribute to the endeavor—a powerful new reason for the disciplines to cooperate and challenge exceptional minds. Above all, more teachers are needed—and needed now—in the research and development of AI as an instructional tool.

There is no doubt that ICAI can greatly assist in teaching and helping people to learn as well as produce more in their endeavors. Although it may take longer to see results than enthusiasts claim, predictions of its benefits have been accurate thus far. Of the various components of ICAI, expert systems are most advanced.

Paul Harmon sees intelligent job aids gradually becoming the dominant medium in training for business, industry, and government. He predicts that they will continue to replace the unintelligible manual or the teacher trying to explain complex systems. Nevertheless, he raises a warning flag:

> To the degree that we develop intelligent job aids that ask questions and then recommend solutions, we "deprive" users of the experience of "messing" with a problem until they figure it out. In other words, we deny the users the rich period of experimentation that normally leads to the development of an expert. By automating troubleshooting and problem solving we will undoubtedly increase the quality and consistency of human performance in the near term. In the long run, however, we may find that we will need more sophisticated simulation programs (more education rather than training) to create the experts who will ultimately create and update the intelligent job aids that most employees will increasingly depend on.[25]

We will use the new intelligent technological abilities to aid in job performance, but their use must not preclude our learning and creative exploration as human beings. Will we *depend* on them or simply *use* them and learn the fundamentals on our own? There is a seventeenth-century dictum that applies: man's "right reason" must judge and control so that the new discoveries can serve for the real and long-term benefit of all.

Generally thus far, the new instructional technologies are proving advantageous in bringing essential knowledge and up-to-date information to the work force. And they can deliver it in a cost-effective manner at the place of work and at the time it is required. Without increasing their use and improving further the quality of technological instruction, there is no way we can meet the needs of America's workers today and every day ahead as changes interrupt the accustomed routines. Those changes force adjustment in education and training patterns that go beyond customary teaching routines. We must draw on all resources for learning.

PART

II

THE ADULT

STUDENTS

4

TRAINING TECHNICAL WORKERS

$\mathbb{A}$t first glance the training in place for the work force is extensive and includes some of the newer resources for learning. Although inadequate to the total task, the programs sponsored by large corporations, unions, government (both federal and state), and the military comprise a solid base on which to build. And colleges are increasingly providing instruction. Here the focus is on the workers themselves and their opportunities for learning. We examine four large categories of workers in skilled trades and technical fields: construction, offices and administrative support services, information systems, and automated factory processes. We chose these four areas because they are fundamental to the economy, they comprise a large part of the total work force, and each has seen the dramatic effects of rapid technological change.

There was a time when each worker could do his or her own job rather independently; although the worker's performance related to the production of others, it was not as pervasive a relationship as it often is today. Those same communications that are changing instructional methods and the way we conduct businesses are also linking one person's work to another's, frequently in automatic fashion. When one worker performs poorly or inadequately, it can affect many more people, even dangerously so. Thus, while skilled tradesmen and technicians may be the economy's backbone, they also serve as an essential element in its nervous system, connecting the parts and affecting its total performance.

These workers furnish the practical knowledge and labor that convert construction blueprints to finished structures. They operate electronic systems, computers, and communications networks. They fill technical positions in factories and plants and furnish administrative, clerical, and secretarial support in offices.

For all these jobs, the entry level has risen: educational requirements—before employment—mean more than high school graduation. In most instances, postsecondary training is absolutely necessary. And for the many people already employed to keep their jobs, retraining or additional learning is equally vital.

The diverse occupations being considered naturally differ in the training available to workers and in the degree of innovation used. Where the resources are thin relative to demand, and where innovation is lacking, the industry or occupation will inevitably suffer. Instructional technologies and delivery systems described in the preceding chapters are only now spreading in these fields. Some media have entered construction workers' training, more are apparent for office and administrative workers, and significantly more for training factory workers in computer-integrated manufacturing and other automated processes.

Although we point out critical problems, such as the need for more continuing education for journeymen, nevertheless we found real progress toward the improvement and extension of training opportunities. One hopeful development is the growth in collaboration among providers. Especially for technicians in the advancing technologies, local and state governments are joining companies and educational institutions to encourage training. Such efforts, sparked by competition among the states to attract industry, have the beneficial result of serving workers.

More partnerships are appearing between companies and colleges, particularly the two-year institutions that strive to meet business needs. More contractual agreements between unions and management or trade associations are providing cooperative training programs. These are encouraging signs for workers, but much more remains to be done, as will be apparent in the following descriptions of training in four sectors that undergird the world of business.

Construction Trades

Although the construction industry employs almost eight million people, scant formal attention has been paid to training in basic skills and to continuing education. Colleges and universities, labor unions, and trade associations are the dominant providers, and academic degree programs in construction are growing with placement rates high. Some administrators believe they could place twice the number of their graduates in well-paying entry-level jobs.

The labor unions, a potent force in construction, continue to run their well-known apprenticeship programs for training skilled craftsmen and technical workers. So strongly is this training concept tied to construction that at least 60 percent of the 250,000 apprentices in the United States are in construction-related fields. The National Association of Home Builders and the Associated General Contractors promote construction professions, work to expand and strengthen degree programs, and sponsor their own education programs.

Construction is not a technological backwater. Materials that did not exist 20 years ago are now routinely used in commercial, industrial, and home building, and the technology and equipment that have developed alongside them are much more sophisticated than the "day laborer" stereotype implies. Because more qualified and productive personnel must be employed at all levels, training has assumed a new significance in the industry. When asked about trends, trade association officials emphasize the importance of constant training and the need not merely for workers, but quality workers.

Training by Trade Associations.   Most construction companies are small. They band together to conduct training as a way to share the cost. The National Association of Home Builders, which was founded in 1941 and began its first educational seminars in 1947, has over the past four decades developed a program of entry-level, certification, and continuing education for the building trades. In 1983, the association formed the nonprofit Home Builders Institute as an educational arm to provide quality programs, comprehensive construction training, and assistance with job placement.

Today the institute sponsors seminars, workshops, video teleconferences, hands-on training, study tours, and certificate courses. Each year more than 4,000 individuals participate in these activities. In 1967, the trade group launched its Craft Skills Program to train the unemployed and unskilled in carpentry, electrical wiring, plumbing, heating and air conditioning, maintenance, and remodeling. The program is tailored to local needs and standards by a coordinator who recruits participants and helps employers screen applicants. An instructor, usually a journeyman, teaches the classes using a combination of on-the-job training and classroom instruction.

Pre-apprenticeship consists of two phases. A five-week session introduces tool use, safety, materials, math, and sometimes literacy training. The second phase lasts 16 weeks, with students working as full-time employees. On completion, participants may either seek regular positions or enter an apprenticeship program. Four national certification programs have also been created in residential marketing, commercial property building, business management, and registered apartment management.

The Graduate Builders Institute, a premier continuing education program, began in 1985 in Virginia and Pennsylvania and has since been extended to 30 states. State chapters of the National

Association and the Home Builders Institute sponsor it, and local colleges and universities serve as the hosts. Twelve six-hour courses taught by either university professors or industry experts over a period of several days form the nucleus. Certification is earned by completion of 9 of the 12 courses and maintained by taking additional courses over a three-year period. The courses include Building Codes and Standards, Building Technology, Business Management, Computer Applications, Energy Efficient Construction, Project Management, and Sales and Marketing.

The Associated General Contractors have two divisions of training: hands-on (crafts) and hands-off (supervisory and management training). Supervisory training, designed to move craftsmen up to superintendent or project foreman, consists of 20 to 25 hours instruction in costs, planning and scheduling, oral communications, and interpersonal relations. Courses are offered at numerous sites around the country, including community and technical colleges, vocational schools, and association chapters. In Wisconsin and Virginia, community colleges are heavily involved. The association also sponsors about a dozen management conferences during the year for individuals wishing to upgrade their skills and keep abreast of developments in the industry.

Collegiate Programs. Ernie Jones, Training Director of the Associated General Contractors, says that the construction industry has "one of training's best-kept secrets." Collegiate programs in construction engineering and technology have existed for many years at such major institutions as Iowa State University, Texas A&M, and the University of Florida, where the program started more than 50 years ago. There are 22 accredited baccalaureate programs in construction-related areas and more than 40 programs in construction technology and management in other institutions.[1]

According to a 1988 study, the programs are so popular that waiting lists are common and schools have raised admission standards in response. The study draws two principal conclusions:

first, the numbers graduating do not meet industry's needs, and second, more student places must be opened and promoted to attract additional enrollment. Not enough students are transferring from vocational programs in community colleges; more transfers come from other types of collegiate programs. And "little access is provided to . . . those adult learners who wish to return to college directly from the field."[2]

Among the college programs accredited by the American Council on Construction Education, course offerings range broadly from English, computers, and mathematics to air conditioning, management, and structures. Most curricula, however, have four distinct groupings: construction; math, physics, and the sciences; business management; and general education. Most strike a balance between theory and practical application by requiring field work or a cooperative arrangement in which the student attends school half time and works in a construction job half time. Computer literacy is almost a requirement now in most programs, a testimony to the machine's pervasiveness.

Purdue University's 15-year-old program in construction engineering and management conforms to those curriculum divisions and includes a three-year summer internship with an industrial sponsor. In addition to a baccalaureate, programs leading to both master's and doctoral degrees are available in construction engineering.

Unions as Sponsors. Construction unions represent members who make a living in the building industry as carpenters, sheet metal workers, glaziers, boilermakers, electricians, bricklayers and painters, plumbers and pipefitters. Labor unions in this industry take particular pride in their apprenticeship and journeyman programs. As a learning method, apprenticeship has historically justified its effectiveness. From earliest times workers have learned from fathers, colleagues, and those more highly skilled. Medieval crafts were learned from a master, and even today, training on the job is the most prevalent means of gaining skills and often understanding—even though it may not be formally structured. Learning theories, like John Dewey's, have long supported the practice. Companies seldom hazard a guess about the costs of such training; they simply take it for granted as essential and hold supervisors responsible for it.

When unions sponsor apprentice training and continued learning for journeymen, it is of course more organized with requirements. Sometimes they join with the appropriate employer's association to set educational standards and policy guidelines. For example, the International Brotherhood of Electrical Workers, in partnership with the National Electrical Contractors, determines schedules of courses, related instruction, and details of the work process.

Apprenticeship. Although criticized by some as a static approach to training, apprenticeship can be dynamic in its response to change, which is essential if it is to survive. The journeyman and instructor must be up to date with the latest technology-driven changes in production processes and the new materials invented. Otherwise, the apprentice system will perpetuate outmoded practices and obviously not preserve the worker's job.

Ten years ago it was hard to find a machinist with any knowledge of numerical control machines, an electrician with any knowledge of microprocessors or fiber optics, a plumber with experience in handling plastic pipe, an iron worker or operating engineer with the skills required to use laser equipment. Sponsors are incorporating all these skills into apprenticeship and journeyman training programs.

Requirements call for a certain number of hours of work experience and formal classroom instruction. In 1988, federal government minimums were 2,000 hours of work and 144 hours of instruction for an occupation to be considered apprenticeable. Combining theoretical classroom learning with intensive on-the-job practice, training covers all aspects of the trade as apprentices rotate through its various phases. People trained this way tend to remain in their trade, generally enjoy steadier employment, and are more likely to advance to supervisory positions than their informally trained counterparts.

Unions, employers, and trade associations have created sizable trust funds to support apprentice training. The United Association of Plumbers and the National Contractors Association established their training trust fund some 30 years ago and since then have spent more than $50 million from it to underwrite training activities. (This sum does not include money spent by local apprentice committees.) In the case of plumbers, the fund pays instructor salaries, underwrites purchase of the latest training equipment, and provides seed money for advanced journeymen training programs.

National apprenticeship programs have developed their own curricula, which typically use textbooks written by industry members and published privately, student workbooks and lab manuals based on the texts, custom-made audiovisuals, simulations, and so on. Occasionally, programs hire consultants to develop teaching materials according to specifications established by the national committee. Individual sponsors may also either develop their own or use materials available commercially.

New methodologies have emerged, including performance- or competency-based training, individualized or self-paced instruction, and programmed learning. One of the most carefully planned is the Boilermaker Comprehensive Training Program, designed by a private company specializing in the preparation of competency-based systems. The development process included job analysis to identify standards and procedures, surveys at job sites to solicit input from all levels of workers, and consultation with joint committees of contractors and union representatives. Following field testing, the program started across the country. It begins with selection of candidates and proceeds through orientation, classroom studies, on-the-job training, and performance-based testing that monitors apprentice progress. Classroom work is markedly more complex than a few years ago. The emphasis is on applied math and rigging in the first year; afterward, courses continue on mechanical drawing, layout, hand and power tools, construction materials, and blueprint reading.

Effective, up-to-date instructors are the key to successful training. Without high-quality instruction, the apprentice is little more than an observer, picking up what he or she can but missing the systematic knowledge base that a trades worker needs to perform at a professional level. In fact, the qualifications of individuals teaching in apprentice programs are often questioned. One apprentice carpenter described with scorn his classroom experience: the teacher lacked both substantive knowledge and instructional skill, and marking time in the classroom seemed sufficient to fulfill everyone's obligations. Others relate similar experiences, and union officials concede that the classroom component of apprenticeship programs needs to be strengthened. No federal guidelines exist for classroom instruction except for numbers of hours; the content is left to the employer or sponsor.

To improve the level of instruction, the United Association of Plumbers and Pipefitters each year runs a five-day training program at Purdue University.[3] Apprenticeship instructors learn effective teaching methods and gain exposure to and experience with the latest technological developments affecting the industry. During the 32 years of the program's existence, more than 23,000 instructors have received training. A mix of Purdue professors, industry experts, and outstanding members of the Plumbers Association do the teaching. It has been an effective collaboration.

The boilermakers also train their trainers with a rigorous five-day annual seminar series. Prospective trainers who have completed the comprehensive program in the trade are asked to practice their teaching skills. Each one is videotaped while leading a class session, and staff members criticize the performance and give recommendations for improvement.

Lest the criticism of teaching quality be leveled at apprenticeship programs especially, it is well to remember that the problem is not exclusively theirs. Corporations have greatly increased their sessions for teaching how to teach. The military monitors its teachers' performance. As a matter of fact, more attention is paid to teaching skills by all these providers than by the colleges and universities of the established higher education system.

Apprentices on Campus.   A growing and popular approach to craft training is dual enrollment in an apprenticeship and a college associate degree program. One of the leaders in such training is the International Union of Operating Engineers (IUOE), which ran a pilot program with Dickinson State College in North Dakota from 1972 to 1975. It was funded by the Office of Research and Development-Manpower Administration, U.S. Department of Labor. Apprentices received college credit for both classes and supervised on-the-job training. After the grant expired, the union continued the program, and many similar programs now exist. Rhode Island Community College offers associate degrees in labor and technical studies in cooperation with the union. Apprenticeship accounts for 20 of the 60 credits required for graduation, and credits are transferable to four-year labor studies degrees. An Arizona IUOE local has formed an alliance with Rio Salado Community College to offer an associate degree in applied science such as equipment operation and heavy-duty mechanics. Credits can be transferred to a baccalaureate degree in construction engineering at Arizona State University.

The Center for Labor Studies at New York's Empire State College and the Joint Apprentice Committee of the Electrical Industry offer a somewhat different dual enrollment program. To obtain the associate of science degree in labor studies, the apprentice follows courses in the history of the labor movement and current labor issues, complementing the job training and formal instruction received in the apprenticeship program. Required academic courses include analytical thinking, principles of writing, research skills, economics, and world history. It is a basic curriculum for future labor leaders, while apprenticeship leads to a job as well.

Continued Learning for Journeymen.　The term *journeyman* qualifies as an anachronism that needs a modern substitute. Nevertheless, becoming a journeyman takes as long as earning a bachelor's degree, which is an equivalence cited by union officers and a fact not widely appreciated outside the construction industry. A journeyman is roughly in the same position as a new college graduate: he or she has been introduced to a body of knowledge and methods that form a basis for further learning. Just as accountants or computer programmers must stay aware of changes and developments in their fields, the skilled craftsman needs periodic updating. Labor union leaders, employers, trade association officials, and educators in the field recognize the imperative need, and a number of organizations have made significant commitments to this end. Still, opportunities are grossly inadequate. Although the number of journeymen who update their skills is unknown, the various crafts estimate that fewer than ten percent make the attempt. Some states are beginning to mandate continuing training for renewal of journeymen licenses, but the low percentage at present is a discouraging point from which to start and does not bode well for the industry.

The Graduate Builders Institute, mentioned earlier, and the Associated General Contractors both have prestigious programs designed to move skilled craftsmen into supervisory positions. But for craft workers who prefer to remain in their trade, the union is usually the source for updating skills. Some advanced journeyman courses are extensions of apprentice programs, such as the "second generation apprenticeship" recently introduced in Western Canada.

Sheet metal unions and contractors cooperatively sponsor continuing education and watch for shifts in the trade that signal needs for special training. In one instance at least, the problem was not to prepare for the advent of a new material or technique but to regain a lost art. Since renovation of historic buildings was becoming very popular and widespread, courses were designed specifically to teach skills in architectural sheet metal working that have been out of fashion and unneeded for many years. Studies in the lost art are available now in all 50 states and parts of Canada.

Some journeyman training also cuts across traditional craft boundaries. For example, the sheet metal workers, electricians, and painters, along with the National Electric Sign Association, have formed a joint training committee to develop and conduct programs. In Toledo, Ohio, instrumentation is taught to journeymen in the pipe and electrical trades by teachers from both fields. And a few programs take training to the job site, offering it during or immediately after the regular workday. "Drop-in" training has attracted some back to class. Sponsors usually designate one night a week when journeymen (occasionally with their families), employers, and suppliers get together to discuss topics of mutual interest like new equipment, safety, or innovative work methods.

Although all are worthy efforts, a more concerted attack is needed to keep journeymen abreast of technological change. Many other people depend on their knowledge and ability, so they are in a critical position in the work force. Learning opportunities will have to be tailored for their needs and temperament and delivered to them in ways that encourage their participation.

Industry officials note a reluctance on the part of many journeymen to enroll in training that is not immediately applicable to their jobs or that requires a time investment of more than a few class meetings. Community colleges appear to have lost some credibility with journeymen seeking advanced training in their trades, apparently because college requirements exceed their levels of interest and application. Indeed, few ever take advantage of the tuition reimbursement provisions of collective bargaining contracts or of company-sponsored tuition refund policies. Their reasons range from lack of information about programs to no recognition for completing a program. Whether the unions, employers, or both are at fault is irrelevant. Industry participants are interdependent and all must be concerned about the lack of continuing education.

Office Workers and Administrative Staff

With more than 18 million workers, administrative support outstripped all other occupational categories in 1984. Although growth projected to the year 2000 is not so high as for service, management, or marketing and sales, it is still a sizable 20 percent.[4] In the past, these office jobs were a primary entry to employment for women. Although this is no longer necessarily the case, many women still regard administrative jobs as the most accessible route to advancement. Because demand is high, the occupation also offers many opportunities for part-time and temporary employment.

From a training standpoint, administrative occupations are notable because of their increasingly paraprofessional nature, which is largely attributable to the technological revolution in offices. Small computer systems of increasing power; a wealth of powerful software packages for word processing, database management, accounting, and other business applications; and telecommunication advances that make possible retrieval and transmission of data among many sources—these have streamlined or eliminated many lower level administrative tasks and created the potential for roles requiring greater organizational skill, technical knowledge, and communication ability. Many secretarial and administrative workers are now better described as system or information managers.

With the revolution in technology and job function has come a staggering array of training designed to prepare workers to use the machines effectively and fearlessly. Computer-related courses are available from virtually *every* source of training and education. Nor does the training involve only computers. Over the past ten years there has been an accompanying explosion of courses designed to enhance the capability of the secretarial or administrative staff through emphasis on personal development, time management, communication skills, and stress management—subjects designed to appeal to workers who think of themselves as professionals, who can establish their own career goals, and who take responsibility for meeting them.

Corporate Concern. Corporations with large numbers of administrative support personnel often provide their own training, contract with commercial vendors to present courses on-site, or take advantage of discount rates by sending groups to a central facility for training. And employees who are not sent may be encouraged by a company's tuition reimbursement plan to enroll in courses that will improve their skills and make them more valuable. But this route has complications: first, in most corporate tuition payment plans, the course must be job-related, and second, the Internal Revenue Service has shifted its position on the taxability of tuition reimbursement as income, creating confusion. This has discouraged individuals from enrolling. Congress, however, recently granted tax exemption not only for courses related to the job but also for all educational help for courses below the graduate level. This commendable action merits wide attention; it can make a real difference in employee enrollment for education.

The percentage of employees generally taking advantage of tuition plans remains notoriously low—about 9 percent of those eligible—although at least 85 percent of U.S. companies have them. This disparity raises the question of whether companies publicize their tuition programs and encourage employees to take part, or hide the policies in fine print in benefits booklets.

Whatever means a company elects for educating its administrative support staff in the latest office technologies, it must make the commitment. Historically, corporations have spent the most money on managerial training, and this level remains high; advanced technical professional training has been next, and the outlay is increasing; clerical and skilled technicians historically have received less attention, but these categories are climbing as job requirements change.

In response to a survey showing that Digital Equipment Corporation's 6,000 secretaries were receiving less than one day of training a year, Patrick Cataldo, vice-president for educational services, started a program that is both unique and extensive compared to those at most companies. With a personalized training plan, designed with the help of a manager and trainer, the secretary selects from 60 courses and generally takes 4 per year. More than 97 percent of Digital's secretaries have taken classes. At the same time there is an experiment underway to retrain employees no longer needed in manufacturing jobs for secretarial positions, where skilled workers are much needed.

Temporary Services.   In today's market, where demand for skilled secretaries and administrators is high, workers are able to pick and choose their places of employment. Some choose to work independently, contracting with a variety of employers for short-term work, often on a recurring basis. For example, free-lance word processors and bookkeepers gain flexible hours, high pay rates, and independence while giving small companies in particular a way to contain costs. Such "consultants" depend on staying abreast of new developments to keep themselves marketable. This often requires brush-up courses or instruction in the new equipment or software they may encounter in the next client's office.

An alternative is to work as a temporary employee through an agency. The National Association of Temporary Services estimates that 5 million "temps" are employed annually, with perhaps three-quarters of a million working on any given day. Because agencies must worry about their clients' satisfaction and repeat business, sending a qualified, skilled worker to each assignment is essential. While employers maintain that personnel agencies still have too few candidates with sufficient computer knowledge, the largest agencies try to ensure that their temporaries are familiar with all popular software and hardware, either by running their own training sessions or by sending temps to courses operated by commercial vendors.

In the early 1980s, Manpower, one of the country's largest temporary services with 650 offices in the United States and 700,000 annual placements, foresaw a need to provide computer training to 60,000 of its workers each year. In 1982, the company developed Skillware (disk-based customized software), which the student can use without teacher, classroom, or manual. Compatible with computers commonly found in offices, Skillware familiarizes students with widely used business programs. To date, more than 100,000 workers have been trained on Skillware.

Kelly Temporary Services and Olsten Services, among the nation's largest agencies, also offer personal computer training to their temporary employees. Olsten uses self-paced, hands-on training systems, while Kelly has designed a machine called Kee Simulator that mimics a variety of word processing systems. Hal Cornelius, director of Olsten's Special Services, expresses the view of many in the industry: "Software technology never stands still. If you knew DisplayWrite 1, you need to learn DisplayWrite 4."[5]

Both Olsten and Manpower offer their computer training to client companies and thereby add to their line of services. Like many other companies, these agencies have discovered in-house training to be a saleable item to clients, suppliers, and others. This trend is bringing more commercial companies, whose first purpose is not education, into the business of learning.

In urban centers, other competitors in training for administrative personnel, like the American Management Association, offer computer seminars and workshops of a few days' duration at a cost of several hundred dollars per student. And commercial vendors, like Deltak Training, a subsidiary of the National Education Corporation, the largest U.S. education and training company, take many business and computer training courses to on-site or central locations for clients. It is a very big business.

Private and Public School Sponsors. Joining the excessive numbers of graduates with business majors coming from all types of educational institutions are large numbers in training for administrative support functions. Some 200,000 students were enrolled in business programs at proprietary schools in 1987. More than 15,000 certificates and 21,000 associate degrees in secretarial and related fields were earned at community and technical colleges in 1985–1986.[6] The figures do not include individuals enrolled in other programs that lead to administrative jobs, taking correspondence or short courses, or learning on the job.

Privately owned trade school programs commonly offer twelve months of continuous study at a cost of several thousand dollars. The Katharine Gibbs School (now a part of McGraw-Hill), a name long associated with serious and high-quality preparation of young women to be secretaries, charges an annual tuition of $6,500. Books add another $400 to the bill. Lately, the school has added accounting and hotel-restaurant management to the curriculum, and men are enrolling as well as women.

Offering few or no general education courses, proprietary schools concentrate instead on saturation in technical training to get the graduate into the marketplace as speedily as possible. A prime reason for going to a proprietary school is to finish quickly and earn money. As several studies have shown, programs in proprietary schools generally last about half as long as those in the public sector and range in length from 300 clock hours to two years. But proprietary school students often spend twice as long in class each week, must take more laboratory work, and focus exclusively on job training. There are no elective courses and no end-of-semester vacations.

Community colleges naturally approach administrative assistants' training differently. Their mission impels them to provide a more general education than a narrowly focused trade school. Along with introduction to business accounting and word processing concepts, the community college student pursuing an associate degree in, for example, office administration and word processing at Los Angeles City College is expected to complete general education courses in natural sciences, social sciences, and the humanities. The degree takes two years to complete and, for state residents, costs a few hundred dollars a year. Many of the office skills courses taught at two-year colleges, however, are not transferable to four-year academic programs.

Piedmont Virginia Community College's courses in the administrative area are typical of associate degree programs. Students can specialize in real estate, word processing, health care, banking and finance, insurance, data processing, marketing, and management. In two years they must complete 97 credits in general education, office skills, and related business areas. The course titles can be found in almost any community college catalog: introduction to business, human relationships, business mathematics, communications, preparation for employment, typewriting (keyboarding), office procedures, machine transcription, principles of word processing, microcomputers, business management, business law, and a host of electives. Students may also choose a one-year certificate program that omits some of the law, finance, and accounting courses given in the second year.

Piedmont's certificate program is quite similar to that of the Stone School in New Haven, Connecticut, a proprietary institution founded in 1864. Its executive secretary certificate program requires completion of communications, business math, filing, keyboarding, machine transcription, speedbuilding, shorthand, word processing overview, and career development. Stone charges about $7,000 for this 12-month, full-time program. It has a strong placement record for its graduates. In comparison, community college certificate programs that get the graduate into the job market in less than a year usually demand fewer hours in class weekly and keep the student in school for a shorter year than a proprietary school.

A trade school curriculum is closely tied to marketplace needs. School owners stay in touch with company and office needs by attending meetings in the local business community, talking with employers, and watching market changes. Therefore, unlike community colleges, the proprietors can move quickly to drop or add a course. Because proprietary schools' very survival depends on offering job training that can be put to instant use, alterations in the curriculum may need to be made frequently. Changing a community college curriculum is significantly more time consuming, engaging a larger number of people on the faculty and in administration in a negotiated process. Financial considerations are not as immediately compelling to those planning community college curricula.

Whatever the type of institution an individual enters to obtain administrative training, one trend is clear. Not only are word processing and secretarial skills critical, but so is a grasp of language fundamentals and clear communication. It is one of the ironies of the age of the smart machine that individuals responsible for operating more and more complex and sophisticated office equipment often lack basic writing and reading abilities. Some trade schools provide remedial instruction outside the regular course load, but only if necessary to bring a student up to workplace entry-level standards. School owners concerned with showing a profit tend to limit their instruction to the specific skills a student needs to get a job.

An urban business school visited for this report plans to open a basic skills laboratory with computer-assisted instruction for those students who need to improve their reading and writing abilities before passing the entrance test for enrollment in the school's office assistant program. The director believes this is a trend, albeit an expensive one, for the trade school industry, which has found it must pretrain more of its prospective student population. In this respect, trade schools' narrow, market-oriented view of education has put them far behind community colleges. For years community colleges have been running remedial courses and skills laboratories for large numbers of their students.

Full-time or part-time adult education classes taught at local schools are another source of training in business and office services.

For example, the Great Oaks Joint Vocational School District near Cincinnati offers more than 15 occupational programs to adults in the district. A number of part-time classes are available at modest cost, such as computer literacy for those unfamiliar with micro-processors and a beginning Lotus 1-2-3 course. Both consist of 21 hours of instruction over seven weeks for $50. Fees rarely exceed $85 for part-time courses, but full-time programs can be much more expensive. For instance, a 900-hour, 36-week course in infor-mation processing (clerical studies and office procedures, word processing, data processing and data entry skills) costs $1,500 plus book charges.

Government Offices. The federal government is a large employer of secretaries—more than 150,000 at last count. A scarcity of skilled recruits and high turnover in the work force have created severe shortages, causing the Office of Personnel Management to autho-rize premium salary rates to attract and retain people in the secretarial field. Recognizing that pay is not the whole answer, many federal agencies are turning to training and development as a way to professionalize the secretarial occupation, establish a ca-reer path for secretaries, and ensure adequate preparation for the more skilled aspects of this rapidly changing occupation—notably decision making, interpersonal relations, and technology.

Among the new career development programs for secretaries, the Central Intelligence Agency has a comprehensive and clearly defined approach in four steps that require completion of certain courses before advancement to the next level:

- Level I Secretary Trainee. Required: agency orientation, office procedures, correspondence, word processing, time manage-ment, and proofreading. Recommended: typing, shorthand, and pouched communications.

- Level II Secretary. Required: management workshop, stress management, essentials of writing, professional office protocol. Recommended: geography, language training.

- Level III Senior Secretary. Required: effective oral presentation, getting your ideas across, management skills for secretaries, women in the work force. Recommended: leadership styles, advanced writing, area familiarization.

- Level IV. No required courses at the top of the secretarial career ladder, at grades GS-11 ($27,172) and above. Recommended: intelligence issues, briefing techniques, and further language, area, and management study.

In 1987, the Treasury Department established EXCEL, the Executive Committee for Excellence, to encourage professionalism in its support staff. Funded by the deputy assistant secretary for administration, the committee has 16 members from the major units of the department. It is charged with establishing a curriculum for use department-wide, standardizing administrative operations, and including special programs for the professional development of secretaries. After sponsoring a training needs survey, the committee identified five basic courses for support staff: grammar review, basic writing, proofreading, communications, and time management. Outside contractors teach the half- to two-day classroom courses using off-the-shelf materials, but with examples tailored to the Treasury.

From Arlington, Virginia, the General Services Administration (GSA) Training Center sponsors more than 120 practical skills courses open to employees of all levels in federal, state, and local government. The areas cover procurement, information resources, property, supply, and security management. Lasting from one to ten days and given by professionals in the particular field, the courses are usually scheduled in major cities with large civil service populations. The student pays the costs, which range from $145 to $300. To make sure that the material is current and relevant, the GSA center tries to keep a sharp eye on technology and other factors affecting government operations.

Many of the same courses are available through other government agencies, like the Training and Development Services unit of the Office of Personnel Management (OPM). This central federal personnel agency offers more than 300 administrative courses centrally or, given enough participants, on site.

OPM courses often overlap with GSA offerings. For example, a dBase III course is available from both, but GSA requires five days at $300 while OPM takes three days for $450. A Lotus 1-2-3 introductory course costs $210 from GSA and $450 from OPM; each lasts three days.[7] There may be some extenuating circumstances in these cases, but duplication of basic administrative courses is a costly feature of government training. When an agency has specialized needs, a course is warranted. But when different agencies offer precisely the same basic course, often technologically delivered, then efficiency loses, apparently for bureaucratic reasons.

Information Systems Technicians

Essential to all the skilled workers described thus far and, indeed, to the entire work force, are the computer technicians who keep in working order the information systems on which we all depend. They are, in effect, the infrastructure of industry and society. They install, maintain, operate, and repair computerized systems in companies, the military, government agencies, hospitals, universities, and innumerable other institutions. Technicians usually move from a beginner's job to higher levels by adding more complicated functions to their battery of skills. This field hardly lacks training resources. The issues here are not availability but quality and currency, and attracting sufficient numbers of recruits to this type of technical work.

Colleges, commercial vendors, corporations, and the military teach courses that furnish the basic knowledge necessary, and some offer training programs that extend well beyond the fundamentals. Perhaps because electronic technologies are essential in almost every workplace today, the proliferation of courses is to be expected, and every major provider of training is active in the field.

And since the training needed is generic and quite definable, the programs have marked similarities, and more providers can conveniently cross their customary lines to train people from different industries and institutions. There are also instances of cooperative sponsorship like that between Motorola and community colleges.

Although our focus is on the other providers in this category, community and technical college programs are serving many and reach those who could not otherwise get training. A 1987 survey, commissioned by the Carnegie Foundation and conducted by the Center for the Study of Community Colleges at UCLA, reported that 74 of the 95 participating colleges offered classes in electronics technology—a total of 700 class sections. And in one school year, 1985–1986, nearly 16,000 certificates and 11,000 associate degrees were earned in engineering technologies for mechanics and repairers.

The curriculum at the Los Angeles Trade-Technical College illustrates the two-year degree program. Requirements for electronics engineering technicians include electronics mathematics; fundamentals of D.C. and A.C.; electronics and physics laboratories; principles of semiconductors, tubes, and electronic circuits; lasers and opto-electronics; transmitters, computers, test equipment, and related mathematics; and microwave, servo and control systems. Suggested electives include electronics technology, advanced electronics math, television systems, and business data processing principles. The graduate should have greater flexibility in learning, more to build on, and more options for career growth than those coming from one-year programs. Community college curricula, whether called electronic repair or communications technologies, are not unlike programs offered by other providers except for their calendars and generally less concentrated schedules. Otherwise, the distinctions are few.

Across Provider Lines. Trade schools and military training are similar in that both strip technical training to its essentials, limiting or eliminating excursions into theory and general education. Both stress efficient, short-term instruction. The military offers 15 categories of specialization under the heading "Electronic and Electrical Equipment Repair Occupations," and structures each category according to specific learning objectives so that trainees know precisely the tasks they must perform.[8]

In the two specialties most comparable to civilian jobs—data processing repair and electronics instruments repair—the military employs nearly 26,000 people and undertakes training needed to replace about 10 percent of them annually. Since many military uses of computers are similar to civilian uses, the training offered in the two sectors is similar. Computer maintenance training in the armed forces consists of 25 to 35 weeks of classroom instruction and laboratory work concentrating on electronics fundamentals, systems operation, and repair. Trainees then join a maintenance unit or data processing center to work under supervision. On-the-job training supplements and refines the skills acquired during formal training.

The Community College of the Air Force (CCAF) offers an associate in applied science degree to enlisted personnel, the only military institution in the country to do so.[9] The CCAF's degree requirements in electronic engineering technology are the most rigorous of any of its programs, demanding 70 instead of the usual 64 semester hours, and nearly half must be in technical education courses. Correspondence courses, very carefully designed around learning objectives, supplement the training of technical personnel. The Air Force's Extension Course Institute supports the resident study program and job training. Electronics fundamentals, for example, presents an intensive introduction to the field with five volumes of instructional material.

In some cases personnel wanting to satisfy degree requirements can transfer the credits earned through this self-paced study to the Community College of the Air Force. More important, the courses serve to satisfy the educational requirements for promotion in rank. And most significant, the courses are also available to Department of Defense and U.S. Civil Service personnel. This is the type of exchange and sharing of learning materials needed: the military could offer superior courses to civilian as well as military members and make them available widely to workers in industry and students in college.

One of the military's most difficult training challenges is rapid turnover in its electronics systems and equipment. Despite the efficiencies of pragmatic training—without a theoretical basis—it is not enough to train maintenance technicians or operators in a single system that will soon be replaced. They must be familiar with the technologies underlying different generations of systems. But these basic technologies themselves change. Without continual training, technicians become as obsolete as the machines they were originally trained on.

The same statement holds true in industries where machine obsolescence is a fact of life. Many of AT&T's courses are tailored to particular equipment, so presumably the corporation too is faced with the constant challenge. Obsolescence is especially pertinent for the large, multinational corporations that carry on training throughout their companies and on to clients and customers worldwide. If the training is inferior or out of date, they perpetuate mediocrity on a grand scale and slow productivity accordingly.

AT&T trains its own telecommunication technicians, maintenance personnel, and supervisors. In addition, the company "suitcases" training to customer sites and customizes it to meet a client's special needs. The curriculum starts with introductory courses like "Switch and Minicomputer Fundamentals," which is a prerequisite to 12 company-developed curricula. COMCATS, an on-line computerized catalog that gives course descriptions, is accessible to anyone with a telephone and terminal who wants to select an AT&T course. The course is on line only for employees, but the basic telecommunication training is commercially available outside.

Training for electronic fields, particularly at the technician level, has been a popular trade school offering for a long time, and the best schools have stayed abreast of developments and invested in the latest technologies. The high price tag for their courses, school officials say, enables them to afford the advanced equipment that many public community colleges and vocational schools lack. Together with the highly focused nature of the training they offer, the schools market this advantage.

One of the most respected trade schools is the Human Resources Research Organization Technical Education Center, better called HumRRO TEC, in MacPherson Square, Washington, D.C. Opened in 1976 as a unit of George Washington University, it moved off campus in 1981 under its present independent auspices. Roger Williams, who moved with the school from the university and became its director, is a firm administrator, deeply committed to his students and tolerant only of the highest training standards. HumRRO is rigorous, as students attest: several hours of homework each night and intensive training five days a week for 15 months.

The school's demanding instruction pays off. HumRRO's placement rate exceeds 95 percent, and A. B. Dick, Honeywell, Unisys, and other prestigious corporations hire its graduates. To protect students, HumRRO has a training guarantee similar to policies at responsible nonprofit colleges. If, after six weeks of studies, the student is dissatisfied with the school or the electronics field, he or she may withdraw and claim a full tuition refund. The only requirement is that the student maintain a 95 percent attendance record during the six-week period.

Thousands of students attend 36 accredited ITT Technical Institutes in 17 states, where they earn diplomas, certificates, or associate degrees in electronics technology. While most of the schools have no more than 500 students, the one in Fort Wayne, Indiana, enrolls nearly 1,400, many of them from outside the area. They are drawn by the school's excellent reputation and high placement rates. An ITT associate degree requires 18 months to 2 years; a certificate or diploma, 9 to 15 months full time.

Jack Bainter, national director of education for ITT Educational Services, stresses its hands-on approach: at least 50 percent of a student's training takes place in the lab, and much of the theoretical material is taught with interactive techniques supplemented by lectures. The company has recruited highly qualified faculty because of its reputation and because of an instructor salary scale set according to ITT's corporate pay rates.

NRI School of Electronics is a home study school owned by McGraw-Hill's Continuing Education Center for more than 20 years. It was founded in 1914 as the National Radio Institute by a high school teacher named James E. Smith, who gave four of his students extra instruction in wireless radio—six years before the world's first commercial radio broadcast. NRI now claims to be the largest training school of its kind in the world. The company delivers instruction through learning kits consisting of equipment like a computer or stereo that the student takes apart and works with. Interaction with an instructor occurs through mail exchange of consultation forms. Many of the courses also use audiotape cassettes with printed visuals and self-checking quizzes. Eleven training courses, ranging in price from $520 for basic electronics to more than $3,000 for the robotics course, are available.

Another learning product on the market comes from National Compu-Ed, a Texas computer education firm that sends a comprehensive learning package designed to train corporate, university, and government users to become computer technicians. The $1,700 package requires a substantial investment of time. Using an oversized computer motherboard with sockets for more than 100 chips, students build a computer from the chips up and learn about peripherals, operating systems, computer languages, and computer architecture. When finished, the student should be able to diagnose and fix microcomputer problems.

One other example particularly merits attention and commendation. Among its extensive training and education programs, for which Motorola spends more than $40 million annually, there is a one-year, full-time associate degree program in electronics for minority and women employees to improve their career prospects. It is restricted to employees who joined the company in a production or assembly capacity and are now employed in technical positions. Graduates are not guaranteed a promotion but are assured they can resume a job at the same level as that held before enrollment. More than 50 employees enroll each year and receive full pay and benefits. The per-student cost of the program to Motorola is $25,000, including tuition and books.

The company has run the program in cooperation with community colleges near its facilities in Chicago and Phoenix since 1979. Maricopa Community College District campuses in Arizona, the nation's third largest community college system, are the current program sites. Governed by a set of company-formulated expectations and objectives, the cooperative agreement recognizes the company's right to "submit recommendations to 'tailor content' to meet Motorola technician needs" and to determine "electives selected and additional course offerings." Corporate monitoring of a college's performance can be a positive influence, a kind of quality assurance check on physical facilities and instruction. But if the company's oversight is parochial and narrowly vocational, a student-employee's needs may be sacrificed and the college's academic freedom eroded. In the present case, both parties report satisfaction with the arrangement.

Training for the New Factory

Manufacturing, once a strength of the United States in the world economy, has become a weakness for reasons that academics and executives are still debating. Despite the late start on renewed innovation in American manufacturing and the worries that it is economically too little, too late to make U.S. goods globally more competitive, large-scale changes are taking place on the factory floor. But workers, unions, and even management are not necessarily welcoming them with open arms. Training plays a key role in this difficult transition.

A Sophisticated Process. Computer-integrated manufacturing (CIM) and automated manufacturing technologies are flexible systems being adopted increasingly in a range of industries. Their installation brings a whole new set of protocols. They link workers in nontraditional patterns, creating needs for training on a scale that manufacturing companies have not known before. Not even the training necessary to support the first Industrial Revolution is comparable; it was much less demanding on workers' knowledge and usually was limited to a particular task.

CIM uses computers and robots to automate the manufacturing process from design to production and integrates the functions involved in each stage.[10] The flexibility permits use of a single computer-controlled production line to make a variety of products simply by being reprogrammed; it does not have to be retooled. The ability to produce different products as market demand changes, without adding capital investment or large inventories, gains the user strategic advantage.

When a company undertakes the tremendous investment required for installation of one of these systems, it must include major training programs. Workers at all levels must not only learn to use the equipment but also understand the interconnections of the machine system and the processes by which critical information is shared. Workers who had only mechanical production responsibilities now are asked to troubleshoot problems with sophisticated, electronically controlled machinery, share information laterally as well as up and down the employee axis, and understand how the components of the production system work together as a whole.

Given greater responsibility for the smooth functioning of the system, workers find themselves in a new role. They can no longer limit themselves to narrowly defined jobs, leaving managerial authority in the hands of superiors. Workers in a plant with flexible technology necessarily share some of that managerial responsibility. *Industry Week* compares the new CIM worker with one in a traditional manufacturing operation:

- The old worker had specific discrete duties. The new employee needs broader skills.

- The old production worker performed physical labor. Now, manufacturing needs "brains" instead of "brawn."

- The old employee may have required some equipment-specific training, but that was treated as a one-shot deal. Now, workers will be continually learning as technology changes, cross-training occurs, and new systems are installed.

- The old worker was passive. The new one is involved in decision making and works closely with others.

- The old employee was often frustrated and bitter. The new one, if all is managed correctly, will be highly valuable to the company and will have greater self-esteem and job satisfaction.[11]

In 1981, American corporations spent an average of $3,300 per worker on physical assets and $300 per worker on training. Flexible manufacturing technologies are changing that ratio. A study by International Resource Development expects that industrial expenditures on training will more than double in the next ten years. David Hewitt, vice-president of United Research, a management consulting firm, adds:

When you install a CIM machine, it continues to evolve. When you put a traditional lathe in place, that lathe might remain there relatively unchanged for many years. But with CIM you are beginning a process which is subject to software changes and updates, and other changes which have operator impact. So even noncorrective training must continue as the implementation of CIM becomes more sophisticated.[12]

And a manager of manufacturing training at Digital Equipment Corporation agrees: "We have to [train] continually. . . . It's a definite. There's no discussion."

Establishing a training program and gaining full cooperation for it, however, are not easy. A number of corporations that have installed flexible systems without sufficient planning and consensus have learned the hard way that careful preparation of workers at all levels is critical to successful implementation of a new system. Dramatic organizational change inevitably is threatening.

Supervisors, who are often left out of the planning and decision-making process, may be uncommitted to the new way. They may resent the dilution of their authority under a more cooperative management system, and they may not really understand the technology. Workers may justifiably fear that new technology will cost them jobs or dictate changes in job classification and work rules—both the fiercely protected turf of labor unions. Workers on the floor who must make the system operate often put up strong resistance. "I know of one case where a group of about a dozen auto workers simply refused to operate a five-machine flexible manufacturing system after spending several weeks training at the builder's plant," says William Fife, president of Giddings & Lewis in Fond du Lac, Wisconsin.[13]

Programs for New Systems. The auto industry may be the leader in quality retraining programs for manufacturing employees. Since the companies have invested heavily in the advanced technologies, their line workers and others up the line need new skills and understanding to perform their jobs and avoid dismissal. In designing and monitoring the training programs, the United Auto Workers has played a key role. The union's initiative at the bargaining table in 1982 resulted in contractual arrangements for training that are now being carried out jointly with management. Because these programs include more types of training than those directed at manufacturing systems, we discuss them in chapter 7.

Many industries are making large commitments to retraining workers for new manufacturing systems. The United Rubber Workers and Kelly-Springfield Tire Company in 1983 agreed to substantial worker concessions on pay and work hours in exchange for the company's promise to convert its Tyler, Texas, plant from bias tire production to the more technologically advanced radial tire construction. New equipment and processes were essential, as was retraining of Tyler's more than 1,000 employees.

In this case notably, workers themselves became the trainers. It is an educationally sound, cost-effective idea. Tyler selected about 100 hourly employees to be teachers and trained them to develop their courses with methods that included computer-based learning. The employees visited other plants, some in Japan, to improve their knowledge and understanding of radial production and technological systems. After the instructors had obtained approval of their training programs from department heads, they began to teach machine operators in the new systems. In the course of their training, the instructors learned the jobs of other employees, thus gaining a more thorough understanding of the plant's operation. The entire hourly work force received instruction in up-to-date methods, enabling them to retain employment at the Tyler plant or, with their more current skills, to move elsewhere in the industry.[14]

Community colleges, technical schools, and four-year institutions are also updating their manufacturing curricula. Besides training new workers, the postsecondary schools retrain employees already on the production line. CIM, automated technologies, and flexible systems have become cornerstones of the courses.

In 1984, Chattanooga State Technical Community College dedicated what it called the most sophisticated automation training center in any two-year college in the country. The Center for Productivity, Innovation, and Technology, a $3 million investment, houses flexible manufacturing cells, robots, computer-assisted design (CAD), computer-assisted manufacturing (CAM), and automated quality control units. The facility serves three constituencies: students seeking an associate degree in advanced manufacturing technology, workers who must be retrained in order to remain in the work force, and industries needing assistance in solving technological problems. Regional industries are supportive and enroll their employees in courses and workshops as CIM is adopted in their plants.

Milwaukee Area Technical College has a somewhat similar center to further CIM in local industries and give technical assistance to companies installing such technology as well as orientation for their managers and executives. It shares its research facilities with business and other educational institutions. State and local governments and industrial partners have donated equipment, technical assistance, and several million dollars to the CIM center. Grants also have come from the U.S. Department of Education and the National Science Foundation. Of special note is an invitation to smaller companies to pool their resources in support of the CIM program, from which all could benefit. The ambitious program had its inspiration from a program in CAD/CAM in which students with Apple microcomputers ran software developed at the college that simulated the far more expensive CAD/CAM equipment. Today that software is running at more than 700 high schools, colleges, and universities around the country.

The CIM center, opened in December of 1986, expects to graduate 600 a year in the near future. Victor Langer, manager of instruction development, says that current graduates are quickly snatched up by local businesses at starting salaries sometimes in excess of $30,000. This may seem to be an extraordinary wage for someone with a new associate degree, but most of the center's graduates have also had previous work experience.

In the same year another CIM program started at Moraine Park Technical College in southeastern Wisconsin—a progressive state in manufacturing as well as political history. Fashioned after a model proposed by the Society of Manufacturing Engineers, the program has an unusual industrial clientele: an estimated 90 percent of the world's small engine manufacturing (lawn mowers, motorcycles, marine engines) takes place in the region. These plants are moving rapidly to computerization.[15]

Similar initiatives started in the last few years under the aegis of community and technical colleges are testimony to their leadership and service record. In New Jersey, Camden County Community College has constructed a multimillion dollar facility with support from a 1984 state bond issue to underwrite jobs, science, and technology. The CIM program serves six technical colleges around the state where students train during the first year and then go to Camden to complete their degree work. Tri-County Technical College in South Carolina introduced two associate degree programs in 1986—automated manufacturing technology and quality assurance technology, the latter one of a handful of such programs in this country.

Martin-Marietta, Westinghouse, and Stromberg Carlson are among the major employers working with Valencia Community College in Orlando, Florida, on a CIM program involving robotics. Corporate advisers help ensure that classroom and lab training are closely related to the skills needed in the workplace. Queensborough Community College in New York has joined with the New York Chapter of the National Tooling and Machining Association in a program to upgrade the skills of machinists critical to manufacturing. It is an effort to meet the shortage of skilled workers with programming capacity on computerized numerical control machines. Those who possessed this knowledge have been promoted, thus creating the shortage in the lower ranks.

Trends

In all these examples, chosen to indicate the range of training available to skilled trades and technical workers in America, certain trends are apparent along with problems that need to be examined and solutions that must be found. Schools—public and private—offer many opportunities for workers both in preparation and in retraining for different skills or for advanced levels. Community colleges are ahead of other traditional institutions in adjusting curricula to needs and in cooperative training programs with industry.

Partnerships between and among the various providers are multiplying with four-fold benefits. There exist many combinations of government, industry, and academic institutions working together, especially in the more technologically advanced fields that require large investments of money and knowledge. Labor unions and management have started collaborations in health care and in the automotive and other industries. Unions and academic institutions have long had labor studies and special programs like Purdue's with construction workers. Cooperative schemes that bring together knowledge and abilities from different fields can add strength and quality to programs; they pool and extend resources.

Since there are marked similarities in the content of many courses and their objectives, whether for administrative assistants, electronic technicians, or workers on the new factory floor, the question arises: Could these training programs be shared more effectively and reach many workers not being served? At the very least, investigation would reveal course redundancy as in, for example, the various federal agencies. Courses could be compared and superior materials selected for wider circulation. Given the limited financial resources and ever-growing demand—true for all providers—cooperation is a viable answer. It offers the means to enlarge the basic curricula as well as the esoteric specialties emerging with high technologies.

Regardless of the worker's employment category, the trend is indisputably toward multiple skills. The person adept at only one task is on the dangerous road traveled by the "deskilled." That task will all too often be rendered useless by increasingly sophisticated processes built into technical aids. The capacities of new inventions are challenging us to broaden our knowledge and skills as human beings.

One of the most important skills being called for is troubleshooting. Training in problem solving has flourished. The challenge here is to get a sufficient basis in knowledge—that is, the fundamentals and logic of the process. This requires time and instructional programs on a higher level than the short courses aimed at immediate placement. Reliance on the quick remedy in response to crisis will not give the U.S. work force the competent personnel it needs. Nor will it help the individual to hold a position and grow in career development.

Clearly we have many resources and providers for technical training. We have many entrepreneurs with energy and imagination creating ways to learn. The workers who are the foundation of our productivity deserve the best training we can give them.

5

EDUCATING MANAGERS

$\mathbb{M}$anagement, a career for millions of Americans and one to which many more aspire, is also the subject of large-scale educational enterprise, itself a respectable industry. Education for managers usually brings to mind the prestigious M.B.A. programs of elite schools like those at Chicago, Dartmouth, Harvard, and Stanford, whose graduates are wooed by the big corporations and paid astonishing salaries. But far more people receive management instruction in company or government classrooms as part of formal or informal career development efforts. These nondegree courses and programs comprise one of the largest categories of adult education in the United States, and most of them are delivered outside traditional academic institutions.

Once again, the organizations providing the education operate independently, although they are linked by a multitude of contacts. Their goals and purposes may differ, yet they too can learn from each other. Government, the military, and industry in the United States have all suffered from worrisome failings of management. A frank, collaborative, and far-reaching assessment of weaknesses and gaps in management education and ways of correcting them is appropriate at this juncture in the nation's history.

There is disturbing evidence that management education has not worked as well as it could. Despite a sizable rise in the number of undergraduate business majors, the annual yield of more than

60,000 M.B.A. graduates, and the expenditure of billions of dollars and man-hours on teaching managerial skills to hundreds of thousands of corporate and government employees, the competitive performance of the United States has weakened. The decision making of managers is questioned. It is often asked, for example, whether business leaders too readily choose the route of fast profits to the detriment of long-term investment for growth and development. And some observers attribute what they perceive to be our economic decline directly to mismanagement.[1] Whether that is true or not, education bears considerable responsibility for the results.

At a time when the world economy is growing and changing rapidly, the management curriculum should be subjected to a general assessment. Regardless of the sponsor, there is remarkable similarity in the courses being offered. In both the public and private sectors, topics recur in program after program, making management curricula more consistently recognizable than many other types of training. "People-management" courses and, for lack of a better term, "self-management" courses are taught everywhere. Leadership tops the people-management course list. Self-management encompasses topics such as time management, interpersonal skills, and the many different approaches to evaluation of personal strengths, weaknesses, and values. The popularity of the two types of courses indicates a widely perceived need. There are, however, questions about their efficacy and, perhaps as a result, a willingness to try new or purportedly new approaches.

Somewhat less common are courses in strategic analysis and basic financial control, primarily budgeting and resource management. Strategic analysis makes sense as a category of managerial training only if it is broadly construed as examination of an organization's external environment, development or review of an organization's essential goals, and consideration of how to reach those goals. Under this definition, much of the education in the civilian federal government and the military can be classified with courses in the academic and corporate worlds, where strategy is enjoying a boom. Financial control courses are frequently more specific to the organization's practices and procedures, but they also teach concepts that managers in virtually any organization must know to do their jobs. Furthermore, financial control represents a discipline that is fundamental to modern management practice and education.

Over the years the advocates of specialties like accounting, economics, and industry-specific courses have clashed with those who see human relations and people-management as equally vital for the manager. These two early and influential concepts oppose each other on whether management is an art or a science. The effects of the unsettled argument are discernible in contemporary managerial training.

The industrial engineer who first espoused "scientific" management, Frederick W. Taylor, defined it painstakingly through analysis of time, output, and costs—all dependent on system efficiency and specialists' supervision.[2] A different viewpoint known as the "human relations" school became associated with Elton Mayo in the 1930s. Basing his findings on field studies at a Western Electric Company plant, Mayo made a distinction between the economic organization of a business and its social organization. Both contributed equally to the performance of a business. Taking the "total situation" into account presupposed dealing with messy and inexact phenomena, emotions, and social relations. Traditional management specialties and analytical control had to make room for human factors.

The persistent hostility between the two positions finds expression in the colloquial language of organizations. "Bean counter" on the one hand and "touchy feely" on the other condense a wealth of pejorative attitudes and suspicions. The tension between the two perspectives will be evident in the examples and discussion we offer about training for managers.

To assess the contributions of the major organizations educating managers and executives, this chapter devotes a section to each:

the federal government, the armed forces, companies, and universities. We show the scope and complexity of their programs in relation to their particular goals and problems. Nevertheless, the similarities of courses given by the different providers are self-evident, and suggest possibilities for cooperative curricula or transfer of courses in instances that are not industry specific. Many courses in the government's executive training programs reflect the course titles from corporate management centers. As will be shown, however, there are distinct differences in the persons being served and in the organizational structure for training them.

The Federal Government

By private-sector standards, the federal government may be the ultimate conglomerate. Its global organization, with slightly more than 2 million civilian employees, includes more than 280,000 supervisors and managers and more than 9,000 executives.[3] Through a large number of operating units it delivers a vast array of unrelated services and contracts for the manufacture of a vast array of goods. One unit, the Department of Agriculture, is composed of more than 40 agencies and staffs engaged in market regulation, resource conservation, farm income maintenance, commodity inspection and grading, feeding programs, and scientific research.

From a management standpoint, the federal government is a nightmare. Not only are its goods and services unrelated, but they are also regularly changed or added to by a short-term chief executive and an outside organization, the Congress. This sprawling enterprise is subject to uncertainties that have direct impact on the managerial training it undertakes.

It is a truism that training needs the sustained support of an organization's top leadership. Compounding the risks of frequent change at the highest level of the federal government is the even faster turnover of high-level agency appointees. As the top executives of often huge organizations with which they are unlikely to become well acquainted and as the agents of a political agenda that they are expected to install, appointees and their aides are unlikely to give much attention to managerial education. If they do, their usually brief tenures limit the effect of their support.

Federal expenditures for training and the number of participants generally moved upward from 1980 to 1985,[4] but, as is the case in most organizations, government funds for the training function are always vulnerable. As a high-profile political issue, the federal deficit intensifies the normal jockeying for shares of the budget. Funds for management education remain a potential casualty of selective austerity.

Finally, a fashion of recent presidential campaigns has produced a morale problem that is hardly conducive to management development. Presidents Carter and Reagan ran against the government, particularly the executive bureaucracy. "Bureaucrat bashing" undermined federal employees' pride, sense of professionalism, and motivation.

The federal civil service, however, also has a stability that can enhance its internal educational programs. Although many functions of the federal government, including managerial education, may not flourish or achieve excellence in the short run, they may survive to see better days. Finally, civil service personnel are among the few employees in the nation who have de facto lifetime employment. With enough motivation and support, government employees can take a long-term view of their development as managers.

The Federal Training Function.   Until after World War II, training of civilian employees was generally thought to be unnecessary. When agencies began to spend funds on training, they reasoned that the expenditure was a legitimate managerial decision and did not seek Congressional approval. Soon, however, they found themselves in a bureaucratic dispute about the legality of the spending. The Soviet Union's launch of Sputnik in 1958 galvanized all parties to clear the bureaucratic gridlock. Congress promptly passed the Government Employees Training Act of 1958, which authorized a decentralized approach. Agencies were to offer training within standards set by the Civil Service Commission

An executive order issued by President Lyndon Johnson in 1967 directed the commission to pursue centralized training, particularly for civil servants at the executive level. The commission responded by setting up the Federal Executive Institute, a center for advanced management studies (discussed in the next section). The Civil Service Reform Act passed by Congress in 1978 had a greater impact on government management education. According to Alan K. Campbell, administrator of the civil service during the Carter presidency and an architect of the legislation, "We were consciously trying to restore and revitalize the role of managers in the Civil Service System. . . . A corollary of this . . . was to insist on systematic training and preparation for the managerial role."[5] The legislation was informed by the example of large corporations that regarded managerial development and formal training as essential to effective long-term performance.

The Office of Personnel Management (OPM), successor to the Civil Service Commission, and the Senior Executive Service (SES) were two of the more important means established by the 1978 legislation. The SES encompassed the top levels of the civil service. It was intended to upgrade the career appeal and effectiveness of government management. The Reform Act streamlined the promotion process at this level, established a better reward system for senior staff, and mandated formal and on-the-job training for SES candidates and members.

Under the legislation OPM, charged with setting up educational programs that supported the SES, had the choice of operating the programs or having government agencies do so under its supervision. In effect, OPM chose to do both. All the larger federal agencies run their own programs, conforming in varying degrees to OPM guidance,[6] while OPM offers similar courses and programs in centralized facilities. In fiscal 1986, the latest year for which figures are available, government civil servants received training from OPM and federal agencies as follows: of the total number of managers and supervisors, 59 percent had training, while 48 percent of executives and 45 percent of line employees had such opportunities. At least half of all government employees got some training.[7]

To develop and foster management education, OPM undertook research aimed at getting a descriptive model of effective managerial performance. The research yielded the management excellence framework shown in figure 1 describing what government managers do (management functions) and how they do it (effectiveness characteristics). The third dimension, management levels (see figure 2), takes into account the progressively broader duties and outlook as one moves up the organizational hierarchy from first-line supervisor to middle manager to senior executive. The model has provided an organizing principle for management education programs throughout the government and formed a way of evaluating managers' developmental needs. For the latter purpose OPM also developed a management excellence inventory based on the framework.

Whatever shortcomings the framework may have, it is comprehensive and based on investigation of how government managers actually operate. Educational programs guided by such a model are more likely to be responsive to the needs of participants. It can also give coherence to management training programs, which universally suffer from a scattershot approach.

Office of Personnel Management Programs. The Federal Executive Institute is OPM's elite management program. With its own small faculty and 12-acre campus in Charlottesville, Virginia, the institute generally limits participation to new or prospective senior executives, though a small number may come from state, local, and foreign governments or the private sector. A four-week program

Figure 1   The Federal Government's Management Excellence Framework

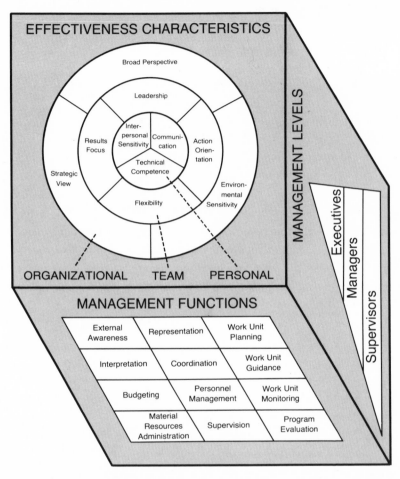

Source: U.S. Office of Personnel Management, *The Management Excellence Framework: A Competency-Based Model of Effective Performance for Federal Managers*, September 1985, p. 2.

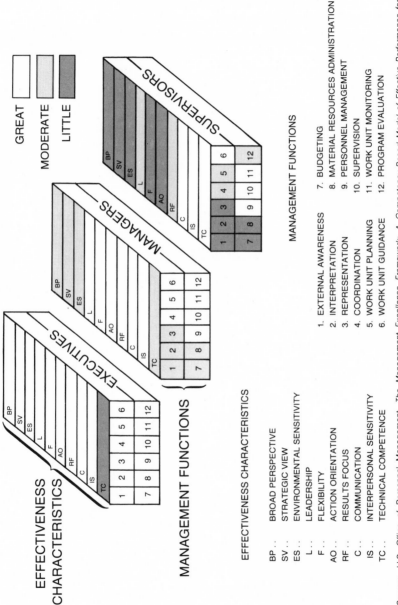

RELATIVE IMPORTANCE GUIDE --

GREAT
MODERATE
LITTLE

EFFECTIVENESS CHARACTERISTICS

EXECUTIVES

MANAGERS

SUPERVISORS

MANAGEMENT FUNCTIONS

EFFECTIVENESS CHARACTERISTICS

BP . . BROAD PERSPECTIVE
SV . . STRATEGIC VIEW
ES . . ENVIRONMENTAL SENSITIVITY
L . . LEADERSHIP
F . . FLEXIBILITY
AO . . ACTION ORIENTATION
RF . . RESULTS FOCUS
C . . COMMUNICATION
IS . . INTERPERSONAL SENSITIVITY
TC . . TECHNICAL COMPETENCE

MANAGEMENT FUNCTIONS

1. EXTERNAL AWARENESS
2. INTERPRETATION
3. REPRESENTATION
4. COORDINATION
5. WORK UNIT PLANNING
6. WORK UNIT GUIDANCE
7. BUDGETING
8. MATERIAL RESOURCES ADMINISTRATION
9. PERSONNEL MANAGEMENT
10. SUPERVISION
11. WORK UNIT MONITORING
12. PROGRAM EVALUATION

Source: U.S. Office of Personnel Management, The Management Excellence Framework: A Competency-Based Model of Effective Performance for Federal Managers, September 1985, p. 8.

entitled Leadership for a Democratic Society concentrates on the theme of "specialist to generalist to leader." The mandate is well taken. Federal agencies are technical and professional organizations that hire and promote on the basis of technical proficiency. Unlike the military or large corporations, the agencies do not identify management candidates early on and groom them for the role.

Many federal managers are promoted for years through the grades of narrow specialties, receiving along the way little if any management preparation, until they arrive at a supervisory or management position. A few simple statistics demonstrate that federal agencies are not fast-track organizations. In one department, 70 percent of first-line supervisors were over the age of 40, and more than half had between 16 and 30 years service. Of middle managers, 34 percent were between 50 and 59, and almost half had 21 to 30 years of service in the department.[8] The institute is a four-week attempt at managerial remediation.

Opinions have varied about its effectiveness. It has been most often faulted for a tilt toward the human relations aspects of management, involving self-evaluation and interpersonal skills. In interviews, however, participants expressed general satisfaction with the program.[9] True, the institute does not emphasize quantitative management techniques; it focuses on personal development, the analysis of leadership abilities, and action-oriented team projects. Each graduate leaves with a plan to be implemented in his or her agency and attends follow-up sessions.

The institute devotes much time to courses with broad implications, such as one on constitutional literacy and others that explore major policy issues and their consequences for government agencies. Adjunct teachers and speakers come from universities and government agencies to join the eight full-time faculty members. A new learning laboratory uses technological instructional aids.

For middle managers, OPM offers training through three Executive Seminar Centers located in Kings Point, New York; Oak

Ridge, Tennessee; and Denver, Colorado. They are residential facilities with classrooms, libraries, and dormitory accommodations. In fiscal 1986 almost 4,000 government employees, nominated by their agencies, were enrolled in center programs.[10] Their curriculum consists of eight management and nine national policy seminars over a two-week period. Management courses scale up from a new managers' seminar on interpersonal relationships and skills to seminars emphasizing general issues like strategy and planning. The topics of the seminars include regulatory policy, national security policy, and the role of the government in technology transfer. Acquainting middle managers with policy and strategy issues is a recognized strength of these programs. The Executive Seminar Centers offer few quantitative management courses, but they make more of an effort in this area than the Federal Executive Institute does.

The centers can take less than three percent of those eligible in the federal government.[11] The small capacity relative to demand would be more understandable if the centers were an elite program. That they are not raises anew the question of costly centralized facilities that compete against the resources of the other agencies devoted to the same purpose. Still, the centers receive generally positive reviews from participants and observers.

A large-scale nonresidential program with some 300 short courses operates at OPM sites in Washington, at ten regional centers and a European facility, and on the premises of host agencies. In fiscal 1986, these courses attracted nearly 150,000 students, of whom many worked in Washington. About 19,000 more took OPM correspondence courses.[12] The grab-bag variety of offerings—from decision analysis to effective listening and memory development, from performance appraisal to COBOL programming—can be attributed to the rough-and-tumble free market in training that exists, paradoxically, in a sector that is generally perceived to be the antithesis of free enterprise.

These OPM courses are not obligatory steps to promotion, and they too compete with agency courses. Moreover, the participants' home agencies are charged a fee, and the courses are expected to pay for themselves. Therefore, courses that find a market survive and those that do not, disappear. Although an unfettered market mechanism has seldom found support among educators as a good way of determining a curriculum, in this instance the results are fascinating. The curriculum consisting of short courses may lack coherence, but it exhibits a balance between functional and general management and between quantitative and nonquantitative approaches.

Presidential Management Interns. A centralized program designed to attract high-quality senior executive candidates from outside the government attests to the concern for improvement in government management. The Presidential Management Intern Program (PMI) was instituted with other civil service reforms in 1978. Eligibility for the two-year internships is very narrowly defined: candidates must be students in their final year of a master's degree program in public administration or a field closely related to it. Interns are, in theory at least, rotated through short developmental positions in the host department or agency, are assigned a mentor, and are required to take part in formal courses and seminars.

For a program designed to attract talent, PMI has some peculiar features. Restricting eligibility to master's candidates in a few fields eliminates a vast number of qualified persons who have taken training in other fields and are not now degree candidates. Successful interns are not guaranteed jobs in an agency or in the government. It is their responsibility to find positions; the host agencies may or may not make places for them, although it is rare for an agency to refuse. And when a presidential intern secures a permanent government job, no special effort is made to accelerate the individual's entry into the Senior Executive Service through further formal education and assignments. PMI does not offer rapid promotion—an idea that may well be alien to the culture of the federal bureaucracy.

Federal Agency Programs. In 1985, the Department of Agriculture conducted a survey of management training in 12 federal agencies that required training for supervisory personnel and offered internal programs to meet the requirement.[13] Most of the programs were confined to formal classroom instruction. At the middle-management level, only four organizations required training, although all but one made internal instruction optionally available. Senior-level executives in all the agencies must take at least some formal management instruction.

Some agencies are more than dutiful in their approaches to management education. Examples are the Internal Revenue Service, the Department of Commerce, and the Treasury Department. The IRS has been notable as one of the few civilian units of the government to rotate its managers through a variety of positions. It is also well known for careful assessment and development of its management personnel. Like banks and financial services companies in the private sector, the IRS faced the task of converting entry-level college graduates into competent professionals within a short period of time. The agency's solution was a formal system of on-the-job training and classroom instruction as well as a mentor system.

The IRS requires independent development plans (IDPs) for both supervisors and middle managers, while most other agencies require IDPs only for senior executives (adhering to the letter of the 1978 Civil Service Act), if they honor the requirement at all. Negotiated between the manager and the mentor, an IDP specifies on-the-job training and formal coursework to improve the person's functional knowledge and managerial abilities. The bureau trains supervisors at seven regional centers using a centrally developed curriculum. Mid-level management programs have three tracks: managing work systems, managing human resources, and continuing professional education.

Senior executive candidates are assigned coaches to help them construct training schedules, to funnel feedback from instructors, and generally to help candidates make the transition to executive positions. A sample of a nine-month-long training schedule for an IRS executive candidate shows 27 different training activities in six cities over a period of six months. Only one of these activities involved an outside supplier, and only one was provided by the Office of Personnel Management; all the rest were within the IRS. Some examples of the activities:

- Nine days of tours, field visits, and participation in meetings to become acquainted with regional office operations.

- Seventeen days spent in teams of four visiting each function of an IRS district office.

- One week spent in teams of two "shadowing" a district director in his or her daily work, with end-of-day debriefing sessions.

- One week observing the data processing functions at national headquarters.

IRS senior executive candidates and those already in the position are also trained in the Department of Treasury's Executive Institute, housed in a federal office building in Washington and supervised by a Treasury advisory panel. Run by a permanent administrative staff, it offers high-powered executive seminars, most conducted by outside consultants. Familiar topics have been presented as well as the exotic "Visionary Leadership" and the mundane "Liability of the Federal Manager." People-management has dominated recent offerings, but the institute has also looked at the future of robotics and at "management tools for the 1990s and beyond." The frequency of the seminars, the presence of well-known outside consultants, and the impressive facility in which they take place put Treasury at the gold-plated end of the government managerial education spectrum.

More typical is the Department of Agriculture. In 1985, the department had 12,604 first-line supervisors, 2,007 managers, and 352 executives. The USDA requires the three grades of managers to participate in training. Supervisors and managers have complained, however, that the training often did not meet their needs, particularly in human resources management. Middle managers have been the most vocal. Quoting from a departmental report,

> Some [managers] stated that they had been promoted up through the ranks to their present positions without being trained in how to perform their managerial or supervisory responsibilities and tasks. Many reported that planned and scheduled training had been canceled because of budget problems. Many who had had training reported that the training was of poor quality, occurred at the wrong time in their careers, or was too general for them to apply to specific situations. We again heard the general cry, "I have never been taught how to supervise or manage people."[14]

Buried in a General Accounting Office report published in 1984 is a similar critical finding about the training the government provides to SES candidates and members. But in this case, those sampled were asked to compare on-the-job training and different types of formal instruction. On-the-job training rated much higher than courses. Of the coursework options, college and university courses ranked first as preparing candidates to a "very great extent." Courses given by federal agencies received a far lower rating.[15]

Another problematic finding of the USDA survey was that most supervisors and many managers regarded their supervisory or managerial duties merely as additions to their basic jobs. Neither departmental training nor the organization itself had made clear that they were now administrators—not specialists—with an entirely new set of concerns and goals. Obviously, managerial training is very unlikely to have a significant impact if the organization it serves has minimized, misunderstood, or overlooked the management function. The finding probably applies equally to many other federal agencies as well as to many companies and corporations. The Department of Agriculture had the good sense—and courage—to survey its employees as a start in mapping change. How many other organizations choose not to know is interesting material for speculation.

The Armed Forces

The Department of Defense (DOD) is one of the largest, most complex, and resource-rich organizations in the world. In fiscal 1987, DOD outlays amounted to 27 percent of total federal expenditures, or 6.2 percent of the country's gross national product.[16] The Army's share of the federal budget was just over $75 billion and the shares of the Navy and Air Force each exceeded $94 billion. The department spends nearly $130 billion annually on military research and development and hardware production and enters into contracts at a rate of 60,000 every day. DOD personnel number in the millions. The uniformed services in 1989 had 2.1 million officers and enlisted personnel, with nearly 1.7 million in the National Guard and reserves, and the department also employs more than 1 million civilians.

The uniformed combat services are the core of this enormous enterprise. No other function of government saw such expansion in funding in the Reagan regime: the military budget nearly doubled, and cumulatively it surpassed a trillion dollars. Recruitment for the volunteer force picked up and retention rates improved. And the educational background of recruits improved sharply.[17] Among those entering the three service academies, the average level on college entrance examination scores was just below that of freshmen admitted to the nation's elite colleges and universities.

A recently concluded study comparing the education levels of Army brigadier generals with those of corporate managers and executives revealed that substantially more officers held master's degrees. The number of officers holding Ph.D. degrees was only slightly less than the number of private-sector executives and managers with doctorates. Nearly 60 percent of the career officers in the Air Force and 25 percent in the Army hold graduate degrees.[18] Career officers today consider graduate study a de facto requirement for promotion to senior levels. But the tacit and therefore unregulated requirement encourages "ticket punching"—the acquisition of graduate degrees in less-than-stellar programs merely for the sake of advancement. Nevertheless, the educational level of the armed forces is rising markedly.

Management Education in the Military.   The lower levels of the officer training system, the service academies like West Point and the Naval Academy at Annapolis, have broadened their requirements and electives from engineering and technical courses to include a great deal of work in the social sciences and humanities. Although the choice would seem unlikely for someone intent on becoming a flag officer, a West Point cadet can major in history or an Annapolis midshipman can major in English.[19]

At the next levels, technical military subjects begin to overshadow "softer" studies. Management-related issues also enter the curriculum. For example, by their tenth year of service, all Army captains must complete training at the Combined Arms and Services Staff School at Fort Leavenworth, Kansas. At the beginning of their studies, conducted by correspondence, less than one-third of the total hours are spent studying management. During the nine-week residential phase that follows, two of the six courses could be considered managerial topics. The major emphasis, naturally, is on military operations.[20] In table 3, we list military schools at the intermediate and senior levels. The officer course at the Army's Command and General Staff School, also at Fort Leavenworth, is representative of intermediate service schools. Its term of 40 weeks is divided into a common curriculum and individual development of elective courses. Two of the six core courses deal with management. Roughly four days are spent on Army techniques for resource management, three days on organizational communication and group dynamics, and slightly less than two days on senior-level leadership. Each student chooses seven electives from more than 100 offerings. Fewer than 20 concern military management and these courses are concentrated in logistics, personnel, and military leadership. The last-named is taught with historical examples rather than through a combination of theory, case study, and practice.

Table 3 Intermediate and Senior Officer Training Schools

Army	Navy	Air Force	Interservice
	INTERMEDIATE SCHOOLS		
Command and General Staff School	College of Naval Command and Staff	Air Command and Staff College	Armed Forces Staff College*
	Marine Corps Command and Staff College**		Defense Systems Management College
	SENIOR SCHOOLS		
Army War College	College of Naval Warfare	Air War College	National War College*
			Industrial College of the Armed Forces*

* These comprise the National Defense University.

** The intermediate school of the Marine Corps is placed here merely for convenience. The Corps has no senior school of its own: Marine officers at that level attend one of the other senior-level schools.

The Defense Systems Management College, an intermediate-level, interservice school located in the Washington, D.C., area, has the special mission of preparing military officers and civil service personnel to function as managers of defense acquisitions programs. They will oversee weapons and equipment development and production worth billions of dollars annually and involving defense contractors who employ thousands of workers on their projects. Major weapons programs can easily last ten years or more from concept development to production and deployment. Government managers of large programs are usually military officers with the rank of colonel (Army and Air Force) or captain (Navy). Both military and civilian deputies report to them. The military program manager generally has had little business training, and in any case serves as a program manager only for two to four years before rotating to the next duty assignment. Managers employed by defense contractors generally have more experience, more business training, and remain with a given program for a longer period.

The services' use of the Defense Systems Management College program is uneven. A 1986 General Accounting Office study found that two-thirds of the Army's program managers had attended the college, compared with 30 percent of the Navy's and 18.2 percent of the Air Force's managers.[21] The 20-week course is designed to conform to the military's definition of temporary duty. If the course were longer, the assignment would be considered a change in duty and the service would have to pay moving and housing expenses. The arbitrary determination of its length compresses the program, making the instruction hours given to complex topics pitifully few: cost proposal estimation, three hours; types of contracts, one hour; understanding financial reporting by defense contractors, three hours; cost principles in defense contracting, two hours; and principles of cost control systems, one hour. According to a recent book on defense acquisition management, the college has also had trouble attracting top-flight faculty.[22] Civilian instructors already working in government must resign their civil service positions, although their teaching appointments last no longer than seven years. Military officers shun the assignment because it is perceived to carry less weight in promotion decisions than field commands.

The year-long programs of the War Colleges and the National Defense University are the pinnacle of the military training system. Discussion of strategy and policies dominates studies on this level, and the three colleges have similar curricular emphases: national security policy, service-specific military strategy, and joint operations strategy, whose inclusion Congress recently mandated. Treatment of executive-level management issues varies according to the service.

The Army War College begins its core curriculum with a substantial if brief two-week course aimed at understanding wartime leadership and management leadership in a large organization.[23] At the Air War College, officers have three courses on executive leadership and management topics that constitute nearly one-sixth of their instruction.[24] And the College of Naval Warfare addresses management only as a component of a required course on national security decision making.[25] Students at all three senior schools choose elective courses such as executive power and influence, power and politics in complex organizations, and civilian personnel management.

Located at Fort McNair in Washington, the National Defense University is charged with promoting a joint multiservice perspective in senior officers selected from the services and in high-level civilian officials. It consists of three institutions: the National War College, the Industrial College of the Armed Forces, and an intermediate school, the Armed Forces Staff College. Each has its own curriculum but all are oriented toward national security policies and strategies with a focus on the command of joint forces. All include international dimensions. The Industrial College is unique in its studies of how decision makers in the defense community can convert available military, social, and economic resources into effective military forces capable of achieving national security objectives. Electives train students in important general and defense-related management areas.[26] The "hard side" of management studies is well represented at the college, but there are no "soft side" courses.

In view of the extensive training programs for military personnel, one wonders why there are so few programs for civilian DOD employees, who fulfill essential roles in the management and operation of the military. The military schools that make up the professional education system admit only limited numbers of civilians. But to increase civilian opportunities, the services run programs designed for nonuniformed personnel. An example is the Army's Management Staff College in Linthicum Heights, Maryland. A 19-week residential course trains Army civil servants and some officers in how the service conducts its business. Five of the nine required courses deal with management systems and techniques from resource management to the Army personnel system. Unfortunately the courses are so inclusive they can yield only a quick view of the designated topics. The course titled "Leadership, Management Techniques, and Corporate Fitness," for example, spans management theory, team building, strategy planning, and physical exercise programs, among other subjects.

Issues in Military Management Training. The sheer size of the defense establishment and the enormous national investment in it are reasons enough to expect good management by those responsible for it. Yet this simple proposition lacks the priority it deserves. The reasons for this have a logic of their own. The military services exist to defend the nation, and their overriding responsibility is competence in tactics, strategy, and military leadership. Management is decidedly subordinate.

Not everyone agrees, however, that the services are realizing even these basic objectives. No fewer than three studies made public in 1988 questioned the intellectual rigor of the programs, the quality of school faculties, the adequacy of joint operations training, and the soundness of strategy courses.[27] The Army is taking steps to improve the faculty, increase the interservice focus, and upgrade strategy training at its War College.[28] But these reforms still leave a dearth of substantive education in management.

Even in leadership training, which fits comfortably among the traditional skills of a military officer, critics suggest improvement and updating. The fondness for case studies drawn from past wars ignores the strategies appropriate to battlefield conditions of the late twentieth century. The heroic exploits of Alexander the Great or even the unassuming, stolid command of Ulysses S. Grant may have little to contribute to modern military leadership training in which technology is a critical element.

The services are technology-intensive organizations. Although this is a characteristic of many large organizations today, the American military continuously absorbs new systems at all its levels. The educational burden of this effort is the need for continuous training of the service personnel who conceive, design, command, operate, and maintain the systems and equipment. That requirement further subordinates management on the military's educational agenda.

But in many assignments, an officer's combat leadership skills and technical prowess do not compensate for a lack of management knowledge and experience. Many studies of weapons acquisitions have found that the government pays much more than it should for weapons and equipment and that poor management is a cause. Officers with cursory management education and limited experience often perform poorly as program managers and stand at a great disadvantage in dealing with defense contractors' more experienced, better-trained representatives. The result has been an inflated bill for American taxpayers.

There are many other officer billets that have a strong but neglected managerial dimension. An example is a Navy engineering duty officer who supervises ship repair. The assignment requires not only engineering knowledge but also the skills and savvy of a good project manager. Engineering duty officers get an excellent technical education but little if any management training. Students in a university program leading to a master's degree and active duty as an engineering officer offered these comments to us on the imbalance:

- Expertise in both engineering and management is required for understanding the requirements for getting a ship from the mind's eye to the fleet.

- A management-business education is as important to the engineering duty officer as the technical education.

- Any corporation that spent as little time and money developing executive managers as is spent by the Navy for senior shipyard managers would likely be unable to compete in the marketplace.

To rectify the situation, the military will have to reexamine the serious managerial responsibilities of many of its officers. As a committed training organization, it will also have to recognize that two-week core courses delivered to all promotable officers, or survey courses delivered to a small number of officers coupled with brief two- to four-year duty rotations, do not add up to competent and confident management of complex projects and organizations. Longer, deeper courses are necessary.

Finally, and crucially, the military will have to alter its promotion system to offer first-rate officers the incentive to gain significant managerial education and elect management careers. The bias toward combat commands and technical expertise in military promotion decisions is a powerful disincentive. The ideal is not a military led by M.B.A. graduates. Just as a hospital needs not only surgeons and technical equipment that works, but also knowledgeable medical administrators, so the military needs effective defense managers to complement its front-line warriors and senior strategists.

Companies and Corporations

Of the billions of dollars U.S. corporations spend on training, the portion that goes to management education is not precisely known. In 1987, however, human resource development managers in *Fortune* "500" companies were asked what percentages of their total resources were dedicated to various types of training. Just over 56 percent of the training money spent in the 179 companies that responded was committed to managerial education and development.[29]

Through the 1980s companies and corporations added to their investment in training and education. From 1988 to 1989, total training budgets rose by almost five billion dollars, or 12 percent, according to a *Training* magazine survey.[30] Most of the increase was in trainers' salaries, but expenditures were also higher for outside services, seminars and conferences, customized as well as off-the-shelf materials, and hardware. Training, including management education, was a growth industry in that decade, and indications are that the growth will continue. Another study yielded strong evidence that over the next ten years companies will expand management training, particularly in-house programs.[31] A recession may cause a revision of these plans, but in the 1980s training and education became inextricably linked with competitiveness, the most potent challenge of the 1990s for American business.

Against this expansionist background, the company status of human resource development staff seems ironic. The whirl and flash and high-tech glitter of training conventions seems hard evidence that company-based education has reached a status equal to that of other business specialties. Away from a meeting of the converted, however, Rodney Dangerfield's trademark line often seems to apply: "I can't get no respect!" As in government, private sector human resource development personnel can lead a skittish and insecure existence. A group of them were asked in a 1987 survey to state their single greatest challenge or problem over the next three to five years. A full half of the respondents mentioned credibility and support from management.[32] The same survey rated human resource development as having the lowest credibility of five company functions. Mediocre performers historically have often been assigned to the training function, a practice lost neither on the individuals shunted off to teach in company classrooms nor on line employees. The practice reflected the opinions and priorities of top executives, who may have been influenced by the old dichotomy between the hard and soft sides of management.

Oddly, training and education *have* gained high credibility and, in the case of managerial and executive education, even prestige, but employees who manage the activity think they have not. The differential status is most pronounced with respect to executive training, most of which is delivered by outsiders. Elevating the in-house function of education either as a career or a career step seems imperative.

One approach is to bring outstanding managers into the training function or rotate them through it. Experienced line and field personnel make up about 75 percent of IBM's educational staff.[33] A frequent guest instructor at General Electric's Management Development Institute is John F. Welch, Jr., company chairman. Of course, the status of corporate educators is not the salient point; effectiveness is. But the status of the company educational function affects the students and teaching staff. A cardinal rule for successful training programs is to start with the CEO's strong and public endorsement.

Students, Sources, and Subjects. The absolute number of production workers and salespeople in the work force far exceeds the number of managers, yet the training commitment to the latter is greater proportionally, and programs are more structured. It can be argued of course that the manager's role is pivotal to company decisions and success, so the attention to his or her development is essential. But it is also probable that the allotment of time and resources to managerial training has simply evolved over the years and has accumulated as managerial specialties multiplied.

Most companies emphasize training for middle managers, which is not surprising considering the conventional business hierarchy.[34] A move from supervisor to middle manager means a shift from overseeing line employees to managing managers. Corporate America clearly appreciates the difficulty of the transition.

However, the percentage of companies training their first-line supervisors seems low. The transition from employee to supervisor can be traumatic and as difficult as the next step upward. In a period of brisk technological and competitive change, more resources should be dedicated to continuing the training of supervisors.

A recent study restricted to executive education in large corporations confirms that about 70 percent of the companies sponsor formal education at that level.[35] Certain industries exceed the average: insurance, 100 percent; retail, 79 percent; banking, 75 percent; and industrial companies, 72 percent. Several of these industries have strong training traditions, in part because they always have hired liberal arts college graduates and others without industry-specific backgrounds.

For management training, those in higher positions are more likely to take courses from outside providers such as consultants and universities, while exclusively in-house training is most frequent for supervisors and others in the lower ranks. One survey shows that the average number of policy-level executives trained per year in a company with at least 50 employees is just over five.[36] The average corporate budget for executive education ranges from $100,000 to $500,000 a year. Thus the average cost per executive is at least $20,000. The figure is useful as a very rough index of the cost of what is considered to be high-quality top-management education.

How can small business take advantage of such costly education? Owner-managers of small companies may not need the same type of instruction as executives of multinational corporations, but they can profit from instruction suited to the scale and scope of their business environment. Most smaller businesses, however, may be priced out of the market. Harvard Business School's Owner-President Management Program, given in three units of three weeks over three years, cost $7,500 per unit in 1988. Other small business programs at leading institutions are also expensive: Stanford, two weeks for $6,300, and the Wharton School at the University of Pennsylvania, five days for $1,595. All of these programs are residential, so the company must be large enough or mature enough to spare the owner or top officer for an extended period.

Serving the management education needs of small business may well be an area in which community colleges, private colleges, and state universities can expand their adult education enrollments and contribute to the economic vitality of their communities. These institutions should be able to offer high-quality nonresidential programs at a modest cost. The Small Business Development Center at the University of Connecticut has launched a program along these lines.[37]

Of the management courses taught in private industry, those oriented toward people-management and self-development are most frequent. The heavy "soft skills" emphasis is a striking characteristic. And the same characteristic dominates a list of learning goals for company managerial education. In table 4, we show the goals ranked according to their importance as revealed by a survey of human resource development managers in nearly 100 companies. Respondents were permitted to mention goals not served by in-house training that they believed should be part of such courses.

Table 4   Learning Goals of Company Management Education

Great Importance	
1. Problem solving and decision making	7. Negotiating skills
2. Understanding manager's role	8. Assuming responsibility
3. Oral communication	9. Delegation skills
4. Interpersonal skills	10. Leadership
5. Listening skills	11. Self-confidence
6. Managing change	12. Self-evaluation

Medium Importance	
1. Giving and taking advice and criticism	6. Time management
2. Motivation	7. Self-awareness
3. Tolerance and trust	8. Generalizing and synthesizing
4. Organizing and summarizing	9. Finance
5. Creativity	10. Stress management

Low Importance	
1. Strategic thinking	7. Writing skills
2. Public speaking	8. Computer literacy
3. Performance appraisal	9. Liberal arts
4. Human resource development	10. Ethics
5. Organizational theory and behavior	11. Social values
6. Career management	

Source: Robert Hahn and Kathryn Mohrman, "What Do Managers Need to Know?" *American Association for Higher Education Bulletin*, October 1985, p. 3.

Why the overwhelming emphasis on soft skills? Although human resource managers might be expected to stress people-oriented skills, the business community presumably would not invest large sums in educational programs for which it did not see a compelling need. Private industry has complained that schools and universities have done a poor job of educating the American work force, which makes it necessary for them to undertake compensatory education. In the instance of basic skills like listening, writing, and speaking, the complaints seem warranted. In other areas, responsibility is harder to assign.

College graduates ought to be at least minimally competent in goal setting, problem solving, and decision making because these activities call on cognitive abilities that traditional education is supposed to develop and deepen. But should colleges and universities teach leadership, team building, management of change, or interpersonal skills? Companies teach these topics as operational or instrumental skills—that is, the goal is a particular performance and outcome specific to the working environment. Colleges and universities are inclined to teach the topics as a body of knowledge, not as behavioral skills. Students who participate in extracurricular activities can experiment with leadership and team-building skills, but for the increasing numbers who must work when they are not at school, such opportunities are few.

Business schools are a special case. They have the dual mission of teaching business disciplines and furthering the behavioral skills and the values desirable in professional managers. Statements by company officials and the implicit statement made by their management curricula are evidence that business schools are not fulfilling the second mission.

Maturity and experience also have a place in the discussion of whether private industry is compensating for weaknesses in the American educational system. An understanding of the managerial role means little without substantial work experience. The same could be said about leadership—with the exception of those rare individuals who seemingly were born to lead—and about motivation, team building, and interpersonal relations. Maturity also contributes to the understanding, self-control, and sensitivity that are part of effective "people skills." It is hardly an accident that work experience has become a de facto requirement for admission to the top business schools. Perhaps many management courses in industry and government are being taught where and when they ought to be.

Some large goals of management education at the executive level are not sufficiently expressed in the list given as table 4. One is management succession. American companies and corporations believe that formal management education enhances the internal pool of candidates for leadership positions. This sort of development activity is advanced not merely by improvement of functional skills, but also by preparation of high-potential candidates as generalists. Much of executive education seeks to cultivate a generalist perspective and a broad view of societal issues. Strategic analysis is a related aspect that human resource managers hold in low esteem, but one that many industry leaders would place high on the list. Cultivation of the longer view, dealing successfully with various interacting factors, and risk-taking in innovation: these are abilities which enhance the vision and leadership needed by U.S. companies.

Another omission from table 4 is the concern for instilling or changing company culture. Many corporations have carefully shaped their organizational values and inculcated them in their employees. Examples of such courses are seen most clearly in the structured sequence of curricula given in management development centers of the large companies.

Corporate Academies. The sometimes spartan, sometimes luxurious company facilities dedicated to management development can be hailed as a prudent expenditure on specialized adult education, an indictment of the traditional educational system, a monument to corporate ego, or any combination of the three. In any case, corporate academies are here to stay and unabashedly serious about their educational mission. The list of companies that have management education institutes or academies is long and growing longer. GE, Xerox, Aetna, Hartford Insurance, IBM, McDonald's, Dunkin' Donuts, Kwik Copy, GTE, Motorola, Holiday Inn, Pacific Telesis, and Ford are just a few. Many companies with their own management academies are suppliers to the educational market.

The IBM Management Development Center is strategically located in Armonk, New York, near corporate headquarters. The four fieldstone, oak, and glass buildings house classrooms and living quarters for new, middle, and senior managers. A separate building is a fitness center. On any given day 80 new managers, 40 middle managers, and 20 executives are in residence. Two features of the IBM programs have general relevance: employee indoctrination and the common core curriculum. The first session of the new supervisors' program describes the IBM approach, and when participants receive instruction, for example, in performance reviews and counseling, they are not taught techniques recommended by researchers, but the mandatory methods that embody the IBM way.

A company far afield from the high-tech business of information systems dispenses similarly unapologetic indoctrination. McDonald's, worldwide purveyor of hamburgers and other fast-food items, uses its Hamburger University to drum into managers the operational procedures and service philosophy of the corporation. McDonald's applies a manufacturing approach to fast food—to maintain quality standards, the preparers must always make the hamburger and the milkshake exactly the same way. Any high-quality product must resemble its paradigm. McDonald's relentlessly promotes an entrepreneurial drive among its store managers, and "QSC"—shorthand for quality, service, and cleanliness.

Core curricula are usually segmented by management level

and show a progressive expansion of scope from the internal and short term to the external and long range. The typical company core curriculum has at least three levels: supervisory, middle management, and executive. The IBM curriculum has five: first-line manager, three middle management levels, and an advanced management school for executives. The supervisors' course emphasizes practical people-management. The three middle manager programs, for new, experienced, and senior middle managers, gradually introduce instruction on external factors such as economics and the business climate, in addition to continuing people-management instruction. The advanced school, lasting three weeks, surveys the corporation, its lines of business, and trends in the external environment that affect the company. The school includes a three-day session built around a simulation of a large corporation's operations.

Although critics speak derisively of mandatory, standardized courses, there are some things that all employees at a given level ought to know, and they ought not to be expected to discover them by trial and error. But standard curricula do have problems: courses can be irrelevant because they do not address participants' needs and the critical issues facing the organization, or because they do not fit with the way the organization actually operates. Detachment of top management from the training function can easily lead to such inappropriate programs (often stillborn). Core curricula can also become ossified just as they do in academia. These dangers require a vigilant management and training staff to ensure that a curriculum admits new ideas and responds to change.

GE's chairman John Welch insists that the company's management institute in Croton-on-Hudson, New York, be a "change agent." GE managers are to be imbued with entrepreneurial values, an orientation toward people, and a leadership style that stresses teamwork. A month-long course for managers includes not only case studies and techniques for formulating business plans, but also exercises dividing participants into teams, critiques of team members' leadership styles, and—among other regimens designed to foster team building—the construction of rafts for racing on the Hudson River.

At Motorola, management education is urgent because of the need to turn the company around. In a five-year period Motorola slipped from first to fourth in world semiconductor sales and gained a reputation for erratic product quality and unresponsiveness to customers.[38] Classroom sessions implicitly and explicitly promote the notions of interfunctional product development, quality, and "total customer satisfaction." The Motorola corporate training center's twist on team building activity is volleyball: rivers are scarce in Schaumburg, Illinois.

Some business academies provide schooling for independent entrepreneurs. At a rural campus near Cyprus, Texas—among geese, ponds, footbridges, and an intense concentration of signs and slogans such as "Earn the Right to Be Proud" and "Tomorrow Belongs to Kwik Kopy"—individuals from every conceivable background learn how to be copy shop proprietors. Some of the teaching is by rote, like the McDonald's drills on equipment and operations, and some of it is basic people-management, customer service, and confidence building. But much of it is old-fashioned sales training—drumming up business daily by all means, door-to-door sales not excepted. The company founder tells the would-be entrepreneurs that he once received a frantic call from a copy shop owner asking for a loan to save the owner's family from eating dog food. The founder claims he answered, "Okay, eat dog food." All Kwik Kopy students are now required to sign a certificate that reads, "I will make my PR [sales] calls. Dog food is for the dogs."[39]

Issues in Corporate Management Education. Although management education has rapidly expanded in private industry, its worth is still unproved. For all the money spent on programs and sophisticated measurement techniques applied to monitor markets and operations, no one knows how effective management education is. Written assessment of participant satisfaction with company courses is common. Post-instruction evaluation of on-the-job performance, however, is rarely if ever done. In the words of one report, "The value of executive education appears to remain largely a matter of faith."[40] Indeed, the study from which this quote is taken turned up a *negative* correlation between formal executive education and corporate performance. In six of the eight industries included in the study, companies without formal education programs had higher average sales or assets per employee than companies with them. This result may be attributable to a faulty sample, but in the assessment vacuum it is unsettling. Of course it is exceedingly difficult to attribute changes in a manager's deportment or performance of duties or particularly his or her "skill" in making decisions to the content of any particular course or training experience. But it would seem that more questions could be asked and more follow-up studies done just to see whether verifiable results are possible. Certainly evaluation of the ways we train managers is essential if corporate leadership is to answer the critics who charge that America's managers are largely to blame for what they perceive as a decline in economic competitiveness.

A second fundamental issue involves organizational change and its effects on management education. Presently, the core curricula relate to hierarchical levels in command-and-control institutional structures. What happens if this structure is replaced by the "flat" organization? Peter F. Drucker envisions an analog to the symphony orchestra, a knowledge-based entity consisting of "specialists who direct and discipline their own performance through organized feedback from colleagues, customers, and headquarters."[41] Cadres of knowledge workers and a senior management with direct access to more relevant information on operations, thanks to more powerful and intelligent information systems, can cause a drastic thinning of middle management. And indeed, traditionally organized companies have already reduced the middle ranks.

The flat organization is likely to make greater use of task forces. It is a very different concept from the traditional pattern of work performed in a linear fashion—that is, passed on from one department to the next in an unvarying sequence. Multifunctional teams, which are groups representing the salient specialties in an organization, are part of new approaches to product development, design, and engineering.

These developments have consequences for corporate management education. The concentration on middle management instruction could change simply because there are many fewer middle managers. But an organization of specialists with a thin layer of middle managers could unravel in cross-purposes. Top management must communicate a clear, inclusive vision of the common purpose. Some management education programs serve this purpose, and many more may have to. If managers' main duty in a flat organization is to lead task forces, education will have to focus on the fluid, dynamic model of a task force leader. The process and authority concepts taught in conventional programs will have to be overhauled, and in all likelihood, so will the way such programs are taught.

An organization with many self-managing specialists and few generalist managers must be concerned about a diminished supply of candidates for senior management jobs. No longer would the organization have an abundance of staff, line, and field management slots for preparing and testing people for general management responsibilities. Ironically, industry may be moving closer to certain characteristics of the federal bureaucracy and may inherit its problem of turning specialists into managers.

Formal instruction cannot fill the void entirely because it cannot substitute for experience. Intensive instruction that does not stop at the classroom door may help. Experienced managers could monitor employees in their jobs and serve as mentors. The approach would be costly and would require the redefinition of a manager's job to include the role of teaching. But it seems reasonable to infer that a knowledge-based organization must also be a learning-based organization in which learning is not confined to company classrooms.

Universities as Providers

University-based executive programs, sharing in the robust health of business education, have proliferated. Many special nondegree programs have emerged for managers returning from corporate halls. In 1986, 14,000 executives attended programs offered by 68 institutions. Over the last quarter century, the growth of general management programs has been remarkable.[42] But these are costly and challenging programs both to launch and to maintain.

Faculty "bench strength" is a prerequisite for an institution to enter the executive market in a serious way. Mid-career managers and senior executives bring to academic programs a show-me attitude that surpasses that of M.B.A. students. Faculty need credentials and experience equivalent to the corporate students, and some silver in the hair does not hurt. The stringent faculty requirements may explain why 75 percent of the accredited graduate business schools have not jumped on the executive education bandwagon.

Residential executive programs last from one to as many as twelve weeks, while nonresidential programs usually go on for a half or full day over a number of weeks. The recent trend has been toward shorter program lengths. As the pace of business has continued to accelerate, companies have become unhappy with the prolonged absence of key managers, even if the absence is to improve their managerial abilities.

The types of courses taught in general management programs have remained remarkably and perhaps questionably stable over the years. Financial management, human resource management, and the nonmarket environment (now subsumed under strategic management) were pivotal topics 25 years ago and they are today. Given the rapid development of overseas competition and the greater appreciation of external factors that affect business (e.g., technological advances and global economic changes), one might expect to see more curricular adjustment. The major shift is in the intensified attention paid to strategic planning. Functional and other specialized courses, often with a strategy orientation, have come into their own as business schools have expanded their executive education repertoire.

Executive education does not come cheaply, as the sampling in table 5 makes clear. When asked, many corporate managers will complain that university-based executive education programs are overpriced, but a larger number of them will complain more vociferously about the prices of profit-making vendors in the market.[43]

Executive Education Issues. Executive education programs have some clear-cut and some ambiguous advantages for academic institutions. A central mission of a business school is to lend intellectual assistance to the business community. Programs for executives transfer current research and thinking to practitioners who are in a position to make effective use of the knowledge gained and to disseminate it widely in their organizations.

Because companies generally winnow from a pool of potential participants their most promising or accomplished managers, students bring to academic institutions an abundance of intelligence, insight, and experience, and the latest news from the frontlines of business. They are potentially a brake on arid, hermetic scholarship. Contact with these students can yield good leads for faculty research, and a program with an excellent reputation can enhance the image of the entire school in the business world.

Revenue is another compelling advantage. Executive programs can equal or exceed the financial contribution of M.B.A. programs, and they can be initiated without adding new buildings or faculty.

Table 5 University Executive Education Programs

Program	Duration	Cost*
MIDDLE MANAGEMENT		
Program for Executive Development Pennsylvania State University	4 weeks	$10,000
Executive Development Program Northwestern University	3 weeks	$8,250
Program for Manager Development Duke University	2 weeks	$5,500
EXECUTIVE		
Advanced Management Program Harvard University	11 weeks	$27,500
Program for Senior Executives Massachusetts Institute of Technology	9 weeks	$28,800
Stanford Executive Program Stanford University	8 weeks	$22,600
FUNCTIONAL		
Financial Management Program Columbia University	1 week	$3,750
Competitive Marketing Strategy University of California, Berkeley	1 week	$2,900
Managing the Next Generation of Manufacturing Technology Cornell University	1 week	$2,750
SPECIALIZED		
Achieving Global Integration Babson College	1 week	$2,700

* For 1990–1991.

Source: List compiled by the Polaroid Corporation, *External Executive Development Programs,*
Corporate Human Resource Development, 1988. Cost figures are updated.

Nevertheless, some schools that have invested heavily in executive
education have built plush, technology-laden facilities dedicated to
corporate instruction. The Wharton School, Duke's Fuqua School,
and Michigan State are recent examples. Wharton's executive education center cost more than $17 million and Duke's $14 million.[44]
Inevitably, a four-star physical facility will become a necessity for
schools that want to compete at the premium end of the executive
market.

Elite schools maintain full-time staffs to oversee the programs and conduct the delicate negotiations for company participants. At this level of adult education, applications are not accepted cold. Well in advance of a formal application, school representatives discuss candidates with company management to ensure an appropriate fit. The application then becomes largely pro forma and rejections are not common. Selection criteria include a desirable level of business experience and a mix of industries and countries. (If school administrators did not exert themselves, the programs at elite schools could be filled with managers from a few large American and Japanese corporations.) Many schools are building executive databases and use direct-mail campaigns to publicize their offerings and broaden the base of client companies. If more schools enter the field and the number of programs continues to increase, marketing efforts are bound to expand and become even more costly.

Direct institutional income is only part of the story. The most adept schools encourage managers and executives to think of themselves not as participants in a short-term nondegree program, but as bona fide alumni. From alumni the schools can ask for help in promoting the institution and, of course, for money, either a personal or a company contribution. Because work in executive education is generally not considered part of the regular teaching load, professors are paid an additional sum for this work and thus can augment their salaries. Moreover, the contacts made in the executive classroom can provide openings for lucrative consulting work, either teaching in-house corporate programs or directly advising company management. Senior business school faculty become a privileged group compared with their junior colleagues and with other faculty in the university.

Another development provoking controversy in the business education community is the customized program, one-of-a-kind or ongoing courses tailored to the needs of a particular company. Such courses remedy frequent company complaints that schools are too theoretical and materials not pertinent to their businesses. On the other hand, companies lose the broadening effect on managers of exposure to peers from other companies.

Academic critics charge that university courses specially designed for individual companies can compromise academic integrity. Business schools have split over the issue. Harvard and Stanford, among others, have rejected customized courses, while Duke's Fuqua School and the University of Michigan have supplied them. For the near future customizing seems poised to win more advocates in business schools and departments.

The Biscoe-Hindman Center for Management and Executive Development at the University of Arkansas, Fayetteville, illustrates deep immersion in custom education. The center will tailor management programs for delivery in its classroom or off site and will tackle the most company-specific topics. Since 1985, the center has run the Walton Institute of Retailing, a two-tiered development program for Wal-Mart stores executives. In the basic program, some 900 store managers and assistant managers annually take part in one-week sessions, primarily on people-management. This program consists of familiar topics mixed with indoctrination on the company's approach and culture. Some segments would be recognizable in any management program, while others are strictly the Wal-Mart way of doing things.

According to a school spokesman, negotiating a balance between what the business faculty wanted to teach and what the company wanted its employees to learn was tough, but in the end both sides gave a little. The second tier of the Walton Institute, for top-level managers, is an extension of the first and is more company-specific. The center's refusal to release information about it suggests a problem encountered in custom programs. Traditional classrooms are by definition open to inquiry, while company programs can be considered proprietary and therefore closed.

Although universities and nonprofit institutes may think of their executive programs as a service to the business community (and they are), the fact remains that the programs—customized or not—are big money makers in a highly competitive marketplace. As such, they may reasonably be seen as part of the larger vendor market.

Vendors and Others

Vendors are a variegated, not to mention vertiginous, assortment of organizations, corporations, associations, small companies, and individuals. Barriers to entry into the management education market are low. An individual with a ten-step method for successful public speaking or a set of exercises intended to facilitate team building has a product to enter the market. The for-profit vendor sector is freewheeling and entrepreneurial, resistant to quantitative survey and generalization.

By most accounts the nonprofit American Management Association (AMA) was the major force in vendor management education before the 1970s, although the Menninger Foundation, the Aspen Institute, and others conducted liberal arts executive seminars. The AMA's presence in the field evolved from management conferences, short workshops led by experienced executives, and the four-week management course that is still the crown jewel. Costing $3,000 for AMA members, the course announcement claims it is practical, "for doers." For managers who are liberal arts graduates, the course "gets down to the nitty gritty of business." For M.B.A. graduates the course will "cut through the theory and jargon and give you usable, concrete skills." Today the AMA's catalog describes 237 seminars out of an inventory of 2,000 covering general management, functional areas, and people management.

The AMA monopoly, however, has been decisively broken. Among the growing numbers of competitors, some nonprofit organizations bear similarities to mainstream academic institutions. The Center for Creative Leadership, headquartered in Greensboro, North Carolina, distinguishes itself with research-based instruction. Its centerpiece is a leadership development program, and one specialized course offered is Leadership at the Peak, a seminar for executives held in a highly symbolic setting—Pike's Peak outside Colorado Springs, Colorado. The center has diversified into general management and new product development, having created proprietary management simulations for both areas.

Another outstanding and unusual program comes from the Western Behavioral Science Institute, mentioned in chapter 2 because of its computerized delivery system for executives anywhere. Its distinction also lies in the high level of participants and the complex global issues studied. The nonprofit American Graduate School of International Management in Glendale, Arizona, conducts a master's degree program enrolling 900 students a year from the United States and foreign countries. The School's Thunderbird Management Center runs customized training courses for client organizations. Many of the 75 to 80 faculty members have had extensive business experience. The focus is on three areas: languages, international studies, and world business.

While academic providers of continuing management education debate whether to customize their program offerings and if so, to what degree, there is no debate whatsoever among for-profit vendors. They think directly in commercial terms and make strenuous efforts to differentiate their products and services. Vendor claims for their answers to management problems are broadcast on a scale ranging from the understated to the clamorous.

Wilson Learning, a John Wiley company, has invested heavily in interactive videodisc technology, which offers the advantages of on-site, on-demand instruction without instructors. A popular program, a five-module series for salespeople, managers, and administrators, has a site license fee totaling $30,000. The Strategic Management Group, founded in 1981 by three Wharton School lecturers, has developed management seminars centered on simulations run on personal computers.

Some vendors add the tried-and-true appeal of celebrities.

Video Arts in Northbrook, Illinois, has gained much attention for making effective management education and functional training videos starring John Cleese, the rubber-legged alumnus of the "Monty Python" television show. Kenneth Blanchard, author of *The One-Minute Manager*, has leveraged the best-selling book into a vendor business, spinning off a group of management seminars—including "The One-Minute Manager Gets Fit." He has teamed with another author-celebrity, Norman Vincent Peale, on a business ethics book that forms the core of another seminar.

Training firms and organizations such as those mentioned are the most easily discerned part of the vendor business. Large corporations that have added training to their business lines mark one extreme among the vendors. The giant corporations can supply a complete package: materials, instructors, classrooms, and accommodations. At the other extreme, a single consultant may have as tangible assets a flip-chart and a few slides. There is no way of knowing how many full- and part-time consultants are engaged in management education, but the number is no doubt large and growing.

A study of vendor literature soon gives one the queasy experience of inflated promises, overselling, and dog-eared ideas. One distrusts definitive answers to complicated management problems that inevitably contain ambiguity, trade-offs, and difficult choices. But it is hard to sell the truth, so vendors often make simplistic claims in advertising the product. And this phenomenon is not peculiar to the vendor business. Ragged quality will likely persist as an issue here just as it exists for all other providers, including universities, which must worry about the caliber of teaching in their many classrooms.

Off-the-shelf materials and seminars account for a large part of corporate spending on outside services and materials. From the customer's vantage point, vendor products and services are holding their own. Lyman Porter and Lawrence McKibbin report that company managers responsible for management education rank vendors below in-house programs but above university programs.[45] And they indicate that companies plan to fill future needs for lower and middle management education from the following sources: in-house programs first, vendors second, and universities third. For executive education, however, vendors are listed as the preferred source, with universities second.

Vendors have advantages as specialists in practical short courses that minimize time away from the job, and they teach on site or at locations convenient to company facilities. Apparently they are doing a satisfactory job of tailoring their sessions to the requirements of companies that continue to engage them.

Agendas for Management Education

Since World War II, continuing management education has developed into a widespread, expensive activity and a growth industry. And the notion of lifelong education has brought management closer to fulfilling the promise of professionalism. Since multidivisional organizations arose, creating a need for professional managers, private industry has come to acknowledge management as a career, not a mere accident of promotion. In fact, U.S. business may have overvalued management. By assigning the highest material and symbolic rewards to management, it has influenced talented and capable employees to leave functional specialties in which they might otherwise have happily remained and conceivably made a greater contribution.

In contrast to the private sector, government has had more difficulty accepting the idea of the career manager, even though the civil service grades offer a ladder of advancement. At least, the path upward is slower and the candidate receives less attention and less grooming for future responsibilities. The civilian agencies of the federal government have enormous management responsibilities, but many lack a clear strategy and a supportive culture. Civil service officials can do only so much to improve the situation; they need unflagging support from politicians.

The federal government is of course the largest conglomerate industry, embracing the widest diversity of functions, purposes, and products. But no matter how different its parts, some rationalization should be attempted for the systematic development and education of its in-house leadership. It is both centralized and decentralized without a plan except in a few agencies. Perhaps the division some corporations are adopting could be a model: up to the middle management level, education is decentralized; at the senior management and executive level, it is centralized.

The armed services face some soul searching about their definition of a military officer in the late twentieth century. Is the management of a multibillion-dollar weapons program worth less professionally than the command of a ship, a fighter squadron, or a brigade? To meet operational requirements, remain at the forefront of technology, and cope with fiscal austerity, the military may need to honor and reward officers who are expert managers. At the same time, the services have to gear up their impressive educational machinery to deliver in-depth management education to the many officers who need it.

Government has lessons to teach industry as well. The organization most committed to continuing education of its leaders is not a *Fortune* "500" company but any of the uniformed services. Although they may be single-minded about battlefield and technical education and too little concerned with intellectual rigor, as some critics charge, the uniformed services nevertheless believe strongly in career-long formal learning, and there is no doubt about the commitment. Moreover, their courses pay consistent attention to strategy—and not only in programs for executives and senior officers but also for junior grades. By comparison, many companies still believe strategy belongs exclusively at the executive level. If strategy is to inform everything a company does, and many observers believe it should, supervisors and managers need to know how to think strategically and need to learn it earlier.

Two more features of government programs deserve wider consideration. Candidates for the Senior Executive Service are assigned mentors who counsel them on career development. Mentor relationships are not popular in private industry. They may develop informally when the conditions and the chemistry are right, but even then the parties may have to contend with others' perceptions of favoritism. A few companies have made sanctioned mentor systems work, but not many have followed their lead. The explanation may have less to do with logistics or the perceived cost of managers spending time counseling management candidates than with the managerial culture as it has taken shape in this country.[46] Whether or not the flat organization becomes the dominant organizational form, a mentor system could enhance managerial development in private industry.

The management excellence framework developed by the federal Office of Personnel Management also suggests a possibility for large companies. An objective study of how an organization's best managers actually manage could reveal findings useful in corporate classrooms. Employee-students would likely grant authority to such profiles and might have a stronger identification with them than other vehicles for describing effective management. The study could show a company's culture and strategy in action—or it might reveal portions of either to be phantom abstractions. Either outcome would be worth knowing.

Corporations and companies whose earnest spending has largely fueled the management education business should ask what, precisely, the money is buying. Technical training can be measured against clear-cut behavioral objectives. This is not the case with management education, but the difficulty is all the more reason to push ahead with assessment efforts. More generally, corporations should recognize their teaching function as an essential business mission. They are in a sense educational institutions.

In theory, universities and business schools should be high-quality producers in the field. They should be concerned that corporate customers often see their effectiveness as lagging behind that of company and vendor education. Is it lagging quality, is it too much abstract or theoretical instruction, or is it some other less essential characteristic? A related question concerns the compatibility of customized courses with the values of an academic institution. Debate on this issue inside business departments and schools as well as in the institution's central administration may be fervent, but it is better that a thorough debate precede, rather than follow, any action.

Some issues cut across the boundaries of institutions engaged in management education. First, it is apparent from examining the curricula that few American executives study technological change and its implications for the workplace. Yet all confront these issues daily. With the exception of the military, there are few course titles on technological change, whether in business school, corporate, or government catalogs. It may be that technical specialists moving into general management are better served by courses that broaden their skills than are managers in the routine pattern who wish to increase their technological knowledge.

Second, courses concerning international aspects of business and management are noticeably absent. These subjects appear, if at all, only for top executives, although many managers are involved in markets expanding abroad. In a good business school there may be one course on "Business, Government, and the International Economy" that treats another country's culture, economics, and politics, but it stands alone even if students favor it strongly. The specialist curricula cannot accommodate more. Nevertheless, educators are devising ways to incorporate the global view into the curriculum. Some schools offer master's programs in international business, others have cooperative programs abroad or urge students to study a foreign language. Faculty also need exposure to other cultures. At least there is concern, if not ready answers to the problem.

And third, a word may be added in support of the so-called soft skills compared with the hard subjects. It is not without reason that corporations stress interpersonal skills and behavioral abilities. There is the fact that competition increasingly lies in services— attention to the customer. Just as new combinations of companies are joining service industries, so the individual company must compete in serving the client. The skills of listening, presentation, negotiation, cooperation in a team or group, and dealing with cultural differences, all take on value in the growing service sector.

Still, the tension between the quantitative and behavioral aspects of management, which developed at the inception of management studies, persists. Courses premised on functional integration are rare and not respected by advanced students trained in specialties. Not realizing what they will need in top management roles, they tend to scorn the generalist and admire the expert. Yet business, government, and the military cannot divide their management needs in this way.

There are individuals, inside and outside academia, whose investigations directly address functional integration. George O. Klemp, Jr., and David C. McClelland have done extensive field work to discover the distinctive competencies of outstanding senior managers.[47] Their institutional sample included corporations, a volunteer organization, colleges, and military hospitals. The results describe a set of interdependent cognitive, behavioral, and affective skills. According to their model, managerial effectiveness depends on integration. This area of inquiry, with its potential for balancing specialization, deserves more attention as managerial curricula are evaluated.

The agendas for management education are crowded with issues of first importance. Curricula need to be reexamined, and the major providers should consider the questions together. Our study suggests that managers are not getting the knowledge necessary for the changing world of international economic competition. In the final analysis, our country's future depends greatly on the quality of leadership from its managers in government, corporations, and the military.

6

UPDATING PROFESSIONALS

The professions in America's economy comprise an impressive percentage of the work force. They command high-level salaries and their performance directly affects economic affairs. Beyond their contributions to the business of living, their services are vital to the well-being of millions of people in our society, and we count heavily on their leadership. So it is crucial that they be aware of the latest information in their fields of work.

While there are some similarities to management education, particularly in courses to improve skills in working with people, the programs for professional persons are unique when the subject matter is specific to their occupation. This complicates the question of who will provide it and adds to the sharp competition among providers.

To indicate the educational opportunities available for professionals, we present three rather disparate groups: engineers and computer scientists, doctors and lawyers, and accountants and bankers. Within each group there are clear relationships, but when they are considered together they reveal a wide range of differences in patterns, methods, and problems. Many individuals operate as independent practitioners or in small enclaves banded together for special services, and the majority practice in the private sector. Because most will have access to computers and such equipment, technological delivery of the latest information is especially practical and being used increasingly to reach them. Professional societies remain a primary resource for training as well as for maintaining standards of performance.

For years the most able practitioners have accepted the responsibility for keeping themselves abreast of new developments in their fields. Professional journals and national associations have served well, and informal exchange with colleagues has been effective. Now, however, the explosion in knowledge and information and the constantly changing specializations complicate the process and confuse the effort. It is no longer possible to assume that on their own initiative professional practitioners will keep up to date. They—like managers and skilled technicians—need continual access to learning.

Changes in the Professions

The challenge of updating one's knowledge may be greatest for the engineer or computer scientist in the advanced technologies that are driving the revolutionary changes occurring in the world of work. But the invasion of those technologies into the practices of other professions creates a constant challenge there as well. The technological transformation of medical practice and the delivery of health care is a well-known phenomenon. And the financial services offered by bankers and accountants are similarly undergoing profound adjustments. Consequently, in all these fields we see the spread and growth of training activities for top professionals.

Other factors are also at work building the demand for further learning. Each profession bears witness to a spectacular expansion in specialties that spin off into ever more narrow niches, and any professional person is hard pressed to keep up with their formation—and their demise as old specialties become obsolete. There is little indication that the growth rate is slowing. On the contrary, in a world of increasing complexity, specialties are bred and take hold: they appear as segments of knowledge that one mind can manipulate.

And the professional's task is further complicated by far-reaching changes in public policies. Tax laws that shift like the sands, for example, must be studied quickly by accountants and lawyers whose clients are affected. The deregulation of banking and the airlines caused dramatic adjustment not only in the industries themselves but also in the professions serving them.

Employers of professionals, like accounting firms and high-tech manufacturers, insist that their workers take advanced and contemporary training. Their future rides on high levels of professional competence, so they have big stakes in keeping their staffs not just abreast but ahead of developments. Investment is increasingly targeted on the engineers, scientists, and technicians who are vital in the high-tech world. In-house training programs are extensive; tuition reimbursement and other allowances are gladly disbursed; and corporate connections with engineering schools, computer science departments, and research centers are spreading.

Comparably, programs under company auspices are growing for the other professions: big corporate law firms sponsor their own training in house, the "Big Six" accounting firms have their campuses and enroll thousands of adults in training classes, and large banks are extending internal and external programs. In subsequent sections we will look at some of these programs in detail.

Mandatory Requirements

A more defined and orchestrated force behind the movement toward more education is the growing public interest in holding professionals accountable for their actions, be they surgeons, optometrists, lawyers, or veterinarians. At issue is public trust and protection. Furthermore, the rise in malpractice litigation in many professional areas has spurred efforts to find ways to measure proficiency regularly. Educational requirements often are the handiest means of ensuring that a person is equipped to continue practicing a profession.

Increasingly, state legislatures are linking continuing education requirements to the renewal of licenses, and professional associations on the state level are also enacting regulations for relicensing. A survey (table 6) shows the growth in mandatory requirements. In 1980, postprofessional study was required of accountants in about two-thirds of the states; eight years later, the requirement was nearly nationwide. Other groups saw even greater increases.[1]

On the whole, the regulations are written in general terms and leave decisions on course content to the administrative bodies and professional organizations. For example, North Dakota's rules for lawyers set forth a general statement of purpose, authorize a commission of seven lawyers appointed by the state bar association to administer the program, and stipulate at least 45 hours of legal

Table 6   Growth in Mandatory Continuing Education Related to Licensure, 1980–1988

Professional Group	Number of States in 1980	Number of States in 1988
Architects	1	1
Certified public accountants	36	48
Dentists	9	14
Engineers (professional)	1	1
Lawyers	9	31
Nurses	11	12
Nursing home administrators	43	45
Optometrists	44	46
Psychologists	8	16
Pharmacists	21	39
Physical therapists	3	8
Physicians	20	23
Real estate salespersons and brokers	14	29
Social workers	10	24
Licensed practical/vocational nurses	11	12
Veterinarians	22	26

Source: The 1980 figures are cited in Ronald M. Cervero and Craig L. Scanlan, eds. *Problems and Prospects in Continuing Professional Education* (San Francisco, California: Jossey-Bass, 1985), p. 49. The 1988 figures are from the "Summer 1988 Newsletter" of Louis Phillips and Associates. The District of Columbia is included as a state.

study (approved by the commission) during three-year intervals. The state bar proposed the rules, and the North Dakota Supreme Court approved them. Lawyers file a report of compliance; failure to do so brings possible suspension of the right to practice.

California, however, exemplifies state legislative action that has moved steadily toward more explicit requirements to control the quality of professional services. Supported by the state associations of realtors and real estate brokers, the legislature first directed the commissioner of real estate in 1976 to adopt regulations prescribing continuing education as a prerequisite for license renewal. Since then, details have been specified within the total of 45 hours of education to be completed during the four years prior to license renewal. At first, only three hours of the total were specified for ethics, professional conduct, and real estate law. Two years later certain hours were set for consumer service and protection issues. In 1986, the consumer protection clause was modified to make room for three hours on realty agency responsibilities, including disclosure and confidentiality. The rules have tightened in specificity.

Mandatory continuing education for recertification has returned large numbers of adults to one sort of classroom or another. As such procedures increase, the business of accreditation multiplies, with agencies, specialty boards, and bureaucracies established in state offices—a growth industry itself. And, as education is the means chosen to satisfy requirements, it becomes a lucrative and therefore competitive field for providers.

Disputes Among Providers

There are at least four kinds of providers of continuing professional education: institutions of higher education, employers, commercial vendors, and professional societies. According to experts who are themselves providers, contention and confusion abound in the arena. Not only has the field expanded rapidly and heated up competitively, but also some of the main providers operate from agendas that have long been in place and habits that are only beginning to adjust to changing demands. The problem is one of turf, territory that one or another provider considers to be its own responsibility as well as a source of income.

Furthermore, the old contentious argument between the corporation and the campus still goes on, complicated by a lack of clear definition of what type of training is wanted for what purpose. Is it specialized scientific or factual material to update practitioners in a particular professional field? Or is it more general human resource development that requires behavioral and attitudinal change to improve the professional's ability in working with others, in personnel management? This latter type of training naturally applies across professional fields and is not necessarily specific to any industry.

The division between the specialized scientific courses and the human relations courses is not unlike the tension seen in management education between hard knowledge and soft skills. Many professionals need both, so providers might sensibly consider their contributions toward one or the other.

Some corporate training officers suggest that higher education should concentrate on sorely needed human resource development, leaving the more technical, specialized aspects to the companies. As Robert Young, president of Lockheed Engineering and Management Systems, says, "We have no trouble hiring and training top-notch technical personnel, but we find that these people often have trouble working as part of a group." His sentiments are echoed throughout technical industries and elsewhere.

Still, executives doubt the university faculty's ability to change and adjust teaching methods and content toward these ends. Badi Foster, president of the Aetna Institute for Corporate Education, says:

Yes, we would put human relations R&D money in the universities, but the faculties will have to overcome 40 years of tradition.

They tend to replicate themselves and even when they want to change, they don't know how. They don't want to even walk by the continuing education offices.[2]

The comment reflects what we have heard before from corporate leaders who find the university world unprepared, unable, or unwilling to meet their training needs. Such criticism, however warranted it may be, does little to illuminate the issues. The effect is to eliminate the universities as providers of some types of training that professional people need.

A closer analysis may prove helpful in clarifying the situation. After all, universities are no more monolithic than large corporations. All have divisions and branches that serve very different functions and purposes. Two university divisions are most pertinent to this discussion: professional schools and programs of continuing education or extension services. The schools of medicine, law, engineering, and business have contributions to make in updating professionals in special subjects or knowledge areas.

Schools of continuing education, being more general in curriculum, could be expected to offer more courses fostering human resource development and skills in dealing with people. Adult educators in such programs might well consider more focus on human relations and managing personnel—and incidentally attract enrollment, since this is a large area of need that no one provider seems to be adequately filling.

We are not suggesting that a practitioner from the field should return to a professional school for human relations skills that the school failed to teach in the first place. Whether medical, legal, or engineering, such schools have not demonstrated concern with this area, except perhaps when schools with training for clinical practice have taken time to aid students in interpreting their personal experience.

The universities' professional schools hold a more secure place in specialized training, but questions about their performance keep surfacing. For example, are the professional schools, particularly those most influenced by the pace of technological change, keeping up so that they can offer the latest information in the field? A voice from the corporate side expresses doubt that the schools are in the forefront:

> Industry has gone ahead of academia. . . . There is a time warp when the product changes so fast it compels industry to provide its own education. . . . Specialization compels reeducation to diversify the usefulness of specialists whose specialties are obsolete.[3]

Whether industry leads or not, and no doubt it does in certain areas, beneficial alignments between academia and industries are growing. Both sides are struggling to reach "the cutting edge," as the popular phrase puts it. Faculty in professional schools and practitioners alike are scrambling to keep up with the pace of advancing knowledge in their fields, and the welter of information aggravates the problem.

The time factor is crucial in the equation for technological personnel. Industry must move quickly, while universities keep a more stately pace. Although the difference is inherent in their purposes and practices, both parties seek more cooperation. The most successful schemes involve specific professional groups for particular purposes that benefit both parties. And they require negotiation at top levels on both sides.

Corporations Sell Their Courses

At the same time, corporations are selling their educational services to each other and on the open market to technological personnel and advanced professionals. Bell South, for example, has expanded its employee and customer training to form an extensive network of learning centers open to the public in nine larger cities of the South. Courses include engineering, telecommunications management, and technologies. The company even sells professional development courses in kits for correspondence study. Bell has trained members of the military, state and federal government employees, and workers from dozens of businesses, small and large. The Southern Association of Colleges and Schools accredits the programs.

Many corporations have joined the vendor market, especially in offering advanced technological training to engineers and computer scientists. Accounting firms sell courses to their clients. The entrance of companies into the business of educating professionals is a phenomenon with far-reaching effects. As demand grows, so does the supply of educational products.

Professional Societies Play Key Role

Competing—and sometimes cooperating—with other providers are the various professional societies. Cooperation among corporations, large universities, and professional societies is outstanding for the technical fields, but many links are still weak. For other professionals, like doctors, lawyers, accountants, and bankers, national professional associations, with their state and local bodies and untold numbers of specialty boards, play key roles as providers of ongoing education. The associations are deeply committed to serving their members' educational needs and particularly so in the professions facing mandatory requirements for state licensure. But they are not always organized to provide it adequately or efficiently, and their rhetoric sometimes inflates the content of their programs.

Here is where the ever-multiplying specializations exert a force toward disintegration of the professional group and hence the effectiveness of large national associations. Critics charge that the focus has grown too narrow as each subspecialty forms its own board or society. The result is fragmentation and difficulty in getting groups to work together for the lifelong education of their professional members. Each is on its own track and tries to protect its turf.

University schools of continuing education or extension services have long offered a variety of programs and individual courses for intellectual stimulation to older adults who want the challenge of learning something new or who want to master a new skill to enhance work performance. But until recently they have not offered work specially designed to upgrade professionals; theirs has been a more general curriculum in which some practitioners have found suitable advanced courses.

In the last decade, these schools have begun to work more closely with professional associations to plan programs in fields such as information technologies, business and finance, and real estate. Certificate programs, for example, are given through Harvard's Extension School in administration and management, applied sciences (including computer science), and public health. Each represents one year of study beyond the bachelor's level.

New York University's School of Continuing Education administers one of the most ambitious and varied continuing education programs in the country. Both certificates and diplomas can be earned in such subjects as personnel management, training and management development, magazine publishing, and bank lending. The courses are aimed at an advanced professional audience needing to develop conceptual and technical skills for promotion. (An undergraduate degree is a prerequisite for admission to a diploma program.)

For their faculty these schools often employ practitioners on a part-time basis so that they can add or drop courses quickly according to market demand. These teachers bring practical experience into the classroom, and they supplement regular faculty who are unable or do not wish to teach a course. This type of expanded course listing serves more people, invites advanced students, and generates income. It also enlarges the universities' place in advanced professional training, which is a fast-growing sector of the commercial learning industry.

From this general view of the various providers, their disputes, and their diversity, we look at the situation in several professions and report on what is happening in training efforts.

Engineers and Computer Scientists

At the moment, engineers and computer scientists have been getting national attention, because of shortages in both fields and because they are vital to technological progress. Moreover, it is difficult to find a profession that the accelerating speed of change has hit harder. According to the National Academy of Engineering (NAE), the average engineer's knowledge depreciates alarmingly from three to seven years after formal education ends.[4] A different source reports that, as of 1986, the half-life of a mechanical engineer's knowledge was seven and one-half years, an electrical engineer's five years, and a software engineer's two and one-half years.[5] Moreover, a career that didn't exist when a person entered college may be in demand by the time he or she graduates, just as another career fades away. This means that engineering faculty have a task as Herculean as practicing engineers to keep up to date.

With such a ratio of obsolescence in knowledge to the typical engineer's career lasting forty years, there is only one solution—more education easily available in many formats that can be wedged into an already hectic work life. In fact, many seminars, workshops, and short courses are widely available as well as some advanced credit and degree programs. But they are not reaching sufficient numbers of engineers.

In June 1988, after months of intensive investigation, NAE's Committee on Career-Long Education for Engineers issued a lengthy report with recommendations for improving delivery of continuing education to the 2.6 million engineers and computer specialists engaged in engineering-related jobs. The committee's report described the situation:

A gulf exists in engineering education today. We have a highly organized and effective system of degree-oriented education and a sporadically effective, sometimes outstanding, sometimes unresponsive, and often murky set of elements that address education needs that begin when a student leaves degree-oriented programs.[6]

Clearly the Academy's committee thought that the needs of engineers were not being met, even though it acknowledged that some efforts were outstanding.

Among the more effective programs are those cited earlier as examples of delivery systems for learning: Stanford's instructional program for Hewlett-Packard and other companies, California State University's program from the Chico campus, and others in Maryland and Virginia aimed at practicing engineers. Fittingly, engineers are being served by telecommunication networks—far more so than other needy professionals. And engineers profit further in advanced education from closer cooperation between university departments of engineering and some of their professional societies. The pattern is unusual compared with other professions, whose associations operate more independently of the universities.

An example of cooperation is the Association for Media-Based Continuing Engineering Education (AMCEE), a university-professional cooperative begun in the mid-seventies with funding from a public-private alliance, the National Science Foundation and the Sloan Foundation. AMCEE advocates, coordinates, and markets short noncredit courses for engineers, scientists, and other technologists. Daily programs are broadcast by satellite from universities, and in 1988 the count was approximately 500 courses in 16 disciplines, reaching an estimated audience of 22,000. The sponsors review the topics annually to keep courses up to date, drop outmoded ones, and introduce new and emerging technologies.[7]

From this creative base came the National Technological University (NTU), consisting of 24 universities in the AMCEE consortium and devoted mainly to master's-level work. Operating from administrative headquarters in Fort Collins, Colorado, the university manages the satellite delivery and coordinates course offerings that go to more than 245 receiving sites for employed engineers. The course enrollments for 1988–89 totaled 3,100. The courses not only come to the workplace, but they can also travel with the engineer who is transferred to another company location. NTU offers seven master of science programs: computer engineering, computer science, electrical engineering, engineering management, manufacturing systems engineering, materials science, and management of technology—all accredited by the North Central Association of Colleges and Schools.

It is an admirable system that takes advantage of technological delivery and carries instruction to people at work—a demonstration of what can be done when industries, universities, and government pool their resources in a combined effort with good leadership. About 60 corporations plus government agencies are sponsors. But the courses are costly and generally reach only large corporations; small companies lack similar access or sufficient means. NTU is trying to solve this problem through regional consortia of small companies.

Additional numbers—many thousands—simply audit courses or view special programs on timely topics. NTU is carrying short "tutorials" led by eminent research faculty and sponsored by the American Association for Artificial Intelligence. Other instructional programs originate from corporate facilities at Motorola, Hewlett-Packard, Eastman Kodak, and NCR in Dayton, Ohio. The network is extending its services and its audience.

Another professional group, the Institute of Electrical and Electronics Engineers (IEEE), has long been concerned with advanced learning. Its satellite series also features experts on the latest subjects and frequently draws sizable numbers of engineers. But these programs are less training oriented and more apt simply to provide exposure to a current topic. Home video tutorials on engineering subjects are selling well, better apparently than IEEE's individual workbook packages.[8]

Major high-tech companies have extensive in-house continuing education through their decentralized delivery systems. Few indeed do not have their own liaison with universities located nearby. Boeing, Martin-Marietta, and Tektronix are among many such companies. Hughes Aircraft founded its own Communications and Data Processing Institute in 1985 to strengthen the capabilities of its professionals in specialties like computer systems analysis and design and business software engineering. Several programs give professional certification.

Creative individuals have established other kinds of nontraditional engineering training programs. One of them is Bernard Gordon, the engineering executive of Analogic, Inc. Trained in the Navy and accustomed to military standards of discipline, Gordon wanted to prepare engineers for effective, competitive leadership. In 1987, he opened the Gordon Institute in Wakefield, Massachusetts, offering a master's degree in engineering management to working engineers chosen by their companies for their leadership potential. The program has degree candidacy status in the New England Association of Schools and Colleges. It lasts a year and is a full-time undertaking for which employers pay the $15,000 tuition *and* are expected to continue salary and benefits, a sizable investment likely to be beyond the resources of many small businesses. Seven students graduated in 1988 and ten in 1989, six of whom were foreign: one was from Siemens in West Germany, another from Toshiba in Japan, and four from the People's Republic of China.[9]

Some universities on their own initiative have broken the mold of traditional engineering schools in order to assist working professionals, and so have attracted corporate attention and support through enrollment. The computer science department and the extension department of engineering and science at the University of California, Los Angeles, offer 18 carefully tailored courses from which individuals design personalized programs. University faculty teach the classes over one or two weeks. In Boston, Northeastern University has professional certificate programs in six technological areas with evening classes for two hours a week over ten weeks. The university makes an effort to accommodate the engineer's work schedule.

Numerous other vendors have joined the growing market. Some are well established, like the Center for Professional Advancement in East Brunswick, New Jersey. From its beginning in 1967 until 1984, the center served more than 100,000 students in 4,000 post-baccalaureate courses. For updating its courses, the center relies on an international network of practicing engineering professionals. Courses, intensive and short, are given at the center or on site for companies in the United States and in Europe. Many other "third parties" of this sort have appeared more recently; where there is a need, someone will fill it and soon an organization is created.

With what appears to be a crowded marketplace of providers, there would seem to be ample opportunities for engineers and computer scientists. Moreover, they are heavily organized professions: *Peterson's Guide* lists 63 engineering professional and trade associations—computer fields not included. Although several are umbrella organizations, most represent specialties and therefore complicate efforts toward concerted action to benefit all engineers.

A more basic problem is motivating individual engineers to take responsibility for their own advanced learning. There are no mandatory state requirements for licensure, and many employers do not put pressure on their engineers to keep up with fast-breaking knowledge. Hence individual initiative is vital. As someone put it, continual study must become a habit, not an option.

These issues troubled the National Academy of Engineering's committee on career-long education and prompted recommendations that could sensibly be considered for any profession. The committee's 1988 report, *Focus on the Future*, called for a national action plan to include:

- Formation of a national advocacy group with representatives from industry, universities, professional organizations, government, and private providers to foster greater coherence in continuing education programs.

- A systems approach whereby an undergraduate degree is seen as the first of several steps in a practicing engineer's career. Further education, which unifies past training and work-in-progress, must be made available to those for whom access is difficult.

- Encouragement from employers, public and private, for advanced training, with education objectives linked to organizational goals. Company policy should link continuing education to recognition, potential wage increases, and professional advancement.

- Adaptation of educational institutions' curricula to advances in technology, so that baccalaureate degrees reflect familiarity with them.

- Increased federal and state government responsibility for continuing engineering education. The committee suggested that the National Science Foundation be given primary responsibility for supporting model programs, innovative use of instructional technologies, and research into career-long education, including better data collection. Congress should review tax laws to determine whether they inhibit participation and whether they create obstacles to universities wishing to offer continuing professional education.

- Strengthening professional organizations' outreach to engineers and promoting their concern for career development. Some actions suggested are: skills identification, proficiency testing, program review and other clearinghouse activities, establishing national on-line databases to provide information on engineering courses and conferences, and business start-up assistance.[10]

Several recommendations reflected and elaborated on concerns expressed in 1982 by the Massachusetts Institute of Technology's study of *Lifelong Cooperative Education* and again in 1985 by the National Research Council's report on *Continuing Education of Engineers*. One cannot fault the profession for failing to examine its problems or to develop sensible recommendations. But we may suggest that it is time for studies to give way to implementing action, particularly since this field is essential to our national well-being.

Attorneys and Physicians

The legal and medical professions are big businesses which account for huge expenditures in our society and control important segments of the economy. In addition, they are increasingly becoming commercial organizations with management problems and marketing concerns. The professional medical or legal practice once was a self-employing and self-centered operation that focused on individual clients and was built on trust or personal loyalty. Today both professions are generally practiced in groups that accommodate the growth in specializations and research knowledge. Their leaders, who require managerial and financial skills, are studying risk management and ethics in continuing education as well as the latest information in their specialties.

Advancing technologies have invaded both professions to a remarkable degree. In law, computer-driven processes handle production and billing procedures; in medicine, they go farther, beyond office routines into diagnosis and the delivery of care. Medical technologies transform hospitals and the treatment of patients. Probably no profession has seen a greater revolution in its practice than medicine—now so dependent on revelations from the latest machine that can see into the human body and report on all it sees. The only element that protects doctors' knowledge from the rapid "half-life" decline experienced by engineers is the stability of the human body. Continuing education for doctors is therefore more additive and cumulative, and in this respect education for lawyers is similar.

Moreover, in contrast to engineers and computer scientists, doctors and lawyers are experiencing a tightening of mandatory requirements for licensing. Lawyers have seen state regulations for continuing education spread from 9 states in 1980 to 31 states in 1988. Similar requirements for doctors, who have strongly resisted them, increased only slightly in the same period. They point out rightly that their re-education occurs daily in doing hospital rounds with other doctors, in departmental boards, in extensive reading, and in frequent conferences. Furthermore, numerous specialty boards yoke ongoing learning to keeping one's status in the registry.

Nevertheless, public insistence on the competence of physicians brings immense pressure for formal and timely updating of skills. Dr. Bruce Bellande of the Southern Medical Association says that the public interest in medical malpractice "horror stories" has driven state legislators to impose requirements for further study as a means of ensuring competence. Within this regulatory thrust, physicians are fortunate in having the powerful American Medical Association to represent them. Much of the existing legislation is based on standards set by the association. And a closely related body, the Accreditation Council for Continuing Medical Education, operates nationally to approve courses or activities that will be recognized to fulfill requirements. State medical societies are part of this process on the local level.

These medical organizations exert strong influence on providers of continuing education, who must seek accreditation to be able to give credit for their educational offerings. As of April 1988, the national council had accredited 470 providers and state societies had designated 1,875 providers, including medical schools, specialty boards, hospitals, state medical societies, voluntary health organizations, drug and equipment vendors, and other commercial providers.[11] Altogether, the number of providers and the annual monetary outlay in this field are enormous. More important, the medical profession—through this approval mechanism—has considerable control over its own continuing education and the quality of the programs recognized for credit.

Some medical schools are particularly generous with course offerings and independent study arrangements (with a faculty monitor) for the practicing physician. Harvard Medical School's department of continuing education, for example, offers some 150 short courses annually to more than 19,000 doctors, making it one of the largest single academic providers. Other large programs are at the Universities of Texas and Michigan, the University of California at Los Angeles, and Stanford.

It is difficult to evaluate the continuing education that doctors get from attending regional and national conferences with workshops and presentations on substantive topics relevant to their practice. But many thousands will attest to their value and point out that here they saw demonstrations of new techniques or equipment and exchanged research findings and opinions with colleagues. Such association meetings have long served the medical field as well as all other major professions.

Doctors have a unique program—also sponsored by their American Medical Association. Since 1968, the Physicians Recognition Award has been given to those who have continued their own learning in activities approved by the association. One, two, or three-year certificates are awarded for 50, 100, or 150 hours of study. In 1987–1988, awards went to some 24,000 doctors. Several states accept the certificates in fulfillment of mandatory requirements.

Unlike the medical profession, with its tidy organizational structure and the all-embracing AMA to watch over continuing education requirements and encourage doctors' advancement, the burgeoning field of law has more masters and different organizations involved. Therefore, less coordination exists nationally;

the profession is more like engineering, in which no coalition operates nationwide to provide cohesion, act as a clearinghouse for offerings, or advocate career-long training.

Yet the legal profession has long expressed concern for continuing education. As early as 1947 the American Bar Association and the American Law Institute agreed on the need. And the latter was to assume responsibility for "a national publication program, continued development of correspondence courses, distribution of continuing legal education information to state bar associations, encouragement of state and local bar associations, and underwriting the cost of their participation."[12]

But it didn't happen that way. Although many activities for further learning were begun, both organizations continued to encourage them and neither apparently played the dominant role educationally. There followed three Arden House Conferences on the subject. The first, in 1958, emerged with a consensus that the bar itself must be accountable for continuing education of practicing lawyers, with each state taking a coordinating role; that programs must emphasize professional responsibilities as well as specialized courses; that training must be available for newly admitted lawyers; and that law schools have a special contribution to make.[13]

Five years later, at Arden House II, participants reaffirmed the consensus of Arden House I and added the need for improving educational programs and techniques along with improving the organization and financing of continuing legal education.[14] Arden House III in November 1987 reflected the same topics and concerns. In fact, the agenda was similar for all three sessions over the 30 years. At least it is evidence of the legal profession's quest for increased competence and excellence, and there has been considerable expansion in related programs and state activities.

Since 1970, the profession has undergone profound change and tremendous growth in the numbers of lawyers. Very large firms have emerged with constantly expanding specialties, offices around the world, and high costs. Thus, even though our litigious society has produced growing demand for legal services, competition has risen sharply, leading firms to pressure members to solicit business, generate billing hours, and strive to retain clients. Of necessity, the burdens of marketing and business planning strategies have fallen on the profession, lending it an unwelcome commercial image. Mounting malpractice insurance costs and the increased threat of litigation or disciplinary sanctions encourage both voluntary and compulsory efforts to enhance professional performance.

Among the professions, lawyers had the greatest increase in state requirements for postprofessional education within the last decade. States vary widely in their requirements. Virginia mandates a minimum of 8 hours annually, while Texas, Minnesota, and Iowa have set 15 hours. Some reporting cycles are two years, like Vermont's; Colorado, Idaho, North Dakota, and others have three-year periods. And, with the exception of ethics (study of which is required in at least six states), no subject matter is generally specified.[15]

Within the legal profession, a debate rages over compulsory versus voluntary continuing education. Proponents of compulsory education say that at least such requirements show a concern about professional standards, and the public can see that something is being done about it. Furthermore, "if one accepts that formal learning experiences—discussions, lectures, clinics, seminars, demonstrations and the like—can be a meaningful way of enhancing knowledge of the law, legal skills, and practice structure, then mandatory continuing legal education is worthwhile."[16]

Opponents retort that lawyers voluntarily keep themselves current (like doctors) and that requirements actually make little difference, for the courses are of dubious quality. "If the goals are to ensure competence, these programs won't do it," according to Frank Harris, administrator of continuing legal education in Minnesota. Inevitably the question of program quality is key to the argument—beyond the issue of professional pride and prestige.

Depending on a state's rules, self-study, writing an article, and participation in firm-based activities can earn credit, although the last named is not yet broadly accepted.

In many states where continuing education is mandatory, the state bar association may establish credit requirements or approve programs, and sometimes the state supreme court appoints a committee to accredit sponsors or courses. Involvement of state supreme courts comes from their licensing and disbarment powers, which may be invoked in cases of noncompliance. Major responsibility for continuing education rests with state bar associations, which also act as providers or sponsors either alone or jointly with state law schools or other independent, nonprofit entities.

In addition, on the national level at least three professional organizations offer programs. There is the Committee on Continuing Professional Education, an arm of the American Law Institute and the American Bar Association; there is the American Bar Association itself; and there is the Practicing Law Institute. The field appears to be amply covered, and members of the bar may consult their national register for course listings by date, subject, and state. [17]

Regardless of the extensive opportunities that seemingly envelop the legal profession, some senior lawyers judge them insufficient. Witness the rapid growth of firm-based or in-house training in large law offices. Here too a national body has recently been created to aid and foster development of training programs: the American Institute for Law Training Within the Office. As law offices have expanded to become big multinational corporations with many hundreds of lawyers, and specializations have become more intensive and complicated, training needs are constantly growing. In the large legal agencies of government and in corporate law departments of big industries, the scene is the same.

The gradual erosion of apprenticeship for the new lawyer entering practice has further influenced the need for continuing education. Only in smaller firms is this sort of training still found to any extent. Here senior partners are mentors, counselors, and advisers to the young initiate. But in today's big and complex law firms, the new member is often instructed only by memo about a particular task. He or she will have little contact with clients or senior members; instead, the frustrated neophytes have to depend on each other for information and help. It is hardly the way to groom potential partners for senior responsibility.

For such reasons, but also for advanced training in fields like trial advocacy or taxation, many law firms have established their own classrooms. Some 70 percent of 256 firms responding to a survey report that they have in-house training, usually informal and sporadic, usually offered only at the home office, and usually not limited to specialty departments. Designed mainly for senior and middle levels, training is very seldom available to new lawyers, though their need may be greater.[18] Considering the ethos or company culture of big law firms computerized on six-minute billing schedules, it is hardly surprising that education programs may result from a partner's chance interest, but seldom from company policy.

Nonetheless, eight major law firms are reported to have hired full-time, professional development directors, and more are moving steadily in this direction.[19] In at least two instances the excessive costs of outside training and doubts about its adequacy prompted firms to start their own education. A related reason was the desire to get new attorneys on billable time as quickly as possible.

Illustrative of programs developed with emphasis on the young lawyers is that of Thelen, Marrin, Johnson & Bridges. Based in San Francisco, with offices in seven cities and 280 lawyers on staff, the firm takes its in-house program seriously and leaves new attorneys joining the firm in no doubt about the path their education will take. New attorneys are given a flow chart showing the succession of courses required during the first five years with the firm. Six months of orientation come first, followed by a business course in the type of law they'll be practicing, and courses on depositions, accounting, and negotiating. An elaborate trial advocacy program comes in the third year of an attorney's career at the firm, with subsequent years taking up client relations and techniques for building the practice.

Before the firm turned to in-house training, it had gone the route of most law firms—new attorneys "carrying the briefcase" of senior partners for a couple of years, learning by osmosis and imitation. Now partners serve as trainers, for example, after they have taken a training course at the National Institute for Trial Advocacy. A committee of partners determines program content. Most of the training takes place in the San Francisco office, but the firm is considering spreading the program to its other offices. Since the inception of the program in 1980, the firm has gained prestige in the community and accolades from clients. The program has also become a valuable recruiting tool.[20]

Another large firm, Baker & McKenzie, based in Chicago, created an office of professional development in 1984. It has 34 offices—several of them overseas—and more than 800 attorneys. Operating training programs in regional offices, the firm appoints a director for each office who is trained to prepare educational programs. The director uses materials, practice manuals, and notebooks on topics like writing and negotiating skills. To promote positive supervisory relationships, Baker & McKenzie conducts special programs for attorneys being transferred to other offices.

In-house training on an organized basis is still rather new and often not recognized for state requirements, but certainly for large offices it establishes its own validity in terms of time and cost. Law firms have the precedent of big corporations to look at when meeting staff educational needs for improving productivity. Moreover, they face a problem similar to that faced by the engineering profession: namely, the fact that training programs do not directly correspond to the pattern by which individuals are advanced and promoted. There is no corollary educational structure that offers courses necessary for professional advancement. Without some promise of advancement, professionals can lack motivation and interest in self-directed study as well as in formal programs. Nevertheless, spokesmen for the law profession insist that careful annual evaluations of firm members take into account knowledge gained through the study of new subject matter. This should result in higher ratings that lead to advancing status.

It is still true that even though conferences are held on continuing education and legal competence and professional responsibility, the reality is that corporate executives emphasize ongoing professional education—particularly for management and advanced technological personnel—more than lawyers do. Even corporate lawyers, whose salaries and responsibilities are equivalent to senior executives in business, tend to be excluded from regular executive training programs.

Despite all the training opportunities, the young lawyer often has unmet needs. And as the workhorse of the firm, he or she is allowed little time to pursue programs that could help. Some cities have special seminars and simulations of court experience for those newly admitted to the bar, but overall too few lawyers get to the course. Attorneys in smaller firms and in rural areas are also underserved, which makes it difficult for them to contemplate, much less satisfy, the stiffening state requirements. For solo practitioners, continuing legal education offers opportunities for discussion and exploration of topics not otherwise available. As lawyers point out, collegiality is a necessity in the profession, and seminars on subjects of interest and importance provide it. So, as in other professions, it is necessary to provide the means for lawyers to learn and progress.

Both the medical and legal professions, like engineering, have expanding telecommunication networks to meet continuing education needs. These networks serve two functions. One gives access to databases, on-line information systems carrying the facts that will build knowledge. This may prove to be the most practical and relevant way to update professionals by providing essential information to meet actual problems in practice and at the time of need when people learn best. The other function, using various media, delivers instruction in the more usual course or study format, which is broader and may be more fundamental in supplying background.

Examples of the first type are LEXIS for lawyers and AMA/NET for the medical profession, which typically offers news on the latest developments, bulletins from the Center for Disease Control, literature searches, data on products, diagnostic assistance, and information on learning opportunities. All this is on line for the doctor who can reach and use a personal computer and modem. Also available are a series of interactive computer activities, including diagnosis and patient management simulations, that will give a doctor confidential feedback on his or her performance and point out where further study may be needed. This series comes closer to the instructional mode; and networks naturally can be used for both functions.

Regionally the Southern Medical Association has supplemented the national network with DIAL ACCESS, a toll-free telephone information source available 24 hours a day. Member physicians can use it to hear any of a thousand tapes, updated every year, on a wide range of topics and diseases. Southern Medical also offers home study courses with audiotapes and booklets on subjects like clinical concepts and anesthesiology. Besides convenience, these courses provide optional examinations to doctors seeking credit for their efforts.

Lawyers are similarly served by the Continuing Legal Education Satellite Network and another from the American Law Institute. They too have computer-assisted instruction and a center that supplies software to 120 law schools. Comments suggest that the younger generation of professionals accepts and uses the new media for learning faster than older practitioners, as might be expected. Confronted with increasing state regulations mandating further training, however, all will need such aids—and more of them—easily available. It will no doubt be an expanding and rewarding market.

Accountants and Bankers

Of the several kinds of professionals being considered, accountants have come closest to a national consensus on what practitioners need and where they will get it, perhaps partly because continuing education is mandatory for accountants in almost all the states. The principal source of this instruction is the American Institute of Certified Public Accountants (AICPA). Nearly half of its 250,000 members are in private industry, and its courses reach three-quarters of the continuing education market in accounting. A few years ago that figure was more than 95 percent, but as more and more states have imposed requirements, commercial vendors have begun to take a share of the action, and large accounting firms are increasing their own training programs. In 1990, AICPA started requiring an annual minimum of 30 hours of instruction for all accountants wishing to maintain membership.

AICPA produces its own courses, in both self-study and classroom formats, centered around five topics: auditing and accounting, taxation, management, specialized knowledge, and advisory services. Self-study materials are in video, audio-with-manual, and book-based forms. Each course has a final test that can be submitted to AICPA for grading and recording. The classroom studies, sold only to state chapters, last up to five days, but most take one or two eight-hour days. More than a hundred classes are available, led by instructors who are practitioners or university faculty, joined when necessary by subject specialists who are not accountants.

Dolores Kivetz, administrator of continuing education support services at AICPA, estimates that more than 3,500 presentations of these courses are given around the country each year. Until a few years ago more personal development courses were offered for improving writing, communication skills, and client relations, but they have been discontinued. Kivetz says that the market for soft, noncredit instruction fell off when mandatory education gained force.

The next largest providers of continuing education are the so-called "Big Six" accounting firms, which devote increasingly massive resources to educating and upgrading their large professional staffs and to selling their training to clients. Their programs feature state-of-the-art facilities, easily adapted and updated modular curricula, and a streamlined decision-making process for implementation. With a large share of the market and very large resources, the Bix Six can give academia intense and unprecedented competition.

Possibly their next step will be to offer undergraduate degrees in accounting in order to guarantee a supply of new employees already imbued with the particular firm's attitudes and precisely trained in its practices and procedures. There is no other profession in which private companies loom so large in regard to continuing education. It remains to be seen, however, whether the training employees receive in these in-house graduate schools offers more advantages than disadvantages in terms of lifelong professional development and personal growth.

Arthur Andersen's Center for Professional Education in St. Charles, Illinois, outside Chicago, is an elegant wooded campus that was St. Dominic's College until purchased by the firm in 1970. Its capacity has grown from 900 students in 1981 to 1,750 at present. There are showplace classroom buildings, well-designed dormitories and a social center, hiking trails, and a golf course. The dining rooms rival the best in corporate America, with well-prepared meals, table service, crisp linens, and fresh flowers.

Virtually every one of Andersen's 30,000 professionals will spend some time training at the St. Charles Center. Enrollment amounts to 300,000 student days per year. Larry Silvey, director of tax education, offers a conservative estimate of 500,000 student days by 1991. In addition, the company has secondary training centers in Switzerland, Spain, and the Philippines. As a division, professional education got $60 million of the 1986 training budget and $97 million for fiscal 1988. The staff consists of 500 persons, 300 of whom are professionals with either line experience as accountants or backgrounds in education. Its mission is threefold: developing professional skills in employees, reinforcing the company culture, and professionalizing the training process. It recruits teachers as needed from field offices worldwide and gives them a three-day preparation at St. Charles, with an overview lecture by division staff and a practice teaching session that is videotaped and then critiqued. Since the employees of Andersen's global operation speak the gamut of languages, from Spanish to Thai to Greek, there is even a training subgroup dedicated to helping non-native speakers handle the all-English training. By putting its professionals through a highly structured and tightly controlled education process, Andersen ensures uniformity among its 150 branch offices in more than 30 countries.

According to the division's Gary Adams, the average Arthur Andersen professional will be required during the course of a career to take some 800 hours of instruction in the firm's training programs. Half of this will be self-paced, computer-assisted instruction at the employee's home office, and the other half will be at St. Charles or one of the other training facilities. The former is presented in modules that take a day or so to complete, woven into and paid as time on the job. Computer-aided material covers basic concepts and procedures; the rest is mostly on paper, including proficiency tests for the various modules to be completed and sent to a central grading and record-keeping office. Some of this work is intended to improve general skills, such as writing and judgment in making decisions.

Training at St. Charles is departmentalized according to the divisions of the company: audit, tax, and management information, which includes consulting services. The first phase covers the core or "mainline curriculum" of an employee's training. It includes one to two weeks working as a member of a project team on the actual problems of a "case company." The teams mix disparate academic backgrounds, learning styles, and cultural heritages and, according to Gary Adams, help to overcome differences and encourage uniformity in the corporate style. The second phase of the training consists of skill-oriented elective courses geared to the employee's practice area, and the last phase, which is encouraged but not required, covers specialized subjects. Current issues like the 1987 Tax Act are addressed. Leaders in industry or government often conduct the seminars, and occasionally a very senior partner of the firm does so.

Anderson claims to hire the best—all recruits are among the top five percent of their graduating classes and are selected for their motivation, initiative, and ability to think quickly—and the company clearly wants to make them still better by investing heavily in their training. Ten percent of Andersen's gross fees are put back into training worldwide each year; it is considered a sound investment in the business-generating potential of managers and staff.

The curriculum is constantly subject to expansion and development. If an idea is introduced and the professional education division can create training to match it, new business is born. From experience the training team has learned to de-emphasize technical concepts by providing more nontechnical training (for example, communications and client relations) early in an employee's career, to target the training better, to organize courses in modules to make efficient changes possible, to field-test instructional materials, and to include computer application training (the bulk of the company's business is now in computer systems). Larry Silvey, who considers university education in accounting to be generally good but often too specialized, says it costs about $12,000 to develop and produce one hour of self-study training and $15,000 per hour for computerized basic training.

Like so many other corporations—accounting or otherwise—Arthur Andersen has become a commercial vendor of education and training. For some years the company has given courses to clients and others and published an annual professional seminar calendar listing for-credit courses given around the country. But lately Andersen has shifted the emphasis away from such external seminars because they were neither very effective in training nor very profitable. Now the focus is on tailoring programs for a particular client's needs. Andersen's staff furnishes curriculum planning, training design, development, and support. With 80,000 clients around the world, Andersen has a sizable potential audience and the opportunity to build an education empire.

Though Andersen is the largest of the Big Six accounting firms, the others are not far behind. Peat Marwick's research and training center in Montvale, New Jersey, is a four-building complex with a fountain, pond, and sculpture on the lawns. Opened in 1987, the facility has 70 full-time employees. Its one-hundred-page course catalog lists more than one hundred courses, some available as self-study packages. Most are finance and financial control courses, but there are offerings in information technology, written and oral communication, and team management. The facilities and courses are also open to outsiders. For seminars lasting two to four days, employees of clients pay fees that range from $400 to just under $1,000. Included in its facilities is a mainframe computer that can link 600 employees in 130 offices around the country. Such training centers are becoming the norm rather than the exception in the corporate world. Touche Ross has built one in Scottsdale, Arizona, and accounting giants Coopers & Lybrand and Arthur Young have facilities, respectively, in southern New Jersey and in Reston, Virginia.

In contrast, there is almost no mandatory continuing education in the banking profession. To be sure, the current troubles of many savings and loan associations and large commercial banks due to poor management and bad judgment would suggest that some sort of ongoing training and professional evaluation is called for. But many bankers can and do use a variety of academically demanding programs.

Like accountants, they have looked to their own ranks for specialized, applied, on-the-job training. The American Banking Association (ABA) has an educational unit, the American Institute of Banking, that has been serving the professional development needs of officers, directors, and employees of member banks for almost 90 years. It is the only industry that has a national education program. Six hundred local chapters and study groups involve 350,000 banking employees annually in seminars, short programs, in-bank training, correspondence study, and diploma and certificate programs. Program materials and curricula for most of these students are prepared at the institute's headquarters in Washington, D.C.

The flagship in this educational sector is the Stonier Graduate School of Banking on the campus of the University of Delaware at Newark, where 300 to 400 bank officers who already have 5 to 12 years of professional experience come from around the country for two weeks each summer of the three-year program. In the first year they study the fundamentals of banking; in the second, functional areas of banking as well as case studies and four elective subjects. The third year includes work on a management simulation project called BankSim, senior seminars covering trends in the banking industry, other electives, and an optional thesis or research project. Extension assignments to be completed at the home bank are required during each year of the program. On completion, students are awarded an ABA certificate rather than a master's degree, but banking industry officials think that the demanding and practical nature of the Stonier program makes it more valuable to the individual and the industry than a traditional advanced academic degree.

Of course, the large banks have their own extensive in-house training programs on which they depend heavily for high-quality performance from their employees. They also select their most promising candidates for professional development and underwrite their advanced studies at leading universities. Manufacturers Hanover Trust Company in New York, for example, sends selected officers to earn the M.B.A. at New York University, the Wharton School, or Columbia in a program combining study and work—at full salary and benefits. And as in other corporations, Manufacturers Hanover executives worry that these officers will leave for jobs elsewhere after training. But they need well-trained talent, so they have no choice.

Next Directions

Continuing education for the various professions is one of the fastest expanding and most profitable areas in the learning industry. Driven by more than the technological changes in our working environment, it reflects the growing mandatory requirements for licensure, the pressure from employers in the competitive world, and the constant evolution of specializations that demand attention.

Foremost is the spread of state requirements. In some instances lawmakers are imposing the new rules, in other cases professional associations are instituting their own standards, and frequently the two groups act cooperatively. In some cases, abuses by professionals have led to public pressure for regulatory action. Whether mandating requirements will be effective in correcting ills remains to be seen, but regardless of the reasons, such regulations encourage more learning and updating of skills.

Furthermore, many professional groups are long accustomed to licensure and to practice standards. They have spawned their own specialty and subspecialty boards, and they have framed certificates and diplomas—beyond academic degrees—on their office walls. We are a credentialed society. And the trend toward higher requirements seems to be accepted without much opposition.

Professional societies and associations, whether medical, legal, engineering, banking, or accounting, generally dominate the field of providers, and in most cases they act as centers for accreditation. But they do not always cooperate for the total benefit of their profession; specialty groups within a profession exert a centrifugal force, fractionalizing the profession into many subunits that claim practitioners' first allegiance. Hence the difficulty in maintaining cohesion for the profession as a whole and coherence in the advanced training programs offered.

The universities' professional schools join the societies in the vendors' marketplace and contribute particularly to updating specialized knowledge. We see some evidence of more flexibility in giving shorter courses at more convenient times—which would answer critics' charges of the schools' inability to adjust to the marketplace. Although nonprofit in nature and attitude, professional schools too are aware of the money to be made in this market. Similarly, university schools of continuing education and extension services have begun to probe this market and present courses taught by professionals in the field.

By far the biggest and potentially most extensive changes, however, are coming from the corporations and companies that are opening their classrooms to each other and selling educational services to other companies. It is not a haphazard operation, which opening doors might imply; neither is it a matter of advertising a list of seminars available. Instead, the vendors are pointedly tailoring courses for customers. Arthur Andersen's shift in this direction is most significant. It reinforces what we have seen in other sectors: the move toward customized training for specified purposes.

In methods being used to update professionals, there is the widest variety. As might be expected for people in advanced positions, motivation and initiative are assumed, so self-study courses—book-based, videotapes, audio with manuals—are plentiful. Such self-paced learning often precedes attendance at the company's campus center or seminars at headquarters.

Instructional technologies and delivery systems are also prevalent for this group and especially valuable in aiding access for the individual or small group of practitioners. As part of this forward look, on-line information systems may prove to be most effective. Often the advanced professional may require only the latest information—not a course—to perform better on the job. But this presupposes that the need is for specialized data or specific information. The on-line system does not supply general educational material such as instruction in human relations.

For courses dealing with interpersonal relations and management, which are often needed by advanced professionals moving into broader responsibilities, one looks to classrooms and interchange with others. Here is a curricular area where schools of continuing education could make a great contribution and gain special recognition. They could also add the dimension of broader studies and consideration of contemporary societal issues that many professionals are missing. In the effort to remain up to date with facts applicable to the job, too often professional specialists fail to encounter the larger issues that require their attention and their contribution. To manage the large enterprises that employ millions of people in our country, we need professionals—as well as those who have made management a career—in the ranks of leadership.

PART

III

THE UNFINISHED

AGENDA

7

MISSING PERSONS

F ar too many adults are missing from the productive ranks of the work force, missing from payrolls other than public support, or employed only part-time in temporary tasks that give neither stability nor opportunities. Too many find themselves referred to as "displaced persons"—displaced by new production methods, by changing corporate structures to accommodate new procedures, or perhaps by "downsizing" as companies become leaner (and some say meaner) to meet tougher competition.

Some adults are held back by racial barriers or physical disabilities or prison walls. Others are restricted geographically in rural areas, where 42 percent are said to have fewer than eight years of school. And many are caught in urban centers of neglect and despair. Whatever their circumstances, the missing contributors to productivity are generally bound by the seemingly endless chains of poverty and unemployment. Locked out of the mainstream, they constitute a huge, costly loss to the work force.

No discussion about improving America's productivity through worker education can ignore this wasted potential of human energies and abilities. It is a monumental fact that millions of people, in the midst of a land of promise, are being poorly served or not at all, and the loss is not theirs alone. The problem demands our full attention because of its magnitude and its effects on the very foundation of our economy. It is a major item on the unfinished agenda before us.

Although a web of social and economic factors complicates the situation, many of these victims share one common trait: they lack basic skills in reading, writing, and arithmetic. Some 75 percent of the chronically unemployed and underemployed are believed to be essentially illiterate. This places them in the "Catch-22" of education and work: they can't get jobs that would offer additional training and advancement because they need remediation; because they need remediation, they lack the resources to seek help from social and government assistance programs. They certainly cannot go to ordinary adult education classes or use the variety of self-education materials available today. The bottom line in illiteracy is easy to calculate—can't read, can't write, can't work at much, and can't live very well.

Even among those in the labor force, estimates suggest, 15 percent are illiterate or insufficiently literate to function well. While most are in the lower echelons of workers, some are in professional and managerial jobs. They cope from day to day, cleverly hiding their disability, but it shows in uneven performance that affects the quality of their work and generally lowers productivity.

The totals are almost unbelievable. From the U.S. Department of Education come the generally accepted figures that 27 million adults are *functionally* illiterate and 45 million only *marginally* literate. Of this total—72 million—programs are serving perhaps four million. Yet each year another 2.3 million (high school dropouts, immigrants, refugees) join the ranks of the illiterate.[1] The message is too obvious: we are on a treadmill, running to stay in the same place.

This chapter focuses on the literacy and basic skills programs available. In this sector of adult education, the providers' roles change because many people to be served are outside the work force. Inasmuch as their needs are a public responsibility, the initiatives come from federal and state programs, plus volunteer and community-based organizations. A look at the efforts under way is discouraging. Their inadequacy is readily apparent when compared with what is needed and what the United States could do with its remarkable resources.

Before describing the programs, we consider three questions that lend perspective on the issues. How many illiterates are there? Who are they? And how much are they costing society? The problem of simply defining literacy has led to wide differences in the numbers projected. This is not to suggest that the problem of illiteracy is less serious than we are told, but to gain understanding about who is measuring what ability and how. What standards for measurement are being used?

Literacy: A Moving Target

In Colonial New England, no doubt, a person who could read the Bible and write a simple letter was considered literate. In 1840, when literacy statistics were first gathered in the U.S. Census, marshals counted the number of persons over 20 years of age unable to read and write. In 1870, the baseline became ten years of age and upward, and writing was considered a more stringent criterion in determining literacy than reading. Still, according to these standards, the American population was "quantitatively among the most literate in the world during the first three quarters of the nineteenth century."[2]

Through 1930, the Census maintained the standard of ten years of age and the ability to read and write, adding "either in English or in some other language." Meanwhile, in 1929 the National Education Association set the reading, writing, and mathematical skills of a fourth-grade student as the minimum standard of literacy. In 1947, the Bureau of the Census held to the fifth grade, and by 1980 the bureau set eighth grade as the minimum level. Today some claim the academic skills of a twelfth grader constitute literacy. The minimum keeps rising, and it will continue to do so as the technological environment challenges our abilities. Repeatedly it is claimed that more than a high-school education will be needed for job opportunities in the years ahead. Basic education cannot stop with minimal literacy.

Today's definitions call for *functional* literacy, which reflects what the U.S. Army learned in World War II, when it found that many draftees had basic skills but not enough comprehension to make them effective soldiers. The functional concept considers a person's competence to meet the requirements of adult living and working. Rather than the narrow technical measure of reading, writing, and arithmetic, it includes comprehension and the ability to use knowledge gained through reading.

Within this context a landmark study was carried out in the early 1970s at the University of Texas to determine the adult performance level. The study classified four basic areas of skill proficiency: communication (reading, writing, speaking, and listening), computation, problem-solving, and interpersonal skills. It assessed these skills as applied to five general knowledge areas: occupational, consumer economics, community resources, law and government, and health. The researchers estimated that one-fifth of the adults in the United States were functioning with difficulty or were incompetent, while one-third were functioning at a minimal level of competence. If this finding is translated into population figures, 23 million were in the former category and 39 million in the latter.[3] When the Department of Education applied this study's findings to more recent population statistics, it determined that 27 million adults are functionally illiterate.

Other studies reveal similar results. The National Assessment of Educational Progress, released in 1986, found that 27.6 million adults "do not read as well as a typical eighth grader." The test asked for completion of simulated literacy tasks common to the home and workplace.[4] In a study on English language proficiency, also in 1986, adults were given a written test using 26 simple questions adapted from government social service forms. Results indicated that some 18.7 million people were illiterate.[5] The numbers here are somewhat lower but it must be noted that the questions were limited in coverage. It was not as broad-gauged as some other tests; for this the results have received criticism.

Nevertheless, the numbers are sobering. Each year some 700,000 high school students receive diplomas even though they are unable to read or write at the ninth-grade level.[6] Clearly, a high school diploma is not a warranty of literacy today. It is not that schools have utterly failed their charge, but the requirements for competent performance are rising, and they complicate the problem of definition. Indeed, the more narrowly one defines literacy the less test and survey results mean as measures of people's competence and ability to contribute.

The functional concept, hard as it may be to pin down, is the only way to judge our preparedness as a people to cope with the changing world around us. Furthermore, if we add *technological literacy* to the definition, many if not most of us will find ourselves in the ranks of the illiterate and the marginally competent. In any case, there are entirely too many educationally handicapped adults, and the numbers escalate as the scale of functional skills takes in more and more sophisticated abilities.

Target Populations

Judging the programs in basic skills becomes more complicated when we consider the mixture of people to be taught and what they need to learn. There are many targets in the population of illiterates. Foremost are welfare recipients and the chronically unemployed; most in both categories are deemed functionally illiterate.[7] Another very large group are the incarcerated, of whom 80 percent have not finished high school. Estimates place most of them among functional illiterates. Add to them subsistence farmers, American Indians on reservations, and each year another one million high school dropouts, many of them Hispanics and African-Americans in inner cities.

Counted in the total are the 1.3 million refugees and immigrants who arrive each year lacking English language skills and sometimes skills in their native tongue. Teaching English as a second language presents no new challenge in America; our history is the story of immigrants coming in waves from many other shores. Massive efforts to assist them have been made in the past when they were a larger percentage of the total population than is the case now, and our national resources then were also weaker by comparison.

These newcomers are considered part of the illiterate population, but they constitute a very different group of individuals to be helped. And they are especially important as recruits for the work force that needs them. It happens that a large percentage of immigrants is in the age group from 15 to 29—the entry age for many jobs. In the U.S. resident population, this age group has declined by 2.3 million since 1980. Therefore, there will be jobs for the young adults arriving from other countries if they can acquire competence in English and basic skills.

The Cost of Illiteracy

No one can presume that the United States' economic position will be improved by the costs of supporting the nearly one-third of the population judged illiterate, whether borderline or functional. One expert pegs it as "running into many tens of billions of dollars annually" for American taxpayers.[8] But the deficit is not just in dollars: it is a deficit in human resources that requires remedy and investment for the sake of our future well-being as a society.

The U.S. Department of Labor's regional office in Atlanta estimated the costs of illiteracy in eight Southern states, using data and projections from the National Planning Association, the U.S. Census, the Bureau of Labor Statistics, and other sources. Of an estimated 12.1 million functionally illiterate adults in the region, the report found that:

- 7.3 million were not in the labor force—costing the economies of those states $31 billion per year in "lost business productivity, unrealized tax revenues, welfare, crime, and related social problems";

- another 3.6 million undereducated adults were employed, costing employers $24.8 billion annually in "lost time, substandard performance, and various employment-related problems"; and

- the final 1.2 million were in the work force but officially unemployed, consuming $1.4 billion per year in unemployment insurance funds.[9]

The report concludes: "Conservatively, adult literacy problems are already costing the Southeast regional economy $57.2 billion annually or $4,727 per adult illiterate. This estimated annual cost amounts to one-fifth of the region's total business earnings in 1985." One wonders how much it would save over time to invest in solving the problems.

Industry, labor, and academia have all invested heavily in training the work force. So have government and the military. But the foundations are undermined by illiteracy, and present programs are inadequate. Since it is clearly a national problem, we look first at the federal level, where some coherent leadership might be expected.

Federal Policies and Programs

Probably very few individuals actually know all the current federal laws relating to adult education. It would be instructive to make a cumulative analysis of the legislation, some of which sounds like a politician running for office, containing "pork barrel" provisions even though the bill's sponsor has long since left Congress. There might be specific allotments that are not applicable in states where the problems differ or are unique. On the whole, programs have proliferated from department to department, with multiple goals and constituencies and no coordination within departments, much less between them.

A 1985 inventory of federal literacy programs conducted for the Federal Interagency Committee on Education listed 79 programs in 14 agencies—8 programs where literacy was the primary objective, 44 where it was secondary to some other goal, and 27 with incidental literacy activities by virtue of policy decisions rather than legislative mandate.[10] Our overview and the examples selected can at best be only partial, but they may suggest some of the problems and promise of Washington's efforts to meet the needs of the missing persons.

Adult Basic and Secondary Education. The largest program is the one for Adult Basic and Secondary Education (ABE/ASE). As part of Lyndon B. Johnson's plan for the Great Society, ABE was authorized in the mid-sixties under the Adult Education Act to help people aged 15 and over get the equivalent of an eighth-grade education by distributing money, technical assistance, and program guidelines to individual states for programs. In 1969, the Act was extended to cover high school completion: the ASE program was to help adults earn the high school equivalency diploma, known as GED for General Educational Development. These programs also include teaching English as a second language. Between 70 and 80 percent of authorized funds go to ABE programs, with the balance going to ASE.

Administered by the Department of Education, the program distributes federal dollars to states by formula grants based on school completion rates among adults; states pass the funds along to school districts and other organizations that actually provide the instruction. In 1978, Congress broadened the range of ABE providers beyond schools to include community colleges, unions, businesses, churches, and other community organizations that could establish a comfortable and appropriate setting for adult learning. Funding has fluctuated over the years, reaching its peak in 1989 when Congress appropriated $162.21 million, which was $12 million *over* the Department of Education's request. Still, this amounted to less than one percent of the department's fiscal 1989 budget. And the picture government-wide is worse: measured as a portion of the gross national product, federal spending on human resource programs fell from 0.85 to 0.45 percent between 1978 and 1988.[11]

While willing to spend relatively little on adult education, the federal government is requiring the states to give more. Their burden has grown steadily since 1979, both absolutely and as a percentage of the federal contribution. Collectively, the states now more than double the federal contribution to adult education efforts. By law, they have been contributing at least 10 percent of ABE/ASE program costs, and their share rose to 15 percent in 1990 and it will be 25 percent in 1992. As William F. Pierce, former director of the Hudson Institute's Center for Education and Employment Policy, points out, "At a time when analysts at every level are saying a trained and upgraded work force is essential for our national economic survival, the Congress of the United States is signaling that the problem is less theirs than ever before."[12]

In 1987, total state and federal spending on adult education at skill levels up to the eighth grade amounted to only $143 per student. A comparison with the nearly $4,000 spent for each pupil in elementary and secondary school in 1986–1987 readily shows that adults are receiving little government support in learning fundamental skills. Furthermore, in terms of the target populations, too few are being reached. Enrollment in federally supported adult education programs in 1986 totaled just over 3.1 million, of whom 28 percent were in ABE, 48 percent in ASE, and 24 percent studying English as a second language. Although the enrollment grew to 3.5 million the next year—the increase being attributed mainly to public awareness—it still represents only 13 percent of those considered functionally illiterate.

Other Federal Literacy Efforts. A garden variety of smaller programs has appeared without a discernible pattern and without perennials that can keep blossoming with a little nurture. Most are small, one-time-only efforts that fade away after a few seasons. Nevertheless, Congress is on record expressing its concern for the people unable to perform in the labor force because of basic educational handicaps, and scores of proposals have appeared as well as bills enacted for their assistance. But there is no overall policy or willingness to commit funds that are commensurate to the magnitude of the problem. No one in Congress has been asking to shift the cost of several submarines or military planes to basic training for workers. Even with decreasing demands for military expenditure, worker training is not high among domestic priorities. Budget constraints are obvious, and unless hard decisions are made, the current small and fragmented programs will continue to constitute our effort.

Reluctance to make difficult choices has resulted in continual calls for private volunteers to help as tutors. It has further encouraged rhetoric about the problem, but no real action. The Reagan-Bush administration responded to the growing public concern over illiteracy largely with pronouncements *ex cathedra*. In 1983, the Adult Literacy Initiative was established in the Department of Education, mostly as cheerleader for literacy programs and disseminator of information about them. It has extolled the virtues of private sector support, better collaboration and coordination across all sectors, and more research on teaching adults to read and write. Although some potentially valuable research was started, the results remain to be seen. The initiative had no legislative mandate and almost no funding authority, so generally it has been able to address only its public relations charge.

A few samples of recent legislation show the size and disparity of efforts—the absence of federal leadership whether congressional or administrative:

Literacy Corps.   Included in the Omnibus Trade and Competitiveness Act of 1988 was a $5 million provision for a "Peace Corps for the 1990s" mobilized to fight illiteracy. In the fiscal 1989 budget appropriations it received no funding.

Volunteers in Service to America.   Reauthorization of VISTA added $2 million to expand student services for work on literacy in low-income communities.

English Literacy Grants.   Realizing that immigrants have problems in learning English and that their instruction consumes a considerable portion of adult education funds, Congress appropriated about $5 million in grants for state programs. The Secretary of Education is also to "develop innovative approaches and methods of literacy education for individuals of limited English proficiency utilizing new instructional methods and technologies," and establish a national information clearinghouse. [13]

Even Start.   Included in the Hawkins-Stafford Elementary and Secondary School Improvement Amendments of 1988, this program gives literacy instruction to parents and their children in school facilities. It is modeled on Kentucky's Parent and Child Education Program for poor families, which has been judged to be quite successful.

Adult Education and Job Training for the Homeless.   Here Congress made two assignments: one to the Department of Education for about $7 million to provide literacy and basic skills remediation, and the other to the Department of Labor, which received a one-time grant of $12 million for demonstration projects serving the homeless.

Education Partnership for Workplace Literacy.   Under the Adult Education Act of 1987, Congress authorized funds to pay 70 percent of the cost of "adult education programs which teach literacy skills needed in the workplace through partnerships" between businesses, unions, private industry councils, and educational institutions and agencies. Intended for demonstration purposes, the appropriation for the program was $11.86 million in 1989.

Legislation has been added to other operative programs, but on the whole it amounts simply to the proliferation of small programs that may not be worth the bureaucratic machinery installed to handle them and report, not to mention the dispersal of assignments within and among departments. Coordination seems all but impossible to achieve.

Other federal initiatives are directed more purposefully toward training for basic jobs, but these efforts, too, are complicated by the widespread need for literacy remediation before job training can be undertaken. We look now at Washington's major efforts in basic training for adult workers: the Job Training Partnership Act and the Welfare-Workfare program.

Job Training Partnership Act. Aimed at economically disadvantaged adults and displaced workers, this 1982 act created the main and largest federal program. Compared with earlier programs, the Job Training Partnership Act (JTPA) gives more funding authority to states and increases private sector involvement through private industry councils (PICs), which do market analyses and encourage local employers to offer jobs and training to the disadvantaged.

Administered by the Department of Labor, JTPA has three major purposes:

Title II-A: Job training for economically disadvantaged youth and adults. Funds for these activities are allocated to service delivery areas through PICs.

Title II-B: Summer employment and training programs for disadvantaged youth.

Title III: Training and re-employment assistance for displaced workers. In 1988, the Economic Dislocation and Workers Adjustment Act replaced Title III and gave PICs a greater role in distribution of funds for dislocated workers.

This is the cornerstone of federal policies that are intended to serve the tremendous numbers of persons missing from the labor force. But the monies allocated are woefully inadequate. In 1989, JTPA Title II funding was $1.78 billion and Title III funds were only $283.8 million. The wide difference in allotment places the emphasis on the economically disadvantaged rather than on the dislocated worker. Certainly both groups need assistance, but the difference is particularly disturbing when we note that this is *the* federal program for displaced workers. There are no others.

By the letter of the law, JTPA authorizes literacy training for participants who cannot be employed without remediation. In practice, however, few participants receive remedial instruction. Of the 1.1 million adults who took part in Title II-A programs in 1985, just 7 percent received remedial instruction.[14] A similar pattern is found among dislocated workers.

JTPA's inattention to basic skills instruction stems from the priority it gives to job placement. Unlike the Adult Education Act, JTPA pays service providers by the numbers of participants placed in jobs, not by the numbers enrolled. While this approach provides a measure of accountability and adds to the employment rolls, it rewards fast, short-term assistance. Consequently, people are more likely to receive job counseling and brief, job-specific training—if any at all—rather than more extensive remedial education and the foundation for new skills.

The argument for this "creaming" process, which helps the best prospects who can most easily be placed in jobs, claims that limited funds make this the sensible thing to do. On the other hand, critics charge that once again the neediest individuals are left out. JTPA does not provide income maintenance during training and puts a very low ceiling on support services like child care and transportation. These factors, combined with weak recruitment efforts in most programs, mean that JTPA is not set up to serve the most disadvantaged.

Congress has recently expressed concern about the legislation and appointed an advisory committee to review it. The committee was also to examine how the program can work more effectively with the education and welfare systems. Evidence from many sources shows that people in the program need literacy instruction. The time has come for a shift in JTPA away from an emphasis on short-term counseling and quick placement. The task requires a long-term investment in basic education and job training.

Welfare and Workfare. The other principal federal effort aimed at the missing persons is the 1988 welfare reform law designed to move people off public support and into the work force. Along with a provision for "workfare"—mandatory community work by welfare recipients—the act creates a Job Opportunities and Basic Skills Training Program administered by the Department of Health and Human Services. Funding was authorized at $3.34 billion but apportioned over a five-year period. States are required to enroll 7 percent of their welfare recipients in education and training programs in 1990 and at least 20 percent by 1995. Various educational institutions are to evaluate the individual's needs and supply appropriate remediation and job training. Proprietary schools are eligible to participate.

While it is too early to ascertain the potential success of the program, some educators have registered concerns and doubts. Jan Hake, coordinator of the California community colleges' involvement with a state program similar to the new federal initiative, says that colleges already working with state and local welfare officials find the costs of extensive individual attention and the program reporting requirements to be exceedingly high. On different grounds, Joseph Murphy, former chancellor of the City University of New York, doubts whether postsecondary institutions can contribute because experience shows "that state agencies, faced with the understandable pressures to reduce the welfare rolls quickly, will usually push welfare recipients into menial jobs or short-term training programs rather than long-term educational options like higher education."[15]

Solutions to these immense, complicated problems require not only a large financial commitment but also a coherent plan linking the efforts. Programs are emanating not only from the Departments of Education, Labor, and Health and Human Services but also from Agriculture, Defense, and the Interior—all directed in one way or another at adult education and training, and many at basic literacy. Recent laws, such as those establishing Even Start and the welfare reform, specify coordination with other programs, but it is not happening even when interagency groups are charged with the responsibility. And before any of the support gets to the people in need, it must go through the further channels arranged, with varying degrees of success, by state and local governments to discharge their part of the responsibility.

State and Local Government Programs

Like the federal government, the states have historically under-invested in adult literacy and basic training programs and are now faced with hard problems. But unlike the federal government, which can simply deploy umbrella policy schemes, the states bear the burden of implementing the mandates, making best use of scant resources, and reconciling rivalries among agencies, providers, and provider-led coalitions.

Spurred by the social and economic costs of functional illiteracy, most states have organized to deliver services on a scale much broader than before. A survey conducted by the Business Council for Effective Literacy in October 1987 found that 30 states had a statewide adult-literacy planning body of some sort. In addition, some 18 major cities have citywide planning mechanisms.[16] But most of these planning groups are still in their early stages. They have no mechanisms for assessing the particular needs of various groups for basic skills, which makes it hard to target resources effectively, develop new services, and refer adults to suitable programs.

Nevertheless, some states are performing admirably under difficult circumstances. The programs of several states seem to be well ahead of federal policies, particularly in coordinating activities. We single out a few examples. California's Greater Avenues to Independence (GAIN) program combines ABE, JTPA, and state and federal welfare funds to upgrade the welfare recipients' literacy skills and train them for jobs. The Los Angeles Unified School District gives basic literacy education to more than 400,000 adults a year, many of them recent immigrants, for which it receives money from the ABE program, from GAIN, from the federal immigration program, and from JTPA. It also generates funds through customized on-site programs, sometimes in basic skills, for companies and other employers.

Michigan's MOST (Michigan Opportunity and Skills Training) takes a coordinated approach to public assistance recipients, referring those who need remediation to appropriate literacy agencies or ABE services. When policy makers in Michigan examined the state's labor force, they discovered that most workers had passed the tenth grade and had some basic skills, but needed extra help to read and write more effectively, solve problems, and work in teams—the constellation of skills increasingly called for in today's jobs. As a result, Michigan aimed its workplace literacy efforts toward these skills. The legislature appropriated more money, the bulk of it flowing to the community college system. Governor George Blanchard also announced a variety of education services available to all citizens through the Michigan Opportunity Card, a sort of credit card for purchase of literacy and other training. In all, more than $81 million in extra funds were allocated to upgrading basic skills in the Michigan labor force.[17]

Massachusetts, facing a severe labor shortage and a state budget crisis, has not sought infusions of new resources but has tried to redirect existing programs. One result of the Commonwealth Literacy Campaign, a multiyear initiative, is the Workplace Education Program operating from the Executive Office of Labor to encourage collaboration among different groups in offering literacy instruction for employed adults. Among the activities sponsored is English as a second language for employees of TJ Maxx, a Worcester, Massachusetts retailer with a large number of immigrant workers. The program is a partnership of the company, the International Ladies Garment Workers Union, and Quinsigamond Community College. Employees are given released time to take instruction at work.

Another program comes from the University of Massachusetts at Amherst, whose employees can obtain instruction in basic skills, English, and high school equivalency courses. The Massachusetts Longterm Care Foundation developed a language program for the region's nursing homes—a response to their difficulty in finding English-speaking workers.[18] The Commonwealth Literacy Campaign also has an agreement with job training program managers to sponsor literacy instruction for welfare recipients to prepare them for entry into the state's Employment and Training Choices program.

Other states are doing remarkable jobs in the face of even greater adversity. Under the leadership of strong governors, they are coordinating programs and bringing limited resources together for more effective action. South Carolina, for example, has improved dramatically in a very short time. It started in 1983 with Governor Richard Riley, who appealed directly to voters with the slogan "A Penny For Your Schools" and got the legislation for school improvement passed. The next governor, Carroll Campbell, moved the focus of reform to adult education. His appeal was also basic: "Education and economic development are inseparable. Education without job opportunity is folly; a good job without education is impossible."

The state's functional illiteracy is widespread—20 percent of adults have less than a ninth-grade education—but concentrated in pockets of rural poverty. South Carolina has launched a concerted attack on many fronts: besides public programs and community college participation, the campaign relies on volunteer literacy efforts supported by a library system providing materials, space for tutors and students, and publicity to encourage illiterate people to come for help.

Many states and local governments are struggling valiantly against the odds. Although success rates vary erratically, some constitute models for other governors to examine for their appropriateness to their own states' problems. One characteristic is notable: progress is most apt to be seen in those states where we find public efforts collaborating with business, labor, community groups, and others in the private sector.

Private Sector Initiatives

On the private front, there is great attention to the problems of adult illiteracy and the lack of basic skills in the work force. But it is often just attention—not action. Scores of conferences have been convened in recent years to talk about joining forces in attacking the problem. Issuing statements of purpose sprinkled with words like "mobilize," "encourage," and "promote," these gatherings, have given rise to other groups, some more focused and effective than others, but at least they have raised public awareness. It's a front-page or cover story: Illiteracy Threatens America's Work Force and Competitive Position. For the most part, everyone wishes to cooperate with everyone else, and it is unclear what exactly is being accomplished.

Of interest is the role of newspapers and publishers: some have been leaders in the campaign and have started real programs. Industrial corporations have provided spokesmen and contributed, but on the whole they are doing little *within* their own companies for their workers most in need. The sizable action programs enrolling large numbers are those sponsored by labor unions, often as part of negotiated contracts with employers. And of course, volunteers comprise a significant group of tutors working at basic levels to teach illiterate individuals. We report briefly on each of these private-sector initiatives.

Publishers and the Media. Naturally newspapers know that it is self-defeating to try to build circulation and sales in a population with growing numbers of nonreaders. Regardless of self-interest, in some cases their sustained efforts and willingness to commit funds take their campaign beyond rhetoric and into action. The Gannett Company, a media and publishing giant, is such a case. Since 1985, when the company began its program, Gannett has awarded more than $5 million primarily to nonprofit organizations in communities its newspapers serve. Of late, the company has shifted the emphasis toward state and national organizations with a Literacy Challenge program in cooperation with *USA Today*, Gannett's national daily paper. The chain makes more grants now to establish permanent services at the state level. The amount of funds disbursed makes Gannett one of the largest contributors from this part of the private sector.

McGraw-Hill has taken a somewhat different approach. A leader in advocacy, Harold McGraw, Jr., set up the Business Council for Effective Literacy (BCEL) in 1983 with initial funding of $1 million. Since then about 50 other organizations—mostly corporate foundations—have joined the council. BCEL does not itself fund programs: it works to get companies involved in financial or in-kind aid to literacy programs, in awareness campaigns, and in helping to research and plan significant programs both on and off the work site.

BCEL's quarterly newsletter reaches businesses, chambers of commerce, educational institutions, and correctional, volunteer, and library agencies at all levels. Coherent and comprehensive, its publications are an excellent source of information about literacy programs across the country. The newsletter updates available figures, lists relevant publications, highlights new corporate programs and funding, and examines activities of government agencies, unions, prisons, and so on. It is a source where a program in Yuma, Arizona, can pick up a valuable idea from a program in Cleveland, Ohio, or a state-level planner in Kentucky can find reason for connecting with a library in Massachusetts. As a promoter, catalyst, and center for information, BCEL provides valuable services.

Others in the publishing field, like Time, Inc., the Chicago Tribune Company, and B. Dalton Booksellers, have made important contributions. The bookstore chain, before its sale to Barnes & Noble, had spent $3 million to recruit, train, and place 34,000 volunteer tutors in literacy programs. Other organizations have focused simply on advocacy and awareness in efforts to draw national attention to the problem. The American Newspaper Publishers Association and the International Reading Association staged a symposium in September 1988 with representatives of government agencies, literacy volunteers, and many others. The assembly took the title of Working Group on Adult Literacy and called on the next president to begin a *systematic* effort to combat illiteracy.

A recent television campaign, Project Literacy U.S. (PLUS), reached 50 million households through public service programs. Its 30-second "documercials" and features such as "Illiteracy, the Silent Nightmare" prompted thousands to volunteer as tutors or to ask for help in becoming literate. Task forces emerged in communities across the country, telephone hotlines were installed, and state funds increased. Such national attention encourages illiterates to come "out of the closet" and find assistance. They are very difficult to recruit except by word of mouth, referral, radio, or television. Many have low self-esteem and little hope: the mother on welfare trying to feed her children, the farm laborer exhausted at the end of the day, or the street person who has just given up.

While consciousness raising is imperative and a necessary first step in mobilizing a national literacy effort, it carries certain risks. One is that superficial attention will lull the public into a complacent belief that something is really being done about the problem. Furthermore, the use of high-profile, dramatized media in promotion also risks oversimplifying the problem. Sally's inability to balance her checkbook or understand how much interest she pays on her credit card does not produce as much shock or sympathy as Mike's serious injury when he is unable to read a safety sign. To be sure, basic illiteracy is most serious, but the more pervasive lack of functional skills presents an even greater problem. The challenge is to carry awareness to the next level and generate long-term private and public sector support for sustained literacy training programs.

The Business Community. The Business Council for Effective Literacy admits frustration with the vague figures it obtains when trying to determine how much money the business community has invested in literacy programs. But it estimates that corporations have put roughly 65 percent of their contributions into grants and in-kind aid to local and state programs, 26 percent into awareness, planning, and research, and only 9 percent into company-based programs for employees. Corporate philanthropy to combat illiteracy seems to be going outside—not into companies' own in-house programs.

Although AT&T alone may spend $6 million a year on remedial courses for employees, and other companies have sizable programs, the general estimate of corporate expenditure on remediation in the three Rs is only $300 million.[19] It is a small percentage of the total they spend on training. Businesses have not become teachers of literacy. Even among the largest corporations, with 10,000 or more employees where training opportunities are greatest, only 30 percent sponsor remedial basic instruction.[20] Observers say this too will change as the labor shortage forces companies to hire less able people.

A few corporations deserve honorable mention. Aetna Life & Casualty, the Planters Division of RJR Nabisco, the Pratt &

Whitney Division of United Technologies, and Motorola have long-established, well-respected programs. One of the best known is Polaroid's program to help employees progress through nine levels of literacy from the most basic to the highly advanced. To determine the content of each training segment, Polaroid has employees familiar with a job identify its tasks and the basic skills needed to perform them. Then the company analyzes the reading, writing, and mathematics materials used in each job and decides which skills are to have priority and which employees it will teach first.

Domino's Pizza takes a slightly different tack, but also combines literacy with job training in the process of making pizza dough—a functional context! Taught with interactive videodiscs, the course has led to development of a second course with the Los Angeles Unified School District. The next one will improve English language skills in the context of better customer service.

Mid-South Industries' program is one other example of a collaborative effort spearheaded by a forward-looking company. In 1986, Mid-South opened a highly automated plant in Annville, Kentucky, where three-fourths of all adults were school dropouts. With start-up funding from Kentucky's Bluegrass State Skills Corporation and JTPA, Mid-South brought dozens of residents to a local training center. Day after day at minimum wage for six months, Mid-South's trainers taught the workers basic skills as well as technical aspects of the manufacturing process. Many trainees earned GEDs during this period, and all learned to operate and understand the company's production technologies.[21]

The U.S. business community knows full well that its future depends on able workers and that basic skills as well as English as a second language will have to be taught. Even as many corporate leaders call for school reform and work with school systems, they must recognize that more company training efforts will be needed for new workers entering and for those already employed who lack the basic skills on which to improve performance.

Labor Unions. At the bargaining table, union leaders are increasing demands for basic training and retraining of their employed members as well as for displaced workers. For the unions, self-preservation is at stake. At their insistence, some large corporations are assuming more responsibility. This new union initiative can turn out to be a very big contribution toward training.

The funds created, particularly in heavy industries like automobile manufacturing, are enormous compared with the total annual federal expenditure for adult education in the ABE and ASE programs, and they are well beyond the portion of JTPA assigned to help displaced workers. In 1986, the United Auto Workers' national contract with General Motors generated $250 million; for tuition assistance alone, the fund had $1,500 a year available for each worker. Ford had a similar agreement that totaled $120 million in that same year. The Chrysler education fund produces about $7,200,000 per year. Comparable contracts exist with Navistar (formerly International Harvester), J. I. Case, and others.

Started mainly to aid the displaced, these programs are devoting more attention to upgrading the skills of those employed to prevent dismissal. The UAW-GM program has underwritten construction of human resource centers, mostly in Michigan, which train a substantial proportion of GM's workers. The first courses concentrated on the technologies associated with modern manufacturing processes such as robotics and statistical process control. But in meeting workers' needs, they missed the mark; in fact, they provoked lawsuits from fearful workers humiliated at having to learn new skills.

After a few such failures, the GM and UAW staffs realized that no one had bothered to find out what workers wanted and needed. A needs assessment of 10,000 hourly workers revealed the truth: respondents overwhelmingly mentioned basic skills remediation, and 85 percent said they would pursue it on their own time if necessary. Further analysis of a sample showed that 40 percent of the

10,000 workers were functionally illiterate. Yet fewer than 50 workers a year patronized the plant's remediation center, which had long been open. The employees' term for the center explained why they did not use it: "the dummy room."

The UAW-Ford Employee Development and Training Center operates from handsome new headquarters on the campus of the Henry Ford Community College in Dearborn, Michigan. The facilities are outstanding and very well designed. Moreover, a teleconference room takes live or prerecorded television broadcasts to every Ford facility. Employees have an extraordinarily broad choice open to them in the Life Education Planning Program that introduces the options and helps them assess their needs and goals. Since its inception in 1982, some 22,000 men and women have taken courses in fundamental remedial skills and English as a second language, for the GED certificate, and for computer literacy, and have participated in outside programs. At colleges, their tuition is prepaid and their choice is not restricted to job-related courses. While Dearborn is headquarters, the programs operate at 35 locations around the country. George Valso, associate director at headquarters, says, "We're not going to sit here in Dearborn and tell them in Nashville or Tulsa what they're going to teach."[22] Hence the curriculum is not standardized.

One important aspect of these programs in the automotive industry is the instructional method that teaches in relation to the job. Having learned perhaps from the workers' refusal to go to dummy classes, the curriculum planners at Ford have reading and writing taught using practical material—information on new car models, company reports, or profiles of Ford executives. Math skills are developed by analyzing sales figures or determining how much concrete would be needed to pave a student's driveway. Unintended benefits have appeared: critical thinking, good problem solving, and teamwork have been bonus results.

The International Brotherhood of Electrical Workers and the Communications Workers of America have initiated national training programs with AT&T. Funded at about $7 million annually, the Alliance for Employee Growth and Development serves AT&T union-represented employees in a variety of ways. The Alliance, relying on third parties to provide the training, works with local committees to inform workers about job markets and educational services. State and federal agencies, particularly the Department of Labor, have cooperated. As of September 1988, there were 120 programs for employed AT&T hourly workers, 25 for workers who had been laid off, and 12 that involved "downsizing" situations including both those employed and those unemployed. Further tuition assistance has enabled workers to enroll at more than 125 institutions across the country, most of them community colleges. The best indication of the Alliance's success—attesting to the need it fills—is that both the company and the union have *pledged to agree* on the terms for it in the next contract: it will not become a defeated bargaining issue. That is significant evidence.

On the national level, at AFL-CIO headquarters, the Human Resources Development Institute assists unions whose members have been laid off. Recently the institute has been testing a Comprehensive Competencies Program—a computer-managed literacy system—at four learning centers. And with a grant from the Labor Department, it is exploring how best to teach mathematics, reading, and other basics. The focus is on proven methods and materials for workers needing remediation before they can complete job training or move up career ladders.

A Local Consortium. By banding together to attack member illiteracy, unions in New York City are accomplishing together what would have been impossible alone. Led by Teamsters Local 237, this group includes the International Ladies Garment Workers Union, the United Auto Workers District Council 65 and Local 259, the American Federation of State, County, and Municipal Employees District Council 1707, the Amalgamated Clothing and

Textile Workers, the Health and Hospital Workers Union District Council 1199, and the Hotel and Restaurant Trade Council. Altogether they represent 300,000 workers in predominantly entry-level industrial and service jobs.

The consortium estimates that one-half of its members are illiterate in English and another 300,000 of their spouses and children are also sadly lacking in skills. The program began in 1985 with grants from state and city agencies, and one year later more than 7,500 had enrolled. Committed to aiding workers before jobs are lost, the consortium is trying to combine the best elements of effective programs:

- The curricula are built around the occupational needs and lifestyles of union members;

- The teachers selected are sensitive to the struggles of adult students and their need for dignity;

- Cooperation with the City University provides faculty and technical assistance;

- The class sites are union halls, factories, housing projects, and churches chosen for convenience and psychological comfort;

- Flexible hours—before, between, and after shifts, and on weekends—are the norm.

That list comprises most of the important ingredients for success in teaching basic skills to adults. The consortium has not neglected research toward better methods to reach more people: an experiment at one site uses an interactive videodisc system designed by the Army to see whether it can improve instruction.

Through union initiatives with employers and in cooperation with government agencies and educational institutions, many thousands of workers are given opportunities that otherwise would not exist. But the opportunities are far from equal in their distribution and quality. Millions more have no access to learning the basic skills and the necessary facility with language.

Volunteers. Volunteer tutors are foot soldiers on the long front lines of the battle against illiteracy. They truly represent private initiative individually expressed. Forming human service groups under the nonprofit auspices of churches, civic clubs, and community organizations, volunteers have long exemplified an admirable American trait, whether it is to give help in a crisis or to teach newcomers the English language. Fortunately they are among us today and as active as ever. But their contribution cannot go far in reaching the millions of people in need.

The greatest number of volunteers are rather loosely organized by local literacy councils affiliated with one of two national associations, Literacy Volunteers of America (LVA) and Laubach Literacy Action. Their structures are similar and, in fact, LVA grew out of the Laubach program, which was the American child of a worldwide organization founded in 1955 by Frank C. Laubach, a Protestant missionary who had developed a simple method of teaching basic literacy and used volunteers to spread his concept of "each one teach one."

Laubach's group is larger, reaching 100,000 adults a year, with a $5.5 million budget that is mostly financed by the sales of its publications—teaching materials, videocassettes, and special books on subjects like first aid, child care, filling out forms, government, and nutrition—all intended to be relevant to students' lives. One called *Pat King's Family* tells about a young wife whose husband leaves her and their two small children. It deals "realistically with everyday problems such as finding a job, budgeting, making friends and dealing with personal problems and feelings."

The curriculum is apparently more standardized with its own materials than that of the Literacy Volunteers of America, although the LVA also depends on sales of its publications. Stressing the individual approach, their tutors use newspapers, cookbooks, driver's manuals—whatever appeals to a particular student. As the smaller organization serving 30,000 students on an annual budget of $1 million, LVA often collaborates with the government's adult basic education program, as well as libraries, prisons, and various agencies.

The tutors are usually well-educated, middle-aged, white females.[23] But there are many exceptions. A project for New York City's homeless counts two of the homeless among its tutors; one of them got his LVA teaching certificate while in prison.[24] Their preparation consists of 18 hours in workshop training and required practice teaching (which can sometimes earn college credit). Although instructional materials vary, the tutors are committed to a "whole language" approach to reading that helps students look for clues in the total context in order to comprehend more broadly instead of concentrating on a narrowly defined reading skill.

Success in these programs must be measured in personal gains, not statistics. One of the most spectacular successes is that of Lauralyn Smith, an illiterate mother of three children, who went for help when she was 30 years old. She herself became a tutor and so inspired her youngest son that he was reading at college level when he was in fifth grade. Then, using an older son's computer, she developed a program based on Laubach's reading texts that is now used at the Adult Education Center in Brainerd, Minnesota. Thirteen years after her first lesson, Lauralyn Smith became coordinator of the Minnesota Literacy Project.

Literacy associations as well as many other volunteer groups have seen remarkable growth both in the ranks of tutors and students in the last few years. The national awareness campaigns and the well-publicized concern of Barbara Bush have shown results in the numbers involved. But volunteer efforts are beset by organizational and financial problems. Many have part-time coordinators on local levels, and they are responsible for raising their own funds. Not many states have emulated South Carolina in taking action. Recognizing that illiteracy underlies many problems, South Carolina organized local literacy councils into a state organization that helps with fund-raising and management, publicity, and coordination with other state agencies and programs.[25]

A Study in Failure

Despite all the human energy contributed by volunteers and the efforts on the part of companies and labor unions to build more collaborative programs with government and educational institutions, the literacy battlefront seems like a quicksand where funds, effort, and people often disappear without a trace. Some learn to read; but more illiterates appear. According to imprecise figures, four million people are being helped each year. But we know that in the Adult Basic and Secondary Education programs, for example, adults are counted on entrance and attendance—not completion—and dropout rates range from one-third to well over half. Statistics generally are unreliable, if they are collected at all. And the problems of definition further complicate the counting. It is a public-policy quagmire for government, a training nightmare for businesses and schools, and a confusing issue for the general public. It should come as no surprise that literacy efforts are largely studies in failure.

We have described the main programs of the federal government and found them wanting; moreover, the new initiatives coming from Congress are fragmented, spread among an array of departments, and too meager to be of real value. Our findings support the conclusions of others concerning federal programs, including William Pierce, formerly with the Hudson Institute:

> These efforts are inconsistent in purpose, utilize different definitions of adult, recognize different age groups, limit the funds to specific target populations, authorize different purposes for which funds may be spent, and do not have uniform data gathering or accountability measures. In short, they represent a fragmented group of mismatched programs, which taken together define this country's policy on adult literacy.[26]

The result is that, while Congress dutifully continues to appropriate funds—with small increases—for the fight against illiteracy, the programs frequently fail to accomplish what was intended.

Higher marks go to the states for efforts to combine and relate programs, to raise additional monies, and so serve more adequately their citizens' basic needs. But the map is spotty: a few states stand out with more enlightened programs and greater resources, while many are mired in ineffectual efforts. The new federalism does not serve all people equally in basic opportunities to learn.

Among private sector initiatives, the role of labor unions is notable for developing cooperative arrangements with large national industries for training and also in forming consortia with others to help in local communities. Corporate leaders are loud and clear in calling attention to the problems of finding workers with adequate skills, but their efforts thus far are directed more toward school reforms than to teaching literacy in their own companies. As noted, less than one-third of the largest corporations, where one finds the most extensive training programs, give remedial instruction.

Our current efforts on the whole are insufficient to the size of the task. And the changing concept of what constitutes *functional* literacy or basic skills for the work force will only increase the challenge. The lowest acceptable level keeps rising, so the need will be constantly ahead of us. We must reach more people through more effective means.

To do this we must first ask, again with insistence, for analysis of instruction methods used for the target populations. The most effective methods should be widely publicized. Newspapers can describe the better methods, not merely give headlines calling attention to the problem. Certain facts are already established: adults learn literacy and other basic skills most effectively in connection with their jobs or in a functional context, and they retain the abilities if they are put to use. The lesson has been learned in many studies.[27]

The military showed it decisively in what was probably the largest research effort ever on overcoming adult illiteracy. In 1966, in an unusual sort of battle, the armed forces joined the War on

Poverty with Project 100,000. Large numbers of marginally literate youths who would have otherwise failed entrance screening were taken into the military. In testing various methods, the Pentagon found that the best results came from instruction in the basic skills combined with technical training for the military jobs to which they were assigned. Thousands of other low-literate soldiers were given intensive instruction in the three Rs—outside the job context—and there was little, if any, effect on their long-term performance.[28]

It is also clear that adults must be taught *as adults* in suitable surroundings, not as older children in the schoolroom. Instructional materials must be at the appropriate level. The armed services abandoned *Dick and Jane* a long time ago and have produced their own *Sailor Sam* and *Private Pete*. More recently, under pressure from Congress and the General Accounting Office to standardize the approach to teaching basic skills, the Army developed JSEP, the Job Skills Education Program, which tests soldiers in basic competencies needed for the most common jobs. And it provides remediation in those skills in which a soldier is deficient.

All tests and most of the tutorials are delivered by computer, although some lessons are paper-and-pencil exercises. The computer tracks the progress of individual soldiers through the program and produces cumulative data on all users. JSEP is not intended to teach an illiterate person to read and write. Nor does it provide job training. But it will, for example, usually improve the reading and mathematical skills needed to use a tank repair manual.

Although evaluations of JSEP thus far are inconclusive (and the Army has not greatly expanded it), an adapted version, "de-greened" for civilian use, is being tested at a technical school in White Plains, New York. The military does offer useful lessons and materials that were, after all, paid for by taxpayers' money. In this instance, the use of the computer is of special importance: technologies must be used to instruct larger numbers of people.

But the costs are still high and programs remain to be developed and fully tested.

Besides the elementary need to examine and extend instructional methods, the attack on illiteracy requires more support from higher education, which has been weak in research and in the preparation of teachers for adult education, particularly in basic skills. There are not many higher institutions that offer training for educators of adults, whether as teachers or administrators.[29] And at those that do, the status of such programs is low. As a result, there is little professionalism apparent in the efforts to create a more literate population.

More vital even than the missing professionals to help guide our efforts is the absence of national leadership. To treat this debilitating ailment in our society, we must turn to the federal government for policies and programs of sufficient scope and magnitude. To fulfill its responsibility the government will need to examine the splintered legislation and reconsider the divisive pattern of allocation to various departments. Vision and consistency are needed to give focus and guidance so that private sector initiatives can also be more effective.

The imperative need to equip the work force in this time of peace is not unlike the military's effort to remain prepared. We must not lose our economic position because of inadequately trained workers and the costly loss of those unable to enter the labor force. America must prepare its adults to make their contribution for the sake of their own lives and for the well-being of the nation.

At present, there is more concern than concerted activity, more awareness than action. As illuminating as a thousand points or a million points of lights can be—and they are testimony to our caring—volunteers cannot be the sole answer to this basic national problem. Nor can other private sectors carry the burden alone. Too many persons will still be missing.

8

EDUCATING WORKERS:
ISSUES AND ACTION

Compared with the disarray on the literacy and basic skills front, the general training programs under employers' auspices give the illusion of being a tidy system, albeit in disparate parts and in need of remediation itself. At least it is a fast developing complex of networks for adult training being built on new alliances and expansion in the learning industry. The networks are further supported by telecommunication that encourages the sharing of instruction, which will also grow as the commonalities of learning materials become more apparent—especially in the classrooms of cost-conscious providers.

Clearly, adults are creating the biggest educational sector in the country and, spurred by economic necessity, their numbers entering classrooms in corporations, in military posts, union halls, government buildings, and on college campuses can only multiply. Delivery systems will take the teacher to the worker and intelligent tutors will assist. Even more significant, the people participating in this educational revolution range from skilled workers to top executives. It requires learning for all of us. In this final section, we examine some of the issues involved, propose possible action, and discuss the priorities that must be set.

New Alliances

Until fairly recently the major providers have largely chosen to go it alone. Now, however, the same competitive forces that are driving the increasing need for training are driving the formation of alliances and other new ways to provide it. Bruno Lamborghini, economics director of Olivetti Corporation, sums up the change in attitude toward adult education and training this way: "A company's competitive situation no longer depends on itself alone but on the quality of the alliances it's able to form."[1]

Partnership and collaboration are words used often in this report. At all levels of training for workers in many types of jobs, more cooperative programs are being put in place. Some that have been going on for years are institutionalized and have fairly well-set patterns. But many, in fact most, of those we have described are new alliances, either improvising with the uncertain, experimental steps of ad hoc partners or dancing with controlled steps in a carefully designed choreography.

Labor and Management. One of the most carefully designed alliances is the rather unusual partnership of labor and management. Although a few unions have had collaborative arrangements with employers' associations for a long time, the training programs negotiated by the United Auto Workers and the Big Three auto companies are of a different nature and larger scope. Nervousness on the part of such old rivals may be reflected in the constant, excessive use of "jointness" to emphasize the notion that neither partner dominates. In a GM-UAW training facility there is a 22-acre "jointness" park, a 13-room joint-education wing, a joint-communications network with 44 television monitors throughout the plant, a joint newsletter and many "joint-employee involvement groups."[2] It is a new relationship being built from foundations of antagonism and hostility, from attitudes of "them versus us."

Small wonder that protective phrases are inserted; that it is happening is a greater miracle.

Such partnerships require teamwork that depends on mutual trust. It means that workers as well as managers have had to adjust attitudes and correct long-held biases. Workers have traditionally been loyal to the union rather than the company, which is now cast in a more cooperative role, more the benefactor, although unions are paying their full share for the training programs.

The issues raised challenge the leadership of the labor movement to adapt to the changing times. They need to move ahead and champion the workers' rights to education and training in order to preserve jobs or to aid workers in reentering the work force. Along this route they will fulfill the legacy of a great figure in their history, Walter Reuther, who said his goal in getting higher wages for the auto workers was to extend the opportunities for educational benefits to them and their families.

Furthermore, as the new worker plays a more participatory role and assumes additional tasks, it will be harder than ever to classify positions according to old job titles. The flexibility inherent in new production processes invades labor's ranks and organizational structure just as it is causing wrenching change in the corporate structure and in the roles of managers. Hierarchy is giving way to more horizontal patterns that spread responsibility.

Academe and Its Partners. Colleges and universities have also formed uncertain, often uneasy relationships with very diverse partners: large and small companies, the military, and government agencies. Two-year institutions, however, have forged ahead in new alliances that are congenial to the purpose of serving their communities. Although faculty who prefer the straight academic path feel discomfort, their opinions have not hampered the general movement toward more work-related training for adults. The community colleges are willing to conduct courses on campus for corporate partners and design courses for delivery at the work site. The partnerships of companies and community colleges seem to be encountering fewer problems of turf and distrust than some other cooperative efforts.

From the universities, business schools and engineering departments have entered into expanding alliances with corporations, each in its own fashion. Medical and law schools are increasing connections to provide updated knowledge to practicing members of their professions. Individual faculty members go out as consultants or teach in the classrooms of corporations, government, and the military. In similar ways, university scientists have undertaken collaborative research with corporate laboratories. Thus their loyalties are divided in serving two or more masters. To an extent, some university walls have come tumbling down. Their organizational structure too is affected.

Certainly society wants and needs the new alliances, but they raise troublesome questions in academic halls. Faculties become split over the issues involved, and administrators have to find alternate ways to manage institutions that are no longer as cohesive as they once were. Colleges hold on to the old habits and regimen of calendar and schedule while at the same time they try to get around them with off-campus programs or courses scheduled at night and on weekends, or with short summer sessions to attract the older adults they court to fill empty classroom seats.

Financial needs promote adjustments, and more higher institutions are eagerly soliciting contracts with outsiders. They offer quick-turnaround, customized courses to fit the audience, on site or on campus, scheduled at the customer's convenience, and often bearing academic credit. In efforts to find new clients and new partners, they too have joined the vendor market in the learning business, but not without considerable stress. Some faculty fear a corporate takeover, if not dictatorship. At issue is the question of who determines the subject matter. This is the essence of academic freedom.

Rather than tack on programs like odds and ends for sale, universities must analyze the purposes of their various programs and consider reorganization to fit functions. In a way, it would simply be an extension of the professional school pattern already operating for business, law, and medicine. Special units with designated faculties could offer instruction in various fields and at various levels needed by adults in the work force or in transition to new jobs. Along with a fresh look at programs, institutions might start with a fresh calendar and also remember that few plants are filled to capacity year-round. As educational centers for society, higher institutions could be more effective and extend their services.

Companies Collaborate. The partnerships appearing among corporations for training purposes present a phenomenon that was hardly predicted and yet could have been partially foreseen as an outgrowth of courses for customers. In effect, large high-tech companies have been forced to teach their clients about the new technologies delivered to them. Customers have to learn to operate the equipment and use it for optimum results. Now businesses are expanding such training to attract new customers. So Digital Equipment Corporation teaches computer courses at the Aetna Institute for their employees and others in the greater Hartford area: two leviathans joined in an alliance for education. Similarly, the big accounting firms have entered the training business to instruct their clients.

Thus corporate campuses grow and flourish. The public is invited, and enrollment makes training a profitable business. In this case, no mission is threatened, no autonomy involved. Training is given strictly on a pay-as-you-go basis. Corporations are simply entering a new business and doing it very effectively indeed. Their entrance into the training market means that a formidable and potentially huge new presence is there.

In other collaborative efforts, corporations are joining each other not directly for economic profit, but to provide advanced technological training particularly for their engineers and computer scientists. We observed the development of the National Technological University for this purpose. Started by many large high-tech companies and the federal government in cooperation with engineering schools at major research universities, it is an outstanding example. Television with satellite delivery takes the professor in his or her classroom to employees at the workplace. This cooperative program does not entail crucial adjustments for the parties concerned; each and all reap the benefits. Admittedly, there has been some grumbling in the universities providing the faculties because their own degrees are not awarded. Instead, it is the National Technological University degree that supersedes as it combines teaching from many different campuses.

Hundreds of companies, as well as individuals from other sectors, have joined in the symposia on artificial intelligence sponsored by Texas Instruments. Many special programs on timely subjects and advanced topics are available, particularly for the scientific and technological communities representing many corporations. Some companies have started programs to serve their employees and found it expedient to invite other companies to join, as in the case of Hewlett-Packard's programs developed with Stanford and California State University at Chico. Through such delivery systems, cooperative efforts flourish and grow. Although these networks usually start out with the technical fields that lend themselves to such delivery, we can anticipate their extension to include many other subjects for different purposes.

Networks Foster Sharing. The various delivery systems described in this report inevitably combine new partners as they link campuses or tie them to companies and government agencies whose employees take the courses. Telecommunication is collaborative, a powerful force bringing people together mentally, though they are physically separated.

Our states are crisscrossed with telecommunication networks, many carrying education and training. And of course there is no technological reason why they should stop at state borders. If Virginia has quality engineering courses on its learning network and the University of Maryland also offers courses in that field, can they not all be made available for a larger audience?

In fact, a worldwide catalog of courses for adults is technically possible and within our means. Teaching by television via satellite delivery may not be the most effective method for learning certain subjects, as has been explained, but it is a practical way to extend the teacher's wisdom to an unlimited audience and incidentally upgrade the teacher's productivity. Surely there can be no objection to sharing knowledge.

Massive networks encircling the globe are developing under corporate aegis. General Electric is building an international telecommunications system that will permit its employees "to communicate worldwide, using voice, video, and computer data, by simply dialing seven digits on a telephone." GE workers in Cincinnati will be able to talk face-to-face with colleagues in France about designs and projects. Combining facilities of AT&T, British Telecom Ltd., and France Telecom Inc., the first stage of the network is in place for Western Europe, Canada, and the United States. By the early 1990s, it will extend to the Far East, Australia, the Middle East, and South America. Assertedly it will be among the largest private systems in the world.[3]

While the original purpose of these networks is for mundane business transactions, companies are realizing their value for training. Some corporations, like IBM, have separate networks for the educational function. The prediction of about 140 such corporate-owned satellite networks by 1992 seems very modest indeed against the current growth rate. Their contribution to helping train workers could be immeasurably valuable.

The Learning Process and Methods

Lest we hail the anticipated extension of delivery systems too heartily in our desire to reach more workers, we must recall the cautionary notes sounded concerning the fit of the instructional method with the purpose of the training. To take the teacher alone—a talking head—on television throughout the world by satellite can mean dooming the instruction to failure. This approach presupposes a passive learner, uniform instruction for all, and a teacher with extraordinary charisma in holding the audience.

But when interactive devices are added and various media combined, the instruction can be exceedingly effective for different learning goals. Some technological aids make it possible for people to learn truly at their own pace, some give learners complete independence, many free them from the tyranny of time and place; others provide direct interaction—without faculty office hours—between the student and the teacher guiding the process.

The Microcomputer. The basic tool in many instances is the microcomputer, whose teaching powers are proving to be formidable. Computer-assisted instruction has produced learning results at least as effective as the usual classroom teaching and, in many cases, it has performed its task remarkably better.

Experiments at Dartmouth with software developed by Apple indicate that the programming can go far beyond the old right-wrong answer approach. According to a professor in the medical school, it functions "in a way similar to the human mind. It has the ability to let the user make all kinds of leaps and jumps and connect things by association." It appears to correct the rigidity of some earlier systems that made it difficult for a student to learn through exploration. According to some Dartmouth professors, the system is easy to use and program; it is modest in cost and readily adjustable with updated material.[4]

In addition to extensive application in science classes, this program offers drills for a course in the Chinese language: the Macintosh computer speaks aloud in Chinese, "pronouncing the character displayed on the screen in a clear, digitally recorded but not unfriendly voice." At the same time, the screen shows the correct order of a character's brush strokes.[5] Yet another application of the program guides the student through a collection of paintings in the National Gallery of Art. Its uses may be limited only by our imagination.

On college campuses across the land, microcomputers are finding their niche in learning and in creating laboratory and library networks worldwide. They can enhance the learning process for those preparing for the work force; they can help establish the solid educational foundation necessary for adults to go on learning. The ubiquitous computer is in many homes, and there are more in offices and at workstations. It is a short step from the facts and information they now carry to materials designed to teach.

Applications of Research. Intelligent aids, particularly expert systems, can now carry instruction when and as the worker needs it. A powerful type of on-the-job training, they create a new concept of apprenticeship for this decade. Like an intelligent tutor or smart assistant, such systems can provide experts' knowledge in troubleshooting or solving a problem and so help to ensure quality performance and hence productivity. Trainers in industry and the military are using intelligent computer-assisted instruction, as in the Navy's STEAMER or Honeywell's MENTOR, with good results.

Research into the learning process and experiments that apply the findings in instructional methods and materials are two areas where extensive collaboration is of paramount importance. Every sponsor of adult training should offer assistance. Trainers can serve as research participants, trying instructional experiments and reporting on the results. Teachers especially are needed in cooperative teams with scientists. In the effort to construct models of human learning patterns, teachers' contributions are essential. Their knowledge is crucial to the quality of the content to be conveyed. Moreover, they are needed *today*, not later as inheritors of the results.

Of course, learning will go on, as it always has, but it must be hastened and improved through all means at our disposal. It must be made more widely available if we are to improve the quality and productivity of the work force in America. Time is not on our side, but technological methods of teaching combined with delivery systems can take us more quickly toward the goal.

As we welcome new instructional methods and recognize their value in adjusting to individual learning styles, we must still insist that the content conveyed includes the foundation for further learning. We dare not neglect the fundamental knowledge on which specialized functions ultimately rest. Our dependence on technical aids can lessen the need to know what the process really is. The simplest example is the little hand-held calculator that performs basic functions for the student. Will the student's brain and memory be exercised to learn and understand the process?

For the more complicated functions performed today in the workplace, it is essential that the fundamentals be understood. These take time to teach and learn. Without them we are in danger of becoming robots, mindlessly performing our tasks. Without the basic knowledge we cannot adjust to the changing circumstances in our jobs and lives. The issue involves the long-range development of human potential (resources or human capital). It cannot be accomplished by fast, narrowly gauged training for quick profitability. The quick fix is our greatest liability. This approach endangers the very basis of our competitive position as a nation.

The Curriculum and Students

Course materials are overwhelmingly generic in nature for the different categories of workers. Whether for the construction trades, office work, information systems, or automated processes in manufacturing, each learning program has its core curriculum—what it is necessary to know and be able to do. Managerial training has marked similarities over all fields at many levels of responsibility. For updating professionals, it is simply current information that is required for each profession.

Catalogues and databases on training from all the providers carry many courses with nearly identical titles and descriptions: computer programming languages, data processing and analysis, inventory controls, general technical maintenance and trouble-shooting, computer-assisted design, processes for problem solving and decision making, negotiating skills, effective listening, conducting a meeting, and making a presentation. None is specific to an industry, a government agency, or a company. They can easily and appropriately go across provider lines to classrooms and individuals.

Share Courses. Learning materials are, of course, not the property of schools, colleges, and universities. And they are seldom proprietary for corporations or even the military, except where a particular process or instrument offers a competitive advantage or where the orientation program to a military service or a company instills its own unique practices and attitudes. For most jobs, however, the training has common features, so that any trainer or human resource development officer would learn a lot from an examination of what is being taught elsewhere and how it is done. Corporate trainers may have some knowledge of what other corporations are teaching technicians or managers, but they are not sufficiently familiar with similar courses taught by the military or civilian government agencies.

Comparative analysis could help sort out redundancy and waste, and informed selection could further improve the quality of instruction given. Even within the boundaries of one provider, the analysis would be valuable. We observed, for example, duplication of a computer programming course in the federal government's curriculum. Moreover, the Office of Personnel Management or the agencies involved might profit from a comparison of the several institutes for executives. Each may be necessary for special purposes, but the overhead expenses of separate campuses and facilities and overlapping general management courses are an extravagance in an era of enormous deficits. Each may be operating at full capacity on a 12-month basis, but if so, the question arises whether another delivery mechanism could provide basic courses and extend opportunities to more government personnel not presently served. Similar questions can be asked of any one of the major providers.

Training Needs. Among the challenging issues before us is how to *project* training needs to be ready for the next change and how to assist workers in learning new fields and gaining advanced knowledge. More than simply performing today's task, it is anticipating and preparing for tomorrow's. The company that leads will employ education as a strategic tool to achieve its goals.

If we consider the fact that most people who will be working in 2001 are now in the labor force, we can recognize that retraining needs far surpass other demands. All workers, including managers and professionals, face the necessity of learning new materials and new skills. All equally require multiple skills, not only those people in the trades or the skilled technicians who must add another string to their bow. Managers are challenged by technological processes and international conditions that were not taught in their business schools. For technical specialists assuming managerial positions, the complementary challenge is to learn more general skills. In government agencies, for example, specialists becoming supervisors require training in managing personnel, in the organization and assignment of work, and in financial aspects of the job. Comparably in the military, officers managing business contracts worth billions of dollars could profit from training to handle such responsibilities. This type of training obviously can be given on an interservice basis and perhaps by using corporate curricula.

Professional, highly specialized personnel find their specialties are fast becoming obsolete or that they require an infusion of new information. The plight of the engineer and other scientists is well known. For other professions, the demands of certification and licensing are driving further learning. These individuals should take responsibility for their own updating, and there seem to be ample opportunities developing for them through their professional associations and universities.

Closely related is the challenge of changing curricula to fit the changing times. Many instructors report that organizing materials in modules makes it simpler to substitute or update blocks of information. Others point out that the process is aided greatly if the learning occurs through computer conferencing in which an expert or teacher on line can insert new material and correct outdated information. Learning materials too are a moving target; they too must be adjusted for the rising levels of technological literacy and the new skills required. A fourth "R" has joined the basics of reading, writing, and arithmetic: readiness for change.

Resistance to changing curricula is an occupational hazard among university faculty members who feel a vested interest in their expertise. They want their turf preserved as it is. Moreover, if changes involve drastic curricular reform, committees will deliberate at length. For whatever reasons, higher education is not noted for speedy adjustment on curricular matters.

This condition, however, does not pertain to other providers of adult learning, who can hire teachers and trainers to fit course needs. Indeed, the entire learning industry, with the exception of universities and colleges, is free of such encumbrances and can introduce new materials as rapidly as possible. In fact their competitive position depends on their initiative and flexibility. The business of learning that is growing exponentially outside colleges and universities is free and eager to meet work force demands.

Expanding Markets for Learning

A review of the adult education market suggests that "vendors" should be considered another major provider along with the traditional sectors of corporations, government and the military, labor unions, and higher education. But since colleges and universities and corporations have entered the vendor market, it becomes more difficult to define. It can no longer be dismissed as a disorganized group of "third parties" seeking their fortunes.

Large high-tech corporations have big marketing departments and divisions to sell "educational services" outside the company. For many it is a new arm of the business, developing as a profitable venture. In other cases, acquisitions and mergers are making large companies larger. The National Education Corporation merged with Spectrum Interactive (performance-based training systems) and then integrated it with another subsidiary, Applied Learning International, that concentrates on *Fortune* "500" companies. Together they comprise the world's largest provider of training. In addition there are 53 National Education Centers offering allied health, electronics, computer skills, and business programs, and their International Correspondence Schools enroll more than 250,000 active students. Through their publishing subsidiary, Steck-Vaughn, training materials are also produced for adult basic education, literacy, and English as a second language.[6]

Powerful entities have joined the small entrepreneurs and consultants who plan and provide for training needs. The expertise assembled with the added resources of large companies suggests that instructional materials and technological media have reached a new level in the marketplace. Education has been a salable item since the nineteenth-century "chain schools" for business and accounting attended by some of our more illustrious corporate ancestors. Profit neither negates nor guarantees excellence, whether it is earned by an entrepreneur, a big company, or a college or university producing customized courses for workers. In a capsule, when AT&T, IBM, Digital Equipment, Bell South and Bell Atlantic, J.C. Penney, Computerland, General Motors, the Big Six accounting firms, McGraw-Hill, and many others started selling information for learning, the ball game made the World Series.

Opportunities: A Skewed Curve

With all the learning available and more that is possible, opportunities are not distributed equitably, or even smartly in our own self-interest as a nation. The curve of adult learning opportunities is skewed in favor of those with the most education. Many in the work force who need the training most, to prevent being laid off, are not receiving it. Although signs of increased attention to production workers are reported, they are a long way from getting the necessary training. Similarly, office and clerical personnel may be learning to use the new machines, but generally they too have a low position on the training scale. Health workers and people in services like retailing are also low on the list.

Many more—those not in the work force—have poor chances of getting there. Above all others, those coming from minority backgrounds, who will be a larger part of the work force in the years ahead, are not getting the preparation needed or chances for training in the low-level positions that many hold. For these young adults, the community colleges, technical and vocational institutes are doing the best job. But, as we mentioned earlier, inordinate numbers of people from Hispanic and African-American origins are converging on the two-year institutions that are the main route open to them for further education. If the proportion transferring to higher institutions does not grow, segments of our population may be concentrated in jobs that offer little opportunity. While the two-plus-two plans to encourage young people to continue in vocational training from the last years of high school through the first two postsecondary years are helpful, a similar plan is urgently needed on a broad scale at the upper end to help transfers go on to four-year institutions.

Federal and State Policies.   Such issues fall squarely in the domain of public policy, both state and federal. The two-plus-two plan, known as "tech-prep," has reached the initial stage of legislation in the reauthorization of the Carl D. Perkins Vocational Education

Act. Besides this constructive detail, the total act proposed is quite remarkable: it is a major rewrite of the older program, it recognizes and addresses the criticism coming from many quarters, and it reflects the winds of change. Even the short title of the bill incorporates the changing view, "Applied Technology Education Amendments of 1989," and the statement of purpose is:

> To make the United States more competitive in the world economy by developing more fully the academic and occupational skills of all segments of the population. This purpose will principally be achieved through concentrating resources on improving educational programs leading to academic, occupational, training, and retraining skill competencies needed to work in a technologically advanced society.[7]

The bill, sponsored by Augustus F. Hawkins and William F. Goodling, and passed by the House of Representatives in May 1989 and by the Senate a year later, constitutes a big step in the right direction. It awaits final passage. Coordination is the prominent theme in the new design, which relates five federal programs: applied technology education, the Job Training Partnership Act, adult education, vocational rehabilitation, and the Wagner-Peyser Act. On the state level, a State Human Investment Council replaces the former advisory or coordinating councils for the separate programs. Funding may be coordinated and designated for problem areas in the particular state. Set-asides are removed, in large part, to permit cooperative programs and eliminate excessive paperwork in reporting. Replacing set-asides is a percentage formula weighted to drive each state's funds toward its neediest citizens. The proposed legislation is sensible, and its concepts are heartening to anyone concerned with adult learning in our country.

The Job Training Partnership Act (JTPA) is also undergoing reexamination so it will fit the coordinated design of the Perkins amendments. But JTPA needs more than increased services to the most severely disadvantaged youth and extension of summer programs to year-long efforts. It needs more than an infusion of literacy training and remedial work for basic skills. Its funding scheme that rewards quick job placement needs overhaul. Critics from all sides comment on "the skimming of the cream" that results in jobs for the most able, leaving the mass of unemployed with little assistance.

Moreover, in emphasizing youth needs, we must not overlook the growing numbers of dislocated workers who already get short shrift in the current program. It is well to remember that JTPA is our government's primary program for job training. The total funds appropriated for fiscal 1990 are less than $4 billion. And the total request for the recast Applied Technology Education Program is $1.4 billion.

Funding for other adult programs is also meager, especially when compared with defense expenditures and the total federal budget. One can only question the values that influence priorities—particularly so in this case where it is obvious that investment in training to get people into the work force means a return of many dollars from welfare and unemployment payments. While the government recognizes the merit of training by permitting a tax write-off for many billions of dollars of training by corporations, the $5 billion budget of the federal government for adult job training in the two major programs is a small contribution, considering the magnitude of the task and its importance to the nation. And still the smaller companies, where most people are employed, have little underwritten support.

Federal Coordination. Remarkable as the thrust may be in the effort to coordinate federal programs within the states, there remains an Achilles' heel in Washington, D.C. The Perkins amendments seek to coordinate federal programs by creating yet one more interdepartmental task force, this one to include the secretaries of the departments that administer one or another of the different programs—education, labor, and health and human services.

Noble as the notion is, the chances of successful coordination are slim. Witness similar interdepartmental committees tried before. The indubitable fact is that each department has its entrenched bureaucracies, staffed and in place to operate their programs. Coordination is difficult enough in one large department, let alone among three.

Therefore, we suggest assigning responsibility for the development and administration of training for the work force to the Department of Labor. It is a major part of the Department's purpose. The largest program, JTPA, is already located here. The Labor Department has the statistical base for the labor force. It houses extensive knowledge about training programs and commissions studies like the large one done recently by the American Society for Training and Development. It can work closely with the Office of Technology Assessment, which has issued many helpful reports concerning industry, technology, and employment.

Vocational education could be reassigned, as well as basic literacy programs for adults. These have been housed in the Department of Education, whose primary concern is and should be for the public schools. Adult programs have at best been a languishing poor relation to those for elementary and secondary school children. Adult basic education has not only often taken a second seat to public school programs, it has also been heavily influenced by their goals and methods, which are apt to be ineffective when applied to the much different needs of illiterate adults.

Moving these programs to the Department of Labor would require a fresh look by relating them to the working lives of adults. The Department of Education might welcome the transfer that would allow it to focus on badly needed reform of the public school system. Moreover, assignment to one department would facilitate the coordinating role of state human investment councils by reducing the accounting burden from several sites to one location in Washington.

The Secretary of Labor has a substantial discretionary grant program designed to support multistate efforts, research and demonstration projects, evaluation, and technical assistance. Under the rubric of evaluation, the secretary could expand advisory relationships with corporate leaders to include training experts from all the major providers. Such a group might sponsor the comparative curricular analysis recommended so that each could see how their colleagues in another setting are training particular types of workers—both in content and method. The similarities of learning materials would become apparent as well as the effectiveness of some technologies for teaching.

On the broader scene, the challenge is to coordinate efforts and provide adult training opportunities on a more equitable and systematic basis, drawing on both public and private resources. Assignment of the task to one department that is already deeply engaged and concerned about it could help. This is certainly not the time for departmental turf battles. It is a time to place authority clearly in one department and hold it responsible for producing the desired results.

Shifting adult education and training to the Labor Department would fit nicely with the combined concerns of Congressional committees: the Education and Labor Committee of the House, and the Senate's Labor and Human Resources Committee. The task before the nation is formidable and requires the enlightened leadership of our government. In many quarters we hear great concern expressed, but what we need is better solutions. Not all the scientific prowess the United States can muster will advance its competitive position without an informed and contributing work force. Speeding up the process of technology transfer from research laboratories to factory floors merely accelerates the rate of change and challenges workers' abilities more. Without additional training, we cannot effectively cope with the pace of discovery.

In the Higher Education Act of 1972, Congress stated: "The American people need lifelong learning to enable them to adjust to social, technological, political, and economic changes." No program or funds accompanied the declaration. As of today, 18 years later, no significant action has been taken toward this goal. One wonders where the United States would stand in the competitive race if the work force had received opportunities for upgrading skills to meet technological needs.

Education must be recognized as a capital investment in which initial costs are amortized over time. This is the accepted theory when we invest in a college education almost guaranteed to boost earning power, and the theory holds for continuing education that requires periodic investments to counter its depreciation. In the end, this nation must make a deep commitment to learning for a lifetime. Our response to the needs of all workers will in large measure determine America's productivity and shape profoundly the position of the nation in an increasingly competitive, interdependent world.

NOTES

PROLOGUE: *The Challenge of Change*

1. Daniel Yankelovich et al., *The World at Work* (New York: Octagon Books, 1985), p. xii. The phrase, taken from the authors' text, is quoted by Cyrus Vance in his Foreword.
2. *Stanford* magazine, December 1989, p. 27.
3. Shoshana Zuboff, *In the Age of the Smart Machine: The Future of Work and Power* (New York: Basic Books, 1988), pp. 9–10.
4. Daniel Yankelovich, "Trends in Our Changing Society: What They Mean for Labor and Higher Education," *Proceedings of the National Meeting of the Labor/Higher Education Council*, sponsored by the American Council on Education and the AFL-CIO, Houston, Tex., September 19–20, 1985, pp. 8–12. See also Daniel Yankelovich, *The World at Work.*
5. Peter T. Kilborn, "Milwaukee Helps Pace U.S. as Innovator for Workplace," *New York Times*, October 12, 1989, pp. A1 and D25.
6. William B. Johnston, *Workforce 2000: Work and Workers for the 21st Century* (Indianapolis, Ind.: Hudson Institute, 1987), pp. 75–76.
7. Ibid., p. 97.
8. *The Forgotten Half: Pathways to Success for America's Youth and Young Families*, final report of Youth and America's Future: The William T. Grant Foundation Commission on Work, Family and Citizenship (Washington, D.C.: 1988).

1. *Classrooms for Adults*

1. Nell P. Eurich, *Corporate Classrooms* (Princeton, N.J.: Carnegie Foundation for the Advancement of Teaching, 1985).
2. Thomas J. Chmura, Douglas C. Henton, and John G. Melville, *Corporate Education and Training*, SRI International, Report No. 753. Fall 1987, p. 2.
3. Anthony P. Carnevale, "The Learning Enterprise," *Training & Development Journal*, February 1989, p. 27. Data came from many sources, including the 1987 U.S. Census Bureau survey of participation in adult education.

4. Joseph Oberle, "Industry Report 1989," *Training*, October 1989, p. 32.
5. Carnevale, "Learning Enterprise," pp. 27–33.
6. Beverly Geber, "Who, How & What," *Training*, October 1989, p. 52.
7. Chris Lee, "The Three R's," *Training*, October 1989, pp. 67–76.
8. Carnevale, "Learning Enterprise," p. 31.
9. Chmura, *Corporate Education*, p. 20.
10. U.S. Department of Defense, Office of the Assistant Secretary of Defense, Force Management and Personnel. *Military Manpower Training Report: FY 1989* (Washington, D.C.: May 1988), p. 6.
11. J. D. Fletcher, "Cost and Effectiveness of Computer-Based Training," in *Proceedings of the 1987 IEEE Systems, Man and Cybernetics Conference* (New York: Institute of Electrical and Electronic Engineers, Inc., 1987), p. 1.
12. U.S. Department of Defense, *Military Manpower*, p. 4.
13. Ibid., p. 5.
14. U.S. Department of Defense. *Defense 89*, "Almanac" issue, September/October 1989, p. 24.
15. U.S. Department of Defense, Defense Activity for Non-Traditional Education Support (DANTES), publication 127 (Washington, D.C.: 1987).
16. Denise K. Magner, "GI Bill Drawing Veterans to Colleges; Influx May Offset Enrollment Losses," *Chronicle of Higher Education*, November 16, 1988, p. A3.
17. Paul Davis Jenkins, memorandum on meeting with Department of Defense training and educational policy directors, March 20, 1987.
18. Bonnie Jo Buck, "Expert System Prototype Developed as Job Aid for Naval Reservists," *Instruction Delivery Systems*, September/October 1987, p. 17.
19. U.S. Office of Personnel Management. *Employee Training in the Federal Service: FY 1986*, unpublished.
20. Ibid. The figure of 2.1 million civilians employed by the federal government includes civilians in the military but not the 700,000 people in the Postal Service.
21. Susan B. Garland, "Beltway Brain Drain: Why Civil Servants Are Making Tracks," *Business Week*, January 23, 1989, pp. 60–61.
22. From a paper on apprenticeship and journeyman training prepared for this report by Ken Edwards of the International Brotherhood of Electrical Workers, January 25, 1988, p. 21.
23. Ibid., pp. 18–19. This estimate comes from the AFL-CIO Building and Construction Trades Department. See testimony of Michael G. McMillan, executive director, AFL-CIO Human Resources Development Institute, to the Subcommittee on Education and Health, Joint Economic Committee, November 19, 1987, p. 6.
24. Jim Schachter, "Back to School," *Los Angeles Times*, January 4, 1988, Part IV, p. 5.
25. National Center for Education Statistics, U.S. Department of Education, Office of Educational Research and Improvement. *Digest of Education Statistics 1988*, Table 219, p. 253.

26. Leobardo F. Estrada, "Anticipating the Demographic Future," *Change*, May/June 1988, p. 19.
27. Mary Crystal Cage, "More Minority Programs Now Emphasizing Efforts to Keep Students Enrolled in College," *Chronicle of Higher Education*, April 12, 1989, pp. A1, A24.
28. Phil Kuntz, "Congress to Take a Hard Look at Vocational-Training Law," *Congressional Quarterly*, March 4, 1989, p. 456.
29. Cynthia F. Mitchell, "Business School Loses Some of Its Luster," *Wall Street Journal*, July 20, 1988, p. 25.
30. R. A. Gordon and J. E. Howell, *Higher Education for Business* (New York: Columbia University Press, 1959), p. 247.
31. "Facts in Brief: Nearly Half of Doctorates Are Awarded in Science," *Higher Education & National Affairs*, April 10, 1989, p. 3. Percentages later in this paragraph also come from this source.
32. "Number of Women Students Enrolled Part-Time Rises," *Higher Education & National Affairs*, October 5, 1987, p. 6.
33. "Grown-Up Boomers," *New York Times, Education Supplement*, January 4, 1987.

2. Delivering Instruction

1. Digital Equipment Corporation. "Reaping the Benefits of VAX Network Technology," *EDU Magazine*, Winter 1988/1989, p. 41. Other facts in this section come from a telephone interview on March 27, 1989 with Mr. Marlowe Froke, general manager, University Division of Media and Learning Resources, University Park, Pa.
2. James Botkin, Dan Dimancescu, Ray Stata, with John McClellan, *Global Stakes: The Future of High Technology in America* (Cambridge, Mass.: Ballinger, 1982), p. 136.
3. *AFL-CIO News* (captioned photograph), September 5, 1987, p. 5.
4. National Training Fund of the Sheet Metal Workers and the Air-Conditioning Industry. *Windows on the Future: National Training Fund 15th Anniversary Annual Report, 1971–1986* (Alexandria, Va.: 1986), p. 16.
5. James F. Gibbons, "Tutored Videotape Instruction," *The Stanford Engineer*, Spring/Summer 1984, vol. 9, p. 13.
6. Ibid., pp. 14–15, 17–18.
7. Ibid., pp. 15–16.
8. Ron Zemke, "The Rediscovery of Video Teleconferencing," *Training*, September 1986, pp. 38–39.
9. Alan G. Chute, Mary K. Hulick, and Craig A. Palmer, "Teletraining Productivity at AT&T," paper presented at the Association for Educational Communications and Technology Annual Convention, Atlanta, Ga., February 26, 1987.
10. Zuboff, *Age of the Smart Machine*, p. 365.
11. Susan J. Shepard, "A Network of Minds: The Online Phenomenon," *Language Technology #5*, January/February 1988, pp. 28–33.

12. Tony Pompili, "Computer Conferencing Links Far-Flung Pan Am Pilot Union," *PC Week*, July 21, 1987, p. 1.
13. Zuboff, *Age of the Smart Machine*, p. 371.
14. "Management Update, DEC: A Down-Easter Goes International," *Network World*, March 27, 1989, pp. 29, 35–36.
15. John Markoff, "A Supercomputer in Every Pot," *New York Times*, December 29, 1988, pp. D1 and D4. A more recent statement announced the beginning of the countrywide network. See *New York Times*, June 8, 1990, pp. 1 and D4.
16. Beryl Bellman, "Distance Education at WBSI: IEF/SMSS and BESTNET," paper presented at the Electronic Networking Conference, Philadelphia, Pa., May 1988, pp. 10–19.
17. A list of these companies and information about their networks is presented in *BusinessTV*, March 1988, pp. 16–17.
18. Kevin Kelly, "Why Business is Glued to the Tube," *Business Week*, March 27, 1989, p. 160.
19. P. Davis Jenkins, memorandum on conversation with Don Elias, manager, Media Communications Group, Digital Equipment Corporation, Bedford, Mass., July 8, 1988.

3. The Intelligent Tutor

1. Graham P. Crow, Jim P. Papay, and John LaBarbera, "New Technology Assessment Project," *Proceedings of the 1988 Conference on Technology in Training and Education (TITE '88)*, Biloxi, Miss., March 1988, p. 561.
2. "AI Satellite Symposium: Knowledge Technologies at Work," *AI Interactions*, January/February 1989, p. 1.
3. Gordon I. McCalla and Jim E. Greer, *The Practical Use of Artificial Intelligence in Automated Tutoring Systems: Current Status and Impediments to Progress* (Saskatoon, Canada: University of Saskatchewan, Department of Computational Science, 1987), p. 2.
4. John R. Anderson and Brian J. Reiser, "The LISP Tutor," *BYTE*, April 1985 reprint, p. 1.
5. W. Lewis Johnson and Elliot Soloway, "PROUST: An Automatic Debugger for Pascal Programs" in *Artificial Intelligence and Instruction*, ed. Greg P. Kearsley (Reading, Mass.: Addison-Wesley, 1987), pp. 49, 66–67.
6. Seth Chaiklin and Matthew W. Lewis, "Will There Be Teachers in the Classroom of the Future?" *Directions and Implications of Advanced Computing (DIAC-87) Proceedings* (Palo Alto, Calif.: Computer Professionals for Social Responsibility), p. 122.
7. McCalla and Greer, *Practical Use of Artificial Intelligence*, p. 2.
8. William J. Clancey, "Intelligent Tutoring Systems: A Tutorial Survey" in *Current Issues in Expert Systems*, ed. A. van Lamsweerde and P. Dufour (New York: Academic Press, 1987), p. 46.

9. McCalla and Greer, *Practical Use of Artificial Intelligence*, pp. 18–19. The authors project the characteristics for an ICAI system that are reflected in this text.

10. James D. Hollan, Edwin L. Hutchins, and Louis M. Weitzman, "STEAMER: An Interactive, Inspectable, Simulation-Based Training System," in *Artificial Intelligence and Instruction*, p. 132.

11. McCalla and Greer, *Practical Use of Artificial Intelligence*, p. 20.

12. J. D. Fletcher, "Intelligent Training Systems in the Military," in *Defense Applications of Artificial Intelligence: Progress and Prospects*, ed. G. W. Hopple and S. J. Andriole (Lexington, Mass.: Lexington Books, in press).

13. Arthur L. Slater, "Developing a Prototype Expert System Tutor for Training Electronics Maintenance Technicians," *Proceedings of the 1987 Conference on Technology in Training and Education (TITE '87)*, Colorado Springs, Colo., March 1987, p. 506.

14. Ibid. The Training Development Branch referred to is in the 1872 [sic] School Squadron of the Air Force Communications Command.

15. Ibid., pp. 506–512.

16. Hollan et al., "STEAMER," p. 127. The STEAMER system was developed primarily under contract to Bolt, Beranek and Newman.

17. Paul Harmon, "Intelligent Job Aids: How AI Will Change Training in the Next Five Years," in *Artificial Intelligence and Instruction*, p. 165.

18. Ibid., pp. 189–190.

19. Gold Hill Computers, Inc. *Application Portfolio*, 4th ed. (Cambridge, Mass.: Gold Hill Computers, Inc., 1988), p. 27.

20. Beverly Woolf and Pat Cunningham, "Building a Community Memory for Intelligent Tutoring Systems," *Proceedings AAAI-87 Sixth National Conference on Artificial Intelligence*, vol. 1, pp. 82–83. The Recovery Boiler Tutor was also described in an excellent article by Peter R. Kirrane and Diane E. Kirrane, "What Artificial Intelligence is Doing for Training," *Training*, July 1989, pp. 37–43. The authors mention its use in more than 80 plants.

21. Gold Hill Computers, Inc. *Application Portfolio*, pp. 39–40.

22. Greg P. Kearsley, *Authoring: A Guide to the Design of Instructional Software* (Reading, Mass.: Addison-Wesley, 1986), p. 4.

23. Ok-choon Park, Ray S. Perez, and Robert J. Seidel, "Intelligent CAI: Old Wine in New Bottles, or a New Vintage?" in *Artificial Intelligence and Instruction*, p. 24.

24. J. D. Fletcher, "Cost and Effectiveness of Computer Based Training," Proceedings of the 1987 IEEE Systems, Man, and Cybernetics Conference (New York: The Institute of Electrical and Electronic Engineers, Inc., 1987), p. 2.

25. Harmon, "Intelligent Job Aids," p. 189.

4. Training Technical Workers

1. Based on conversations with Ernie Jones, training director of the Associated General Contractors, July 1988.

2. Donald R. McNeil, "A Study of Construction Programs in American Colleges and Universities," draft 4 of a report prepared for the Home Builders Institute, April 8, 1988, p. 3.

3. *Union Labor: Commitment to Excellence* (Washington, D.C.: UA-NCA Training Trust Fund, undated).

4. William B. Johnston, *Workforce 2000: Work and Workers for the 21st Century*. (Indianapolis, Ind.: The Hudson Institute, 1987), p. 97.

5. Quoted in Patricia Mandell, "Temporary Workers: Keeping Pace with the PC," *PC Week*, April 28, 1987, pp. 55, 60, 64. Figures given for the National Association of Temporary Services, Manpower, Inc., and Olsten Services are from this source.

6. *Digest of Education Statistics*, Center for Education Statistics, 1987, pp. 191, 288.

7. Memorandum from Ann Brassier, October 11, 1989. This memorandum appended "A Report on Training and Development in the Federal Government," an unpublished report commissioned for this study.

8. U.S. Department of Defense. *Military Career Guide: Employment and Training Opportunities in the Military* (Washington, D.C.: 1987), pp. 136–151.

9. *Community College of the Air Force General Catalogue*, 1987–1988, pp. 73–74.

10. Manufacturing Studies Board, Commission on Engineering and Technical Systems. *Human Resource Practices for Implementing Advanced Manufacturing Technology*, report of the Committee on the Effective Implementation of Advanced Manufacturing Technology (Washington, D.C.: National Academy Press, 1986), pp. 1–3.

11. John Teresko, Thomas M. Rohan, and Therese R. Welter, "Firing Up Support for CIM," *Industry Week*, November 2, 1987, p. 86.

12. Ibid., p. 92.

13. Ibid., p. 70.

14. Patrick W. Dolan, "Training for New Technology: The Union's Role," discussion paper prepared for Work in America Institute, August 1985, pp. 22ff.

15. "Moraine Park Technical College: Looking to the Future," *Community, Technical, and Junior College Journal*, vol. 58, no. 3, December/January 1987–1988, pp. 52–53.

5. Educating Managers

1. Robert H. Hayes and William J. Abernathy, "Managing Our Way to Economic Decline," *Harvard Business Review*, July–August 1980, pp. 67–77.

2. Alfred D. Chandler, Jr., *The Visible Hand: The Managerial Revolution in American Business* (Cambridge, Mass.: Harvard University Press, 1977), p. 276.

3. Memorandum from Thomas H. Loftis, acting assistant director, Office of Training and Development, U.S. Office of Personnel Management, August 1988.

4. U.S. Office of Personnel Management, *Employee Training in the Federal Service*, *FY 1985* (Washington, D.C.: 1987), p. 9. These are the latest figures available.

5. Ann Brassier and Jim Ludwig, "A Report on Training and Development in the Federal Government," unpublished report, commissioned for this study, 1987, p. 49.

6. For a study of relations between OPM and the agencies, see U.S. General Accounting Office, *Progress Report on Federal Executive Development Programs* (Washington, D.C.: 1984).

7. Memorandum from Thomas H. Loftis, p. 6.

8. U.S. Department of Agriculture. "Supervisory, Managerial, and Executive Training and Development in USDA: Status and Recommendations," unpublished internal report, 1985, Appendix A.

9. Howard Webber, "Recruitment, Career Development and Training in the U.S. Federal Civil Service: Report of a Study" (Webber is a British official who spent a year studying here; the text draws on sections 58 and 59 of his unpublished report for Her Majesty's Prison Service, 1987).

10. U.S. Office of Personnel Management, Management and Oversight Division, "Annual Report of the Office of Personnel Management Training and Development Program, FY 1986," internal report, 1986, p. 2.

11. U.S. Office of Training and Development, *Programs of the Executive Seminar Centers, 1988* (Washington, D.C.: 1988), pp. 4–25. Also see this source for the preceding facts given in the text.

12. U.S. Office of Personnel Management, Management and Oversight Division, "Annual Report, FY 1986," p. 2.

13. U.S. Department of Agriculture, "Supervisory, Managerial, and Executive Training," pp. 3, 4.

14. Ibid., p. 15. Also see p. 5.

15. U.S. General Accounting Office, *Progress Report*, appendix II, pp. 15, 18.

16. J. Ronald Fox with James L. Field, *The Defense Management Challenge: Weapons Acquisition* (Boston, Mass.: Harvard Business School Press, 1988), p. 6. Also see pp. 5, 7, 8 for text references in this section.

17. U.S. Department of Defense, Office of the Assistant Secretary of Defense. *Population Representation in the Military Services, FY 1986* (Washington, D.C.: August 1987), pp. II-13, II-14.

18. "The Military's New Stars," *U.S. News & World Report*, April 18, 1988, pp. 35–37. The study by the Center for Creative Leadership involved 163 Army officers, 139 senior executives, and 1,002 managers.

19. Richard Halloran, "Military Academies Are Becoming Even Tougher on Body and Mind," *New York Times Magazine*, May 22, 1988, sec. 4, p. 1.

20. U.S. Army. *Command and General Staff College Catalog, Academic Year 1988–1989* (Fort Leavenworth, Kans.: May 1988), pp. 147–148.

21. Fox, *Defense Management Challenge*, p. 188.

22. Ibid., pp. 228, 229, 231.

23. U.S. Army War College. *Core Curriculum: Course 1, The Senior Leader* (Carlisle Barracks, Pa.: 1988).

24. U.S. Air Force, Air University. *Air War College Bulletin, 1987–1988* (Maxwell Air Force Base, Ala.: 1987), pp. 6–90.

25. U.S. Naval War College. *The Naval War College Catalog, 1986–1988* (Newport, R.I.: 1986), p. 18.

26. U.S. Department of Defense. *National Defense University 1988–1989 Catalogue* (Fort Lesley J. McNair, Washington, D.C.: 1988), p. 44.

27. Richard Halloran, "Troubling Ratings on Military Education at Top," *New York Times*, September 20, 1988, p. A20.

28. Richard Halloran, "Army Strengthening and Modifying the Way It Teaches the Art of War," *New York Times*, August 13, 1988, p. 5.

29. Eric Stephan, Gordon E. Mills, R. Wayne Pace, and Lenny Ralphs, "HRD in the *Fortune* 500: A Survey," *Training and Development Journal*, January 1988, p. 30.

30. Jack Gordon, "Budgets," *Training*, October 1989, p. 42.

31. Lyman W. Porter and Lawrence E. McKibbin, *Management Education and Development: Drift or Thrust into the 21st Century?* (New York: McGraw-Hill, 1988), p. 249.

32. Stephan et al., "HRD in the *Fortune* 500," p. 31.

33. Harry B. Bernhard and Cynthia A. Ingols, "Six Lessons for the Corporate Classroom," *Harvard Business Review*, September–October 1988, p. 42.

34. "Who's Corporate America Training and to What Extent?" *Training*, Datapage, 1987. Survey of U.S. companies with 50 or more employees. Usable responses: 2,409 (1987).

35. Anthony J. Fresina and Associates, *Executive Education in Corporate America* (Palatine, Ill.: Anthony J. Fresina and Associates, 1988), p. 2. The sample includes 300 of the *Fortune* 500 companies.

36. "Who's Corporate America Training and to What Extent?" *Training*, ibid.

37. "Courses for Small Business," *Litchfield County Times*, September 19, 1986, p. 55.

38. "Motorola Sends Its Work Force Back to School," *Business Week*, June 6, 1988, p. 80.

39. Thomas Petzinger, Jr., "Kwik Kopy College," *Wall Street Journal*, Small Business Franchising special section, June 10, 1988, p. 17.

40. Fresina and Associates, *Executive Education*, pp. 59, 205.

41. Peter F. Drucker, "The Coming of the New Organization," *Harvard Business Review*, January–February 1988, p. 45.

42. *The Bricker Bulletin on Executive Education*, vol. VI, no. 1, Spring 1987.

43. Porter and McKibbin, *Management Education*, pp. 273, 290.

44. Leslie Wayne, "Attaché-Case Education Is Enriching Everybody," *New York Times*, Education Life special section, January 4, 1987, p. 72.

45. Porter and McKibbin, *Management Education*, p. 291.

46. Abraham Zaleznik, "Managers and Leaders: Are They Different?" *Harvard Business Review*, May–June 1977, pp. 67–78.

47. George O. Klemp, Jr., and David C. McClelland, "What Characterizes Intelligent Functioning among Senior Managers?" unpublished paper, McBer and Company, undated.

6. Updating Professionals

1. Ronald M. Cervero and Craig L. Scanlan (eds.), *Problems and Prospects in Continuing Education* (San Francisco, Calif.: Jossey-Bass, 1985), p. 49, and "Summer 1988 Newsletter" from Louis Phillips and Associates, Athens, Ga.

2. *A Call to Action: A Report of The National Conference on Continuing Professional Education* (University Park, Pa.: The Pennsylvania State University, 1986), n.p.

3. Ibid., quoting Robert DeSio, former IBM director of University Relations.

4. *Focus on the Future: A National Action Plan for Career-Long Education for Engineers*, report of the Committee on Career-Long Education for Engineers (Washington, D.C.: National Academy of Engineering, 1988), p. 1.

5. Ibid., pp. 10–11, citing a 1987 report of the National University Continuing Education Association.

6. Ibid., p. 35.

7. R. Lee Martin, "Career Obsolescence: Can It Happen to You?" *Manufacturing Engineering*, February 1988, p. 50. This source also provides facts on the National Technological University.

8. Ron Schneiderman, "Continuing Education: No More 'Nice-to-Know,'" *Microwaves & RF*, March 1988, pp. 38, 41.

9. Tammi Harbert, "A West Point for Engineers," *High Technology*, September 1986, pp. 67–68. Other information in this section is based on conversation with Gordon Institute personnel, November 10, 1988.

10. *Focus on the Future*, pp. 39–47. Our text paraphrases and summarizes the report's recommendations.

11. Arthur M. Osteen and Michael Gannon, "Continuing Medical Education," *Journal of the American Medical Association*, August 26, 1988, pp. 1105–1109.

12. Ralph G. Wellington, "MCLE: Does It Go Far Enough and What Are the Alternatives?" paper prepared for Arden House III Conference, November 1987 (Philadelphia, Pa.: ALI), p. 2.

13. *Continuing Legal Education for Professional Competence and Responsibility Since Arden House II: Selected Articles on Professional Competence and Responsibility from the ALI-ABA CLE Review* (Philadelphia, Pa.: ALI-ABA Committee on Continuing Professional Education, 1984), pp. xiv–xv.

14. "Call of the Conference: National Conference on the Continuing Education of the Bar," Arden House, November 13–16, 1987 (Philadelphia, Pa.: ALI), p. 1.

15. Wellington, "MCLE," pp. 7, 8.

16. Ibid., p. 9.

17. Austin G. Anderson, *A Plan for Lawyer Development* (American Bar Association, 1985), p. 189.

18. American Institute for Law Training Within the Office (AILTO) Survey Returns. Memorandum from Richard D. Lee to AILTO Governing Board, September 12, 1985.

19. Ibid. Information updated by telephone conversation with Richard D. Lee, new director of professional development, Morrison and Foerster law firm, San Francisco, June 13, 1989.

20. Beverly Geber, "S.F. Law," *Training*, October 1987, pp. 86–98.

7. Missing Persons

1. "Adult Functional Illiteracy: On the Verge of Crisis," *BCEL Newsletter for the Business Community*, September 1984, p. 2.

2. Lawrence A. Cremin, *American Education: The National Experience, 1783–1876* (New York: Harper & Row, 1980), pp. 490–492. Cremin refers to the work of Michael G. Mulhall, *The Progress of the World in Arts, Agriculture, Commerce, Manufactures, Instruction, Railways, and Public Wealth Since the Beginning of the Nineteenth Century* (London: Edward Stanford, 1880), p. 88.

3. Adult Performance Level Project, Norvell Northcutt, director. *Adult Functional Competency: A Summary* (Austin, Tex.: The University of Texas, Division of Extension, 1975), p. 6. See also Paul M. Irwin, *Adult Literacy Issues, Programs, and Options: Updated 08/04/86* (Washington, D.C.: Congressional Research Division, Education and Public Welfare Division, 1986), pp. CRS5–CRS7.

4. "Measuring Illiteracy," information sheet from New Readers Press of Laubach Literacy Action, Syracuse, N.Y., January 1987.

5. Jack A. Brizius and Susan E. Foster, *Enhancing Adult Literacy: A Policy Guide* (Washington, D.C.: Council of State Policy and Planning Agencies, 1987), pp. 19–21. This was the controversial English Language Proficiency Study.

6. Frank H.T. Rhodes, "A Neglected Challenge," address given to the Academy for Educational Development in New York City on May 14, 1987 (New York: Academy for Educational Development, 1987), p. 8.

7. Harold W. McGraw, Jr., "A Message to Corporate CEOs," *BCEL Newsletter for the Business Community*, September 1984, p. 1.

8. Harold W. McGraw, Jr., "Banishing Illiteracy: The Challenge We Must Face," *New Jersey Bell Journal*, Winter/Spring 1988–1989, p. 18.

9. Richard A. Mendel, "Meeting the Economic Challenge of the 1990s: Workforce Literacy in the South," report for the Sunbelt Institute (Chapel Hill, N.C.: MDC, 1988), pp. 14–15. Mendel cites U.S. Department of Labor, *Looking to the Year 2000: A View from the Southeast* (Atlanta, Ga.: 1988).

10. Mary E. Kahn, *Literacy Management Information Project Report* (Washington, D.C.: The Washington Consulting Group, Inc., 1986), vol. 1, pp. 8–10.

11. Commission on Workforce Quality and Labor Market Efficiency, David Crawford, director. *Investing in People: A Strategy to Address America's Workforce Crisis* (Washington, D.C.: U.S. Department of Labor, 1989), p. 15. The commission updated information given by Gary Burtless, "Public Spending for the Poor: Trends, Prospects, and Economic Limits" in *Fighting Poverty: What Works and What Doesn't*, ed. Sheldon H. Danziger and Daniel H. Weinberg

(Cambridge, Mass.: Harvard University Press, 1986), p. 37. The data include all "human capital" programs for hiring, training, and general education.

12. William F. Pierce, "A Redefined Federal Role in Adult Literacy: Integrated Policies, Programs and Procedures," draft paper prepared for the Southport Institute for Policy Analysis, Washington, D.C., October 13, 1988, p. 51.

13. Ibid., p. 79.

14. Sar A. Levitan and Frank Gallo, *A Second Chance: Training for Jobs* (Kalamazoo, Mich.: W. E. Upjohn Institute for Employment Research, 1988), pp. 60, 68. See also U.S. General Accounting Office, *Dislocated Workers: Local Programs and Outcomes Under the Job Training Partnership Act* (Washington, D.C.: March 1987), pp. 36, 37, 47. This confirms the fact that remedial education is not a high priority, and similar facts are given in U.S. Congress, Office of Technology Assessment, *Technology and Structural Unemployment: Reemploying Displaced Adults* (Washington, D.C.: February 1986), pp. 64–65.

15. Scott Jaschik, "Welfare Reform-Agreement Creates a New Role, and Problems, for Colleges and Trade Schools," *Chronicle of Higher Education*, October 5, 1988, pp. A1, A30. Ms. Hake's observations are also drawn from this source.

16. "State Planning Update," *BCEL Newsletter for the Business Community*, January 1988, p. 8. Information in the next paragraph is also from this source.

17. Jack A. Brizius, "The State Role in Adult Literacy Policy," background paper prepared for the Project on Adult Literacy of the Southport Institute for Public Policy, Washington, D.C., December, 1988, p. 16.

18. Wendy L. Deans, "Business, Government and Education Unite for Literacy," *Connections*, Winter 1988, pp. 19–23.

19. Ron Zemke, "Workplace Illiteracy," *Training*, June 1989, p. 35.

20. Chris Lee, "The 3R's," *Training*, October 1989, p. 68.

21. Mendel, "Workforce Literacy in the South," p. 30.

22. "Unions: Bread, Butter and Basic Skills," *BCEL Newsletter for the Business Community*, October 1987, pp. 1, 4, 5.

23. David Harman, *Turning Illiteracy Around: An Agenda for National Action: Working Paper No. 2* (New York: The Business Council for Effective Literacy, 1985), pp. 16–17.

24. Barbara Pitts, "VOA Provides Literacy Services to the Homeless," *The Reader* (a newsletter of the Literacy Volunteers of America), May 1987, p. 8.

25. South Carolina Literacy Association, *1988–89 Objectives and Programs* (Columbia, S.C.: 1988), p. 5.

26. Pierce, "Redefined Federal Role," p. 62.

27. Gary B. Hansen, "A Follow-up Survey of Workers Displaced by the Ford San José Assembly Plant Closure," paper presented at the IRRA meeting in Chicago, Ill., December 28, 1987.

28. Thomas G. Sticht, William B. Armstrong, Daniel T. Hickey, and John S. Caylor, *Cast-off Youth: Policy and Training Methods from the Military Experience* (New York: Praeger, 1987), pp. 92–94.

29. Pierce, "Redefined Federal Role," p. 30.

8. Educating Workers: Issues and Action

1. "Gaining the Competitive Edge," position paper of the American Society for Training and Development, 1988, p. 11.
2. Jacob M. Schlesinger, "Costly Friendship: Auto Firms and UAW Find That Cooperation Can Get Complicated," *Wall Street Journal*, August 25, 1987, p. 1.
3. Calvin Sims, "Global Communications Net Planned by G.E. for Its Staff," *New York Times*, May 31, 1989, pp. D1–2.
4. Paul Susca, "Teacher in the Dorm Room," *Dartmouth Alumni Magazine*, March 1989, pp. 34–38.
5. Ibid., p. 36.
6. National Education Corporation. *1988 Annual Report*, pp. 2–4.
7. U.S. Congress. House. *Applied Technology Education Amendments of 1989*, 101st Cong., 1st sess., 1989, H.R. 7, Rept. 101–41, p. 24.

INDEX

A. B. Dick, 126
ABE/ASE. *See* Adult Basic and Secondary Education
Access to training, 1–2, 18–20; in corporations, 18–21, 161–163; in educational institutions, 29–35; in the federal government, 25–26; in labor unions, 26–28; in the military, 21–25; in proprietary schools, 28–29
Accountants: and continuing education, 13, 211–215
Accreditation: of medical education, 202; of professional education programs, 197; of proprietary schools, 32, 198
Adams, Gary, 213, 214
Administrative staff. *See* Office workers
Adult Basic and Secondary Education [ABE/ASE], 230, 245, 251
Adult education: and basic skills, 223–254; compared to traditional classrooms, 1; demand for, 11; and economic growth, 2–3, 10; government policies and programs for, 229–240; growth of, 1, 35, 255; obstacles to, 36; providers of, 36, 134–135, 189–195, 256–261, 267–268; and telecommunications, 37–70, 260–261. *See also* Access to training; Illiteracy; and specific types of institutions, e.g. Vocational schools
Adult Education Act, 230, 235
Adult Education and Job Training for the Homeless, 233
Adult Literacy Initiative, 232

Aetna Institute for Corporate Education, 190
Aetna Life and Casualty, 69, 166; and basic skills education, 243
AFL-CIO, 28; and retraining, 247
African-Americans: and access to training, 19
Agriculture, 44, 140, 149, 150–151
AI. *See* Artificial intelligence
Air Force. *See* U.S. Air Force
Air War College, 155–156
Alcoa Laboratories, 42
Aldo [expert system], 78–79, 89
Alliance for Employee Growth and Development, 247
Allstate Insurance, 47
AMA. *See* American Management Association
Amalgamated Clothing and Textile Workers, 248–249
AMA/NET [telecommunications network], 210
American Assembly of Collegiate Schools of Business, 33
American Association for Artificial Intelligence, 96, 197
American Banking Association [ABA], 216
American Bar Association, 205, 206
American Council on Construction Education, 106
American Federation of State, County, and Municipal Employees [AFSCME], 247–248

American Graduate School of International Management, 177
American Institute of Banking, 216
American Institute of Certified Public Accountants [AICPA], 211
American Institute for Law Training Within the Office, 206
American Law Institute, 204, 206, 210
American Management Association [AMA], 116; and management education, 176
American Medical Association, 202, 203
American Paper Institute, 90
American Society for Training and Development, 18, 19, 26
American Telephone & Telegraph. *See* AT&T
Analogic, Inc., 198
Anderson, John R., 76, 81, 96
Annenberg School of Communications, 48
Apple Macintosh, 44, 57, 133, 262
Applied Learning International, 268
Apprenticeships, 12, 13, 95; at colleges, 110–111; in construction trades, 103, 106, 107–110; in electrical industry, 110–111; and expert systems, 263; and labor unions, 47, 103, 107; and lawyers, 206
Arden House Conferences, 204
Arizona, 110, 128
Arizona, University of, 58
Arizona State University, 110
Arkansas, University of, 175
Armed Forces. *See* Military
Armed Forces Staff College, 156
Army. *See* U.S. Army
Army War College, 155
Arthur Andersen [accounting firm], 212–215, 218
Arthur D. Little, Inc., 90
Arthur Young [accounting firm], 215
Artificial intelligence [AI], 12, 53, 58, 70, 71–98, 260; American Association for, 96, 197; and commercial markets, 96–97; defined, 71–72
Artificial Intelligence Center, 72
Asian-Americans, 34
Aspen Institute, 176
Associated General Contractors, 103, 105, 111
Association for Media-Based Continuing

Engineering Education [AMCEE], 196–197
Asynchronous computer conferencing, 57–65
AT&T, 27, 51, 55, 56, 68, 268; and updating skills, 125; and basic skills education, 246–247
Attorneys. *See* Lawyers
Audiographic conferencing, 55–57
Augusteijn, Marijke, 76
Auto industry, 27, 28, 131, 245–246, 247–248
Automation, 129, 131. *See also* Computer-assisted manufacturing [CAM]; Computer-integrated manufacturing [CIM]
Automotive Satellite TV Network, 67

Baker & McKenzie [law firm], 208
Bank Street College, 78
Bankers: and continuing education, 13, 215–217
Banking: associations, 69; and ICAI systems, 90
BankSim, 216
Basic skills, 9–10, 20, 224, 230–234, 268; and computer conferencing, 64; curricula, 246, 248; Job Opportunities and Basic Skills Training Program, 236; and office workers, 119; and volunteers, 249–250. *See also* Illiteracy; Literacy
BCEL. *See* Business Council for Effective Literacy
Behavioral training, 32–33
Bell Atlantic, 268
Bell Laboratories, 51, 55
Bell South, 192–193, 268
Bellande, Bruce, 202
Bentley-Nevada, 42
Bilingual English and Spanish Telecommunications Network [BESTNET], 65–66
Biscoe-Hindman Center for Management and Executive Development, 175
BITNET, 63
Blanchard, George, 238
Blanchard, Kenneth, 178
Bluegrass State Skills Corporation, 244
Boeing Company, 68, 198
Boilermaker Comprehensive Training Program, 108
Boston University Medical School, 56
Brown, John Seely, 81

Brown, Peter, 63
Burton, Richard, 81
Business Council for Effective Literacy
    [BCEL], 237, 241–242, 243
Business education. *See* Management educa-
    tion
Business schools: mission of, 164

CAD. *See* Computer-assisted design
CAI. *See* Computer-assisted instruction
California, University of, at Los Angeles.
    See UCLA
California Institute of Technology, 48
California State University at Chico, 41,
    49, 196, 260
CAM. *See* Computer-assisted manufactur-
    ing, 133
Cambridge Teleteaching Group, 55
Camden County Community College, 134
Campbell, Alan K., 142
Campbell, Carroll, 239
Campbell Soup Company, 78, 89
Career-Long Education for Engineers,
    Committee on, 195
Carl D. Perkins Vocational Education Act,
    31
Carnegie Foundation for the Advancement
    of Teaching, 123
Carnegie-Mellon University [CMU], 75,
    78, 81, 96
Cataldo, Patrick, 115
CCAF. *See* Community College of the Air
    Force
Center for Creative Leadership, 176–177
Center for Disease Control, 210
Center for Labor Studies, 110
Center for Productivity, Innovation, and
    Technology, 132
Center for Professional Advancement, 199
Center for Professional Education, 212
Center for the Study of Community Col-
    leges, 123
Central Intelligence Agency. *See* CIA
Certification: in construction trades, 104–
    105
Chaiklin, Seth, 78
Chase Manhattan Bank, 69
Chattanooga State Technical Community
    College, 132
Chicago, University of, 137
Chico. *See* California State University

Chrysler Corporation, 245
CIA [Central Intelligence Agency], 120–
    121
CIM. *See* Computer-integrated manufactur-
    ing
Cimino, Aldo, 79
City University of New York, 236
Civil service: access to training, 17, 25–26,
    120–122, 125, 140–151; Government
    Employees Training Act, 142. *See also*
    Federal Executive Institute; Federal gov-
    ernment
Civil Service Commission, 142
Civil Service Reform Act, 142, 149
Clancy, William, 80
Cleese, John, 178
CMU. *See* Carnegie-Mellon University
COBOL [computer language], 147
Cognitive science: and artificial intelligence,
    72, 75; and modelling, 80–81; and teach-
    ers' expertise, 82–83; and PETITE/IV,
    84–86
College Board, 35
College-Level Examination Program, 24
College of Naval Warfare, 156
Colleges and universities: and adult educa-
    tion, 30, 257–259; enrollment in, 35; and
    labor unions, 135; and management edu-
    cation, 171–176; and professional
    education, 190–194; and telecommunica-
    tions, 41, 260–261; and telecourses, 52
Colorado, University of, 76
Columbia University, 51, 217
Combined Arms and Services Staff School,
    153
COMCATS [AT&T training catalog], 125
Command and General Staff School, 153
Commonwealth Literacy Campaign, 238,
    239
Communications: 6, 34; revolution in, 4, 12
Communications and Data Processing In-
    stitute [Hughes Aircraft], 198
Communications Workers of America, 27,
    28; and basic skills education, 246
Community College of the Air Force
    [CCAF], 23, 124
Community colleges, 12; and basic skills
    education, 239; Center for the Study of,
    123; and construction trades, 105; and
    cooperation with business, 31, 102, 128;
    cost of, 30; growth of, 29–30; and man-

Community colleges (cont.)
agement education, 162–163; as providers of adult training, 29–31; and training for office workers, 117–119. See also specific community colleges
Competition: among lawyers, 204–205; among states, 3, 102; in national markets, 6, 20; Omnibus Trade and Competitiveness Act, 233; in world markets, 2, 14, 138, 184
Comprehensive Competencies Program, 247
CompuServe Information Service, 58
Computer-assisted design [CAD], 132
Computer-assisted instruction [CAI], 91–95
Computer-assisted manufacturing [CAM], 132. See also Automation
Computer-integrated manufacturing [CIM], 129; and college curricula, 133, 134; impact on workers, 129–131. See also Automation
Computerland, 268
Computer science, 13, 34, 66; continuing education in, 195–201
Computers, 71–95; and audiographic conferencing, 55–57; and asynchronous conferencing, 57–65
ComputerWorks, 51
Connected Education, Inc., 61
Connecticut, University of, 163
Construction Education, American Council on, 106
Construction engineering: collegiate programs in, 105–106
Construction trades, 103–113
Continuing education: schools of, 194–195. See also Adult education
Continuing Legal Education Satellite Network, 210
Continuing Professional Education, Committee on [for lawyers], 206
Control Data Corporation, 89
CONVOCOM, 43
Cooker Maintenance Advisor, 79
Coombs, Norman, 60
Coopers & Lybrand [accounting firm], 215
Cornelius, Hal, 116
Corporate Education Network, 48
Corporation for Public Broadcasting, 48
Corporations, 18–21, 36, 159–160; and asynchronous computer conferencing,

63; attitudes towards training, 114–115; and colleges and universities, 31, 123, 134, 257–258; and labor unions, 132, 256–257; and management education, 159–160; and proprietary schools, 118–119; as providers of adult education, 259–260, 267–268; and satellite networks, 67–69; and tutored video instruction [TVI], 48–49; and videoconferencing, 54. See also Small businesses
Craft Skills Program, 104
Curricula, 10, 264–267; for accountants, 213–215; in construction trades education, 106–111; for factory workers, 128–134; for government employees, 143–148; for information systems technicians, 122–128; for managers, 13, 138–139, 163–168, 171–172, 174–176; for office workers, 113–121; reform of, 68, 157–159, 168–171, 178–184, 264–267; in service academies, 153

DANTES, 23
DARPA, 91
Dartmouth, 137, 262
"Data superhighway," 63
Datapro Educational Services, 94
Decentralized workplaces, 8
Defense Activity for Non-Traditional Education Support [DANTES], 23
Defense Systems Management College, 154–155
Delaware, University of, 216
Deltac Training, 117
Department of Agriculture [USDA], 140, 149; and training for management, 150–151
Department of Commerce: 24; and management education, 149
Department of Defense [DOD], 24; and Air Force training programs, 124–125; and asynchronous computer conferencing, 63; budget share, 152; and civilian training, 156; and ICAI systems, 91; and management education, 153–159
Department of Education, 133; and adult basic and secondary education, 230–231; and literacy assessment, 224, 226
Department of Health and Human Services: and basic skills education, 236; and training, 26

Department of Labor, 110, 247; and costs of illiteracy, 228–229
Department of Naval Personnel, 44
Dewey, John, 107
DIAL ACCESS [telecommunications network], 210
Dick, A. B., Company, 126
Dickinson State College, 110
Digital Equipment Corporation, 44, 62, 63, 66, 67–68, 268; and CAI systems, 94; and training for factory workers, 131; and training for office workers, 115
Displaced workers, 13, 115, 223, 234; programs for, 247. See also Obsolescence, Workers
DisplayWrite [software], 116
Domino's Pizza, 54; and basic skills education, 244
Drucker, Peter F., 169
Duke University, 173
Dunkin' Donuts, 166

Eastman Kodak, 197
Economic change, 14
Economic Dislocation and Workers Adjustment Act, 234
Education Partnership for Workplace Literacy, 233
Educational Progress, National Assessment of, 22
Electrical and Electronics Engineers, Institute of [IEEE], 197–198
Elementary and Secondary School Improvement Amendments, 233
Empire State College, 110
Employee Development and Training Center [UAW-Ford], 246
Encyclopaedia Britannica Educational Corporation, 29
Engineering: and continuing education, 13, 34, 51, 195–201; and expert systems, 72; and service academies, 153; Ph.D. degrees awarded in, 33–34; professional and trade associations, 199; and tutored video instruction, 51; and audiographic conferencing, 55
Engineering, National Academy of, 195, 199–200
Engineering Science Program Exchange, 94
Engineers: attitudes towards continuing education, 199–200

English [language], 59, 153; and CAI systems, 91; competence in, 226–227; as a second language, 50, 230, 239, 244, 268
English Literacy Grants, 23
Evaluation: of apprenticeship programs, 109; of corporate management education, 168–169; of electronic technologies, 69–70; of ICAI systems, 96; of teachers' performance, 110; of vendor programs, 178–179. See also Accreditation
Even Start program, 233
Executive Committee for Excellence [EXCEL], 121
Executive programs, 171–176. See also Management education
Executive Seminar Centers, 146
Experiential learning [theory], 77
Expert systems, 12, 72, 78–79, 86–88, 263; and insurance industry, 89

Factories. See Manufacturing
Federal Communications Commission, 41
Federal Executive Institute, 142, 143, 147
Federal government: training for civilian employees, 17, 25–26, 120–122, 125, 140–151; programs for adult education, 14, 229–237
Federal Interagency Committee on Education, 230
Fenwick, Dorothy, 32
Fife, William, 131
Financial management, 139
Financial services industry, 68; PORTSIS, 93
Financial support, sources of, 18, 24, 130; for programs in colleges and universities, 133, 172–174; for students, 34
Fletcher, J. D., 22
Flextime, 7
Florida, 134; University of, 105
Ford Aerospace and Communication Corporation, 76
Ford Foundation, 33
Ford Motor Company, 3, 166; and basic skills education, 245; UAW-Ford Fund, 27
Fort Leavenworth, 153
Foster, Badi, 190–191
Fund for the Improvement of Postsecondary Education, 66

Fuqua School of Business Administration [Duke University], 173, 175

G.I. Bill, 24
GAIN, 238
Gannett Company: and literacy, 241
GAO. See General Accounting Office
GED. See General Educational Development program
General Accounting Office [GAO], 151, 155, 253
General Dynamics, 42
General Educational Development program [GED], 230, 244, 246
General Electric: and management education, 161, 166, 167–168
General Motors, 28, 268; and community colleges, 31; and basic skills education, 245–246
General Services Administration [GSA], 121
Geometry Tutor [computer program], 76
George Washington University, 126
Giddings & Lewis, 131
Glenn, Jerome, 61
Gordon, Bernard, 198
Gordon Institute, 198
Goroff, Dan, 55, 56
Government Employees Training Act, 142
Grace Commission, 25
Graduate Builders Institute, 104–105, 111
Graduate schools of business administration, 171; advantages of, to host institutions, 172–174
Grant, Ulysses S., 157
Graphics: and ICAI systems, 86–87
Great Oaks Joint Vocational School District, 120
Greater Avenues to Independence [GAIN], 238
Greer, Jim, 74
GSA. See General Services Administration
GTE, 166

Hake, Jan, 236
Harmon, Paul, 87, 88, 97
Harris, Frank, 205
Hartford Insurance, 166
Harvard Medical School, 51; and continuing education, 203
Harvard School of Business Administration, 137; and customized courses, 175; Owner-President Management Program, 162
Harvard University, 55–56
Hawkins-Stafford Elementary and Secondary School Improvement Amendments, 233
Health and Restaurant Trade Council, 248
Henry Ford Community College, 246
Hershey Medical Center, 44
Hewitt, David, 130
Hewlett-Packard Corporation, 41–42, 49–51, 68, 196, 197, 260
Hierarchy: and management education, 169–171; and management systems, 5–6, 129–130, 237
Higher education. See Colleges and universities
Hispanics: and access to training, 19, 30, 65–66
History, 153; and asynchronous computer conferencing, 57; and CAI systems, 92
Hitachi Central Research Laboratories, 50
Holiday Inn, 166
Home Builders Association. See National Association of Home Builders
Home Builders Institute, 104, 105
Honeywell, Inc., 89, 126, 263
Hughes Aircraft, 198
Human resources: development of, 160–161, 164, 264; management of, 139, 150–151
Human Resources Development Institute, 247
Human Resources Research Organization Technical Education Center [HumRRO TEC], 126
Humanities, 57, 153

IBM, 68, 161, 268; Management Development Center, 166, 167
ICAI. See Intelligent computer-assisted instruction
IDPs. See Independent Development Plans
IDS-American Express, 69
IEEE. See Institute of Electrical and Electronics Engineers
Illiteracy, 9, 20; campaigns against, 230, 232, 233–234, 237–244, 249–250; and computer conferencing, 64; costs of, 228–229; persistence of, 251–254

Illiterates: identification of, 227–228; numbers of, 224, 226–227
Immigrants, 13
Independent development plans [IDPs], 149–150
Industrial College of the Armed Forces, 156
Information science, 34
Information systems, 10, 122–128
Institute for Defense Analysis, 22
Institute of Electrical and Electronics Engineers [IEEE], 197–198
Instructional design, 73
Instructional Television Fixed Services [ITFS], 41, 45, 49, 50
Insurance industry, 47, 69; and expert systems, 89; and management education, 166
IntelliCorp, Inc., 91
Intelligent computer-assisted instruction [ICAI], 74, 91, 95, 263; and conceptual knowledge, 77; and creative thinking, 75, 85–86; evaluations of, 96; future development of, 97; and teachers, 81
Interactive video, 47; and the U.S. Air Force, 83–86
Intermountain Community Learning and Information Service, 45
Internal Revenue Service [IRS], 114, 149–150
International Brotherhood of Electrical Workers, 27, 107; and basic skills education, 246
International Correspondence Schools, 268
International Executive Forum, 62
International Ladies Garment Workers Union, 239; and basic skills education, 247–248
International Resource Development, 130
International Union of Operating Engineers [IUOE], 110
Iowa State University, 105
IRS. See Internal Revenue Service
ITFS. See Instructional Television Fixed Services
ITT Educational Services, 127
ITT Technical Institutes, 126–127
IUOE. See International Union of Operating Engineers

J. C. Penney Company, 67, 268
J. H. Jansen Company, 90
Jamestown Community College, 66
Jansen, J. H., Company, 90
Job Opportunities and Basic Skills Training Program, 236
Job Skills Education Program [JSEP], 253–254
Job Training Partnership Act [JTPA], 234–236, 244, 245
Job training programs, 233
John Hancock Company, 69
John Wiley & Sons, 29, 177
Johnson, Lyndon B., 142
Jones, Ernie, 105
Journeymen, 111–113
JSEP. See Job Skills Education Program
JTPA. See Job Training Partnership Act

Katharine Gibbs School, 117
Kearsley, Greg, 92
Kee Simulator [computer hardware], 116
Kelly Temporary Services, 116
Kivetz, Dolores, 211, 212
Klemp, George O., Jr., 183
Knowledge engineering: 79–81, 85
Kolb, David A., 77
Kwik Copy, 166

Labor Studies, Center for, 110
Labor unions, 26–28, 31, 46–47, 103, 106–107, 131; and academic institutions, 135; and apprenticeship programs, 13, 103; and asynchronous computer conferencing, 60; and basic skills education, 239, 245–247; and management, 256–257; and retraining, 131, 132
Lamborghini, Bruno, 256
Langer, Victor, 133
Language instruction, 50, 58–59, 153, 262; and CAI systems, 91–92; English as a second language, 230, 239, 244, 268
Laubach, Frank C., 249
Laubach Literacy Action, 249–250
Law Enforcement Television Network, 67
Lawyers: continuing education for, 13, 203–210
Leadership for a Democratic Society, 146
Learning process, 5, 70, 71–72, 75, 80–81, 82, 93, 261–264
Learning-Style Inventory, 77

Levinson, Paul, 61
Lewis, Matthew, 78
LEXIS [telecommunication network], 210
Licensing regulations, 188–189, 202, 205
Life Education Planning Program, 246
Linguistics: and artificial intelligence, 72
LISP [computer programming language],
    75–76, 87
Literacy: changing definitions of, 225–227,
    252; curricula, 246; and ICAI systems,
    81; technological, 227
Literacy campaigns, failure of, 251–254
Literacy Corps, 233
Literacy Volunteers of America [LVA],
    249–250
Little, Arthur D., Inc., 90
Local government: and adult education,
    237
Lockheed Engineering and Management
    Systems, 190
Los Angeles City College, 118
Los Angeles Trade-Technical College, 123
Lotus 1-2-3 [software], 120

McBer and Company's Learning-Style In-
    ventory, 77
McCalla, Gordon, 74, 78, 82
McClelland, David C., 183
McDonald's, 46; and management educa-
    tion, 166
McGraw, Harold, Jr., 241
McGraw-Hill, 29, 117, 268; and CAI sys-
    tems, 94; and literacy, 241
McGraw-Hill Continuing Education Cen-
    ter, 127
Macintosh. See Apple Macintosh
McKibbin, Lawrence, 178
Management education: in colleges and
    universities, 33, 171–176; in companies
    and corporations, 159–171; curricula,
    163–168; in the federal government, 140–
    151; in the military, 152–159; reform of,
    157, 178–184; suppliers of, 137, 139–
    140, 176–179
Management Staff College [U.S. Army],
    156
Management systems, 5
Manpower, Inc., 116
Manufacturers Hanover Trust Company,
    217
Manufacturing, 5, 20, 128–134

Manufacturing Engineers, Society of, 133
Maricopa Community College District, 128
Martin Marietta, 134, 198
Maryland, 45; University of, 42
Massachusetts, 45; and adult education
    programs, 238–239
Massachusetts, University of: and basic
    skills education, 239
Massachusetts Institute of Technology
    [MIT], 86, 201
Massachusetts Mutual Life Insurance Com-
    pany, 47
Master of Business Administration. See
    M.B.A. programs
Mathematics: and audiographic conferenc-
    ing, 56; and ICAI, 75–76; and
    manufacturing, 20; and mixed media in-
    struction, 66; and videotaped instruction,
    46
Maxx, TJ, 239
Mayo, Elton, 139
M.B.A. programs: 137; growth of, 33
MCI, 42
MCNC, 53
"Mechanical Universe," 48
Media-Based Continuing Engineering Edu-
    cation, Association for, 196
Medical schools: and CAI, 262; and contin-
    uing education, 13, 202–203; and tutored
    video instruction, 51; and videoconfer-
    encing, 54, 56
Menninger Foundation, 176
MENTOR [expert system], 89, 263
Merrill Lynch & Company, 68–69
Michigan, University of, 175; and continu-
    ing medical education, 203
Michigan Opportunity Card, 238
Michigan Opportunity and Skills Training
    [MOST], 238
Michigan State University, 173
Microcomputers, 262–263
Microelectronics Center of North Carolina
    [MCNC], 53
Mid-South Industries: and basic skills edu-
    cation, 244, 252–253
Military services, 21–25, 36; and asynchro-
    nous computer conferencing, 60; and
    ICAI systems, 83–87; and management
    education, 153–159; research and devel-
    opment, 152; service academies, 152; and
    training for information systems techni-

cians, 123–125. *See also* Department of Defense; Service academies
Milwaukee Area Technical College, 132
Minnesota Literacy Project, 250
Minorities, 9; and access to training, 20, 30; technical education for, 128
MIT. *See* Massachusetts Institute of Technology
MONY, 69
Moraine Park Technical College, 133
MOST, 238
Motorola: and basic skills education, 244; and engineering education, 197; and management education, 166, 168; and technical training, 123, 128
Mountain Bell Telephone, 28
Mueller Associates, 89–90
Multinational corporations, 2
Murphy, Joseph, 236

NAE, 195
NASA, 26
National Academy of Engineering [NAE], 195
National Aeronautics and Space Administration, 26
National Assessment of Educational Progress, 226
National Association of Home Builders, 64, 103; and training, 104, 105
National Association of Temporary Services, 115
National Association of Trade and Technical Schools, 32
National Commission of the Public Service, 26
National Compu-Ed, 127
National Contractors Association, 27, 108
National Defense University, 155, 156
National Education Centers, 268
National Education Corporation, 116, 268
National Electric Sign Association, 112
National Electrical Contractors, 107
National Gallery of Art, 263
National Guard, 152
National Institute for Trial Advocacy, 208
National Radio Institute, 127
National Research Council, 33–34
National Science Foundation, 62, 64, 133, 196, 200

National Technical Institute of the Deaf, 60
National Technological University [NTU], 43, 196–197, 260
National Teletraining Center, 55
National Tooling and Machining Association, 134
National University Teleconference Network, 45
National War College, 156
Naval Academy, 153
Naval Warfare, College of, 156
Naval Weapons Center, 42
Navy Personnel Research and Development Center, 86
Navy. *See* U.S. Navy
NCR, 68, 197
New England Mutual Life Insurance Company, 47
New School for Social Research, 61
New York, City University of, 236
New York University, 217
"Nickel Fund," 28
NRI School of Electronics, 127
NTU. *See* National Technological University

Obsolescence: of equipment and systems, 125–126; of professional knowledge, 186–187, 195; of workers' skills, 6, 8, 125, 129
Office of Personnel Management [OPM], 25, 120, 121–122, 142–143, 150, 265; Executive Seminar Centers, 146–147; and research, 143, 181
Office of Research and Development-Manpower Administration, 110
Office workers, 113–121
Oklahoma State University, 45
Olivetti Corporation, 256
Olsten Services, 116
OPM. *See* Office of Personnel Management
Optel Corporation, 55, 56
Orientation programs, 10
Owner-President Management Program, 162

Pacific Telesis, 62, 166
Pan American Airways, 60
Parent and Child Education Program, 233
Parker, Janice, 32

Peale, Norman Vincent, 178
Peat Marwick [accounting firm], 215
PENNARAMA [educational TV network], 43
Penney, J. C., 67, 268
PENN*LINK [educational TV network], 44
Pennsylvania, University of, 162; Wharton School, 173, 217
Pennsylvania Education Network, 44
Pennsylvania State University, 44
PepsiCo, 46
Perkins, Carl D., 31
Personal development training, 114, 146
Personnel management. *See* Human resources management
Petersen, Donald, 3
PETITE/IV [Prototype Electronic Technician Intelligent Tutor with Interactive Video], 83–86
Physical sciences: and videotaped instruction, 46. *See also* name of specific discipline
Physicians: and continuing education, 13, 54, 201–203, 209–210
Physicians Recognition Award, 203
Physics, 48
Piaget, Jean, 81
Piedmont Virginia Community College, 118
Pierce, William, 251
Platform Manager's Assistant, 90
Plumbers and Pipefitters, United Association of, 108, 109
Plumbers and Pipefitters Union, 27
PMI. *See* Presidential Management Intern Program
Polaroid, 62; and basic skills education, 244
Porter, Lyman, 178
PORTSIS [computer software], 93
Postal Service, 47
Practicing Law Institute, 206
Presidential Management Intern Program [PMI], 148
Productivity, Innovation, and Technology, Center for, 132
Professional Advancement, Center for, 199
Professional associations: and continuing education, 193. *See also* name of specific association
Professional education: growth of, 217; obsolescence of, 13, 186–189, 195;

providers of, 12, 45, 94, 189–195, 217–218, 267–268
Proprietary schools, 12, 28–29, 32, 268; accreditation of, 32; and office workers, 117–119
PROUST [computer programming tutor], 76
Purdue University, 106, 109, 135

Queensborough Community College, 134
Quinsigamond Community College, 239

Radar: and ICAI systems, 89–90
Recertification, 34, 188–189
Recovery Boiler Tutor, 90
Reddy, Raj, 96
Remedial training, 9; by corporations, 20
Research: and training programs, 10, 12, 143, 181
Retirement: 8
Retraining, 185–219; in automobile industry, 131; and CAI systems, 95; and community colleges, 31; and job mobility, 115, 150–151; need for, 5–6, 8, 35, 102, 135–136, 158, 186–189, 195, 266–267; video programs for, 37. *See also* Obsolescence
Rhode Island Community College, 110
Riley, Richard, 239
Rio Salado Community College, 110
RJR Nabisco, 243
Robots. *See* Automation; Computer-integrated manufacturing
Rochester Institute of Technology, 60, 66
Rockwell International, 68
Roe, Terry, 86

San Diego State University, 65–66
Saskatchewan, University of, 78
Satellite networks, 67–69, 210, 260
School Improvement Amendments. *See* Hawkins-Stafford Elementary and Secondary School Improvement Amendments
Schulz, David F., 7
SEC [Securities and Exchange Commission], 68
Secretaries. *See* Office workers
Senior Executive Service [SES], 142, 148, 151, 181
Service academies: academic standards of, 152; curricula, 153

Servicemembers Opportunity Colleges, 24
SES. *See* Senior Executive Service
Shanahan, Joseph, 24
Sheet Metal Workers Union, 47, 111
Silvey, Larry, 212–213, 214
Skilled trades, 12; training for, 101–136
Skillware [software], 116
Sloan Foundation, 196
Small businesses, 7, 19, 31, 43; and computer-integrated manufacturing [CIM], 133; and management education, 162–163
Smith, James E., 127
Smith, Lauralyn, 250
Social sciences, 153
Society of Manufacturing Engineers, 133
Socratic Series Courseware, 55–56
Soloway, Elliot, 76, 81
South Carolina, 54, 134; and basic skills education, 239–240, 250
Southern Medical Association, 202, 210
Spectrum Interactive, 268
Springfield Tire Company, 132
Sputnik, 141
SRI International, 18
Stanford University, 49–51, 136, 175, 196, 260; and continuing medical education, 203
State government: and adult education programs, 231, 237–240
STEAMER [expert system], 86–87, 96, 263
Stone School, 118
Stonier Graduate School of Banking, 216
Strategic Management Group, 177
Stress-management training, 114
Stromberg Carlson, 134
Supervisors: training of, 105, 131, 149, 161, 162, 166
Symbolics, Inc., 86

Takada, Masasumi, 61
Taylor, Frederick W., 139
Taylor Business School, 32
Teachers, 263; and ICAI systems, 74, 82; and telecommunication technologies, 38, 48–56, 61; and training for basic skills education, 254
Teamsters Union, 247
Technical institutes, 17
Technology, 37–40; and continuing education, 65–67; evaluation of, 69–70; and

literacy, 227; and professional education, 186–187, 201–202; and training, 3–4, 12, 35–36, 101–136
Tektronix, 198
Telecommunications, 37–70, 260–261; networks for professionals, 210
Telecourses, 51–52
Television, 41–45; training programs, 29, 37–38
Temporary employees, 115–116
Tennant, Harry, 72–73
Texas, University of, 203, 226
Texas A&M University, 105
Texas Instruments, 42, 53–54, 68, 72, 260; and "Aldo," 79
Thelin, Marrin, Johnson & Bridges [law firm], 207
Thunderbird Management Center, 177
Time-management training, 114
TJ Maxx, 239
Touche Ross [accounting firm], 215
Trade associations, 104–105. *See also* specific trades
Trade unions. *See* Labor unions
Travelers Insurance Company, 47
Treasury Department, 121; Executive Institute, 150; and management education, 149–150
Trial Advocacy, National Institute for, 208
Tri-County Technical College, 134
Troubleshooting, 84–85, 136, 263
Tuition subsidies and refund plans, 8, 34, 112, 114; and the IRS, 114
Tutored video instruction [TVI], 48–52

UAW [United Auto Workers], 27, 28, 131, 256; and basic skills education, 245–246, 247–248
UAW-Ford Employee Development and Training Center, 246
UAW-Ford Fund, 27
UAW-General Motors "Nickel Fund," 28
UCLA [University of California at Los Angeles], 123, 198–199; and medical education, 203
Unemployment, 2, 224; and retraining, 133
Unions. *See* Labor unions
Unisys, 126
United Association of Plumbers and Pipefitters, 108, 109
United Auto Workers. *See* UAW
United Research, 130

United Rubber Workers, 132

U.S. Air Force, 155; and ICAI systems, 83–86; Community College of the, 23, 124–125; Extension Course Institute, 124

U.S. Army, 60, 152, 155; and basic skills education, 253; Command and General Staff School, 153; Management Staff College, 156. *See also* War College; West Point

U.S. Defense Advanced Research Projects Agency [DARPA], 91

U.S. Government. *See* Federal government

U.S. Naval Weapons Center, 42

U.S. Navy, 152, 155, 263; College of Naval Warfare, 156; Department of Naval Personnel, 44; Naval Academy, 153; Naval Weapons Center, 42; and project management, 158; and STEAMER [expert system], 86–87, 96, 263

U.S. Postal Service, 47

United Technologies: and basic skills education, 244

United Telecom, 62

Universities. *See* Colleges and Universities

University of Arizona, 58

University of Arkansas, 175

University of California, Los Angeles [UCLA], 123, 198–199

University of Colorado, 76

University of Delaware, 216

University of Florida, 105

University of Maryland, 42

University of Michigan, 175; and continuing medical education, 203

University of Pennsylvania, 162

University of Saskatchewan, 78

University of Texas, 203, 226

Updating. *See* Retraining

USDA. *See* Department of Agriculture

Utah State University, 45

Valencia Community College, 134

Valso, George, 246

VAX hardware and software, 44, 94

Veterans Administration, 25, 26

Video. *See* Interactive video, Television, Tutored video instruction, Videoconferencing, Videotapes

Video Arts, 178

Videoconferencing, 52–55

Videotapes, 46–48

Vocational Education Act [Carl D. Perkins Vocational Education Act], 31

Vocational schools, 12, 32; and adult education, 120

Volunteers in Service to America [VISTA], 233

Walton Institute of Retailing [University of Arkansas], 175

War Colleges, 155–156, 157

WBSI. *See* Western Behavioral Sciences Institute

Welch, John F., Jr., 161, 167

Welfare recipients, 13; and literacy, 227

Welfare-Workfare program, 234, 236–237

West Central Illinois Education Telecommunications Corporation [CONVOCOM], 43

West Point, 153

Westcott Communication System, 67

Western Behavioral Sciences Institute [WBSI], 62–63, 65; and management education, 177

Western Electric Company, 139

Westinghouse, 134

Wharton School, 162, 164, 177, 217

Williams, Roger, 126

Wilson Learning, 17

Women, 9; and access to training, 19, 30, 35; and business schools, 33; technical education for, 128

Workers: and access to training, 18–19; attitudes towards training, 112, 114, 131; attitudes towards work, 7; diversity of, 8–10; educational level of, 9; and management, 130; minorities, 9; and new technologies, 5, 6, 8, 125, 129–131; retirement of, 8; as trainers, 132; women, 9

Workplace Education Program, 238

Workplace Literacy, Education Partnership for, 233

Wright, Leslie, 42

Xerox, 81, 86, 166

Yale University, 76, 81

Yankelovich, Daniel, 7

Young, Arthur, 215

Young, John A., 50

Young, Robert, 190

Zuboff, Shoshana, 4, 61

DATE DUE

OC 25 04			